D0765829

THIS BOOK IS DEDICATED TO THE MEMORY OF
THE 255 MILITARY PERSONNEL AND THREE
CIVILIANS WHO DIED FOR THEIR COUNTRY
ON THE FALKLANDS, AND IN PARTICULAR TO
MY NAMESAKE, WELSH GUARDSMAN IAN DALE

The Liberation Monument, Stanley

MEMORIES

OF THE

FALKLANDS

 *Edited by Iain Dale*

Published in Great Britain 2002
by Politico's Publishing
8 Artillery Row
Westminster
London SW1P 1RZ

www.politicos.co.uk/publishing

A catalogue record of this book is available from the British Library.

ISBN 1 84275 018 6

Printed and bound in Great Britain by St Edmundsbury Press

All photographs courtesy of the Press Association unless indicated otherwise.

CONTENTS

ACKNOWLEDGEMENTS

This book has been a pleasure to edit. I would like to thank the following for their help and advice: Mark Cann of the British Forces Foundation, Sir Rex Hunt, Sukey Cameron of the Falkland Islands Government Office in London, Denzil Connick, Rick Jolly, Field Marshal Lord Bramall and Tony McNally.

In addition, I am grateful to the following for allowing me to use previously published material: Baroness Thatcher, Sir John Nott, Richard Villar, Carol Thatcher, Lord Tebbit, Charles Laurence, Max Hastings and Sir Henry Leach. I am also indebted to the *Portsmouth News* for allowing me to quote from their Falklands features and also to the *Sunday Telegraph*.

I would also like to pay tribute to Jim Love, a Falklands veteran, who has allowed me to reproduce one of his superb and evocative poems about the war. Further examples of his work can be found at http://www.postpoems.com/members/giajl.

At the beginning of each entry, I have used the name by which the contributor was known in 1982, rather than necessarily use their present-day title. So Lord Blaker of Blackpool, as he now is, is titled Peter Blaker.

Iain Dale
February 2002

ABOUT THE BRITISH
FORCES FOUNDATION

We owe an enormous debt of gratitude to the men and women of our Armed Forces who are often called on to serve in difficult circumstances around the world. If, through the efforts of this Foundation, we can relieve some of the pressures under which they work, then we not only demonstrate our thanks to them but we also contribute towards the better efficiency and morale of all those who serve this country.

Baroness Thatcher LG OM FRS

Jim Davidson set up The British Forces Foundation three years ago to provide morale-boosting entertainment to Britain's Armed Forces on Operations. Believing passionately in the sacrifices our Servicemen and women make, he formed a charity dedicated solely to protecting and boosting their morale in times of need.

With the support of HRH The Prince of Wales, Baroness Thatcher and an array of high profile Trustees from the Armed Forces, diplomatic corps and world of entertainment, the charity has already put on some spectacular shows. Filmed on HMS *Invincible* and broadcast on BBC1 on Christmas Day 2000, 'Homeward Bound for Christmas'"saw a host of celebrities such as Martine McCutcheon and Sir John Mills perform to the men and women of our Armed Services. In September 2001, Status Quo gave a rip-roaring show to 12,000 service personnel and their families in Germany. To name a few. It is difficult to imagine yet nonetheless essential to appreciate just how important these shows are.

Today the work of the Foundation is more important than ever before.

Your support to The British Forces Foundation sends out a very clear and positive message to the men and women of our Armed Forces. It says you care and support what they are doing and the sacrifices they are making.

Jim Davidson OBE

Your support is greatly appreciated. Thankyou.

FOREWORD *by Iain Dale*

On 2 April 1982, I was on holiday, visiting friends, the Weber family, in the German spa town of Bad Wildungen. I was 19, and was on an Easter break from my degree course in German at the University of East Anglia in Norwich. After dinner, we sat down to watch TV. I watched incredulously as the newsreader told us of the Argentine invasion of the Falkland Islands. Unlike most people in Britain, I had a vague idea of where the Falklands were, due to my childhood stamp collection. My German friends assumed that they lay off the coast of Scotland. Herr Weber, a veteran of the Russian front in the Second World War, said: 'It'll all be settled by diplomacy.' I remember vividly replying: 'I doubt it very much. Margaret Thatcher is not known as the Iron Lady for nothing. I think there'll be a war.'

'No, no,' replied Herr Weber. 'There will be a compromise. They'll bring in the United Nations. People don't fight wars over small colonies any more.'

'Trust me,' I said. 'You don't know Margaret Thatcher.'

A few weeks later, back at university, I was asleep in my room one morning when there was a knock at the door. 'Oh, you're still alive then,' an anonymous voice said. Still half asleep, I didn't really think anything of it and dozed off again. A few minutes later, the same thing happened. 'Glad to see you're still with us,' said my next-door neighbour. Strange, I thought.

Later on, in the kitchen, someone asked if I had seen the papers yet. I said I hadn't. 'You ought to,' came the reply.

I remember it as if it were yesterday: turning to page two of the *Daily Mail* and seeing my name. Killed in action in the Falklands.

But it wasn't me. It was Welsh Guardsman Ian Dale, aged 19, from Pontypridd.

It was like being hit in the solar plexus. Tears streamed down my face, as they were to do many times over the next few weeks.

Nothing else could have brought home to me the terrible waste of war like this did.

I was the same age. It could have been me.

Not long afterwards, I attended a debate at the university between the president of the Students Union and leading light in the University Labour Club, Mark Seddon (now the editor of *Tribune*), and someone whose name I now forget but who was on the extreme left. I was horrified that such a debate could take place between the soft left and hard left with no other viewpoint being put forward. So up I stood and defended the sending of the Task Force and our right to retake British sovereign territory. That was my first real experience of the cut and thrust of political debate. And I enjoyed it. It was the catalyst for my getting involved in politics – an interest that endures to this day.

For me, the Falklands War was a formative experience. My father was a teenager during the Second World War and even now he is most happy when he is reading about it or watching TV documentaries on it. I remain fascinated by the political, military and personal consequences of the Falklands War. I remember watching the TV pictures of HMS *Sheffield* in flames, of the helicopter rescues from burning ships, with tears welling in my eyes. I remember the sleep-inducing tones of the Ministry of Defence spokesman Ian McDonald at his daily press conferences. I remember the fury that overcame me as I watched the BBC's *Panorama* programme which sought to pour scorn on the war. I remember John Nott announcing the retaking of South Georgia late at night in Downing Street and Margaret Thatcher urging the journalists present not to ask more questions but to 'rejoice' at the news.

But most of all, I remember the sense of relief, national pride and joy that most of the country felt as they watched the Union Jack being hoisted again over Government House in Port Stanley. It was a day that helped Britain regain its national pride, which many felt had been lost 26 years earlier in the depths of the Suez Canal. In my opinion, 14 June 1982 will be seen by future historians as a turning point in British history. It was a day which showed that Britain was no longer a soft touch and had the ability to stand up to aggressors. Most important of all, it demonstrated a resolve to the communist world, and the Soviet Union in particular, which they thought we had lost years before.

This book has no political viewpoint and does not seek to address the rights and wrongs of political or military strategy. It is a collection of personal memories, anecdotes and reminiscences. It's as simple as that.

In the following pages, there are memories from the 'Great and the Good' as well as recollections from people involved in the war whose names are not well known. They include soldiers and sailors who fought in the war, and Falkland Islanders themselves. There are reminiscences from politicians and journalists, too. The fascinating tales recounted here help us to understand the war a little better. Sometimes amusing and sometimes moving, these memories are all informative and thought-provoking.

Royalties from this book are being donated to the British Forces Foundation. We are delighted to be associated with such a worthwhile charity. The BFF is Jim Davidson's brainchild and its aim is to encourage top-class performers from show business to travel the world to entertain servicemen and women in all three services on operations. Davidson says: 'When young soldiers, sailors and airmen are a long way from home, doing their bit for their country, they like to know that people care back here. The appearance of a well-known entertainer helps give them that reassurance – as well as cheering them up, I hope!'

If you would like to support the activities of the British Forces Foundation, please contact it at the following address:

British Forces Foundation
Ancient Lights
23 Bradford Mews
London
W1W 5BL
Telephone 0207 436 3007
Fax 0207 436 2120

You can find out more about the BFF on its website at www.bff.org.uk

One day I shall visit the Falklands.

Iain Dale
London, February 2002

Prime Minister Margaret Thatcher leaving 10 Downing Street for the House of Commons, Saturday 3 April 1982 – the first time the Commons had sat on a Saturday since the Suez crisis in 1956.

MARGARET THATCHER

Prime Minister, 1979-90

Nothing remains more vividly in my mind, looking back on my years in No. 10, than the 11 weeks in the spring of 1982 when Britain fought and won the Falklands War.

It scarcely seems possible that all of this was 20 years ago.

Much was at stake: what we were fighting for 8,000 miles away in the South Atlantic was not only the territory and the people of the Falklands, important though they were. We were defending our honour as a nation, and principles of fundamental importance to the whole world — above all, that aggressors should never succeed and that international law should prevail over the use of force.

The war was very sudden. No one predicted the Argentine invasion more than a few hours in advance, though many predicted it in retrospect. When I became Prime Minister, I never thought that I would have to order British troops into combat, and I do not think that I have ever lived so tensely or intensely as during the whole of that time.

The significance of the Falklands War was enormous, both for Britain's self-confidence and for our standing in the world. Since the Suez fiasco in 1956, British foreign policy had been one long retreat. The tacit assumption made by British and foreign Governments alike was that our world role was doomed steadily to diminish. We had come to be seen by both friends and enemies as a nation that lacked the will and capability to defend its interests in peace, let alone in war. Victory in the Falklands changed that. Everywhere I went after the war, Britain's name meant something more than it had. The war also had real importance in relations between East and West: years later, I was told by a Russian general that the Soviets had been firmly convinced that we would not fight for the Falklands, and that if we did fight we would lose. We proved them wrong on both counts, and they did not forget it.

I shall not forget the evening of Wednesday 31 March 1982. I was working in my room at the House of Commons when I was told that John Nott wanted an immediate meeting to discuss the Falklands. I called people together. John was alarmed. He had just received intelligence that the Argentine Fleet, already at sea, looked as if they were going to invade the Islands on Friday 2 April. There was no ground to question the intelligence. John gave the MoD's view that the Falklands could not be retaken once they had been seized. This was terrible, and totally unacceptable. I could not believe it: these were our people, our islands. I said instantly: 'If they are invaded, we have got to get them back.'

At this dark moment, comedy intervened. The Chief of the Naval Staff, Henry Leach, was in civilian dress, and on his way to the meeting he had been detained by the police in the Central Lobby of the House of Commons. He had to be rescued by a whip. When he finally arrived, I asked him what we could do. He was quiet, calm and confident: 'I can put together a Task Force of destroyers, frigates, landing craft, support vessels. It will be led by the aircraft carriers HMS *Hermes* and HMS *Invincible*. It can be ready to leave in 48 hours.' He believed such a force could retake the Islands. All he needed was my authority to begin to assemble it. I gave him it, and he left immediately to set the work in motion. We reserved for Cabinet the decision as to whether and when the Task Force should sail.

Before this, I had been outraged and determined. Now my outrage and determination were matched by a sense of relief and confidence. Henry Leach had shown me that, if it came to a fight, the courage and professionalism of Britain's armed forces would win through. It was my job as Prime Minister to see that they got the political support they needed.

Saturday 24 April was to be one of the most crucial days in the Falklands story and a critical one for me personally. Early that morning, Francis Pym came to my study in No. 10 to tell me the results of his negotiating efforts in Washington. I can only describe the document that he brought back as conditional surrender. I told Francis that the terms were totally unacceptable. They would rob the Falklanders of their freedom and Britain of her honour and respect. Francis disagreed. He thought that we should accept what was in the document. We were at loggerheads.

It was John Nott who found the procedural way forward. He proposed that we should make no comment on the first draft but ask Mr Haig to put it to the Argentines first. If they accepted it, we should undoubtedly be in difficulties; but we could then put the matter to Parliament in the light of their acceptance. If the Argentines rejected it – and we thought that they would, because it is almost impossible for any military junta to withdraw – we could then urge the Americans to come down firmly on our side. And so a great crisis passed. I could not have stayed as Prime Minister had the War Cabinet accepted Francis Pym's proposals. I would have resigned.

More than ever, the outcome now lay in the hands of our soldiers, not with the politicians. Like everyone else in Britain, I was glued to the radio for news – strictly keeping my self-imposed rule not to telephone while the conflict was under way.

On Sunday 13 June, I travelled back from Chequers to No. 10 via Northwood, to learn what I could. What turned out to be the final assault was bitterly fought, particularly at Mount Tumbledown, where the Argentines were well prepared. But

Tumbledown, Mount William and Wireless Ridge fell to our forces, who were soon on the outskirts of Stanley.

When the War Cabinet met the following day, all we knew was that the battle was still in progress. The speed with which the end came took all of us by surprise. The Argentines were weary, demoralised and very badly led – as ample evidence showed both at the time and later. They had had enough. They threw down their arms and could be seen retreating through their own minefields into Stanley.

That evening, having learnt the news, I went to the House of Commons to announce the victory. I could not get into my own room; it was locked and the Chief Whip's assistant had to search for the key. I then wrote out on a scrap of paper I found somewhere on my desk the short statement, which I would have to make on a point of order to the House. At 10pm, I rose and told them that it had been reported that there were white flags flying over Port Stanley. The war was over. We all felt the same and the cheers showed it. Right had prevailed. And when I went to sleep very late that night, I realised how great the burden was that had been lifted from my shoulders. For the nation as a whole, though the daily memories, fears and even the relief would fade, pride in our country's achievement would not.[1]

SIR REX HUNT

Governor of the Falkland Islands, 1980-85

'How small!' That was my first impression of Stanley, capital of the Falkland Islands and my home for almost six years. I was standing on the flight deck of an Argentine Fokker Friendship. The year was 1980 and the Argentine Air Force ran the only airline operating into and out of the Falkland Islands at the time. I was on my way to take up an appointment with the imposing title: Governor and Commander-in-Chief of the Falkland Islands and their Dependencies, Vice-Admiral of the same and High Commissioner of the British Antarctic Territory. Quite a mouthful. The sky was overcast and visibility poor, so we were making a low approach from the sea. Suddenly, as we skirted round a black squall, the sun broke through and there was Stanley directly in front of us, lit up as if by floodlights. In contrast with the sombre surrounding countryside, the gaily painted roofs gave a cheerful glow to the little town. In the distance, I saw for the first time the distinctive peaks that were to become so well known in 1982: Tumbledown, Two Sisters, Mount Kent, Mount Longdon and Wireless Ridge.

The pilot showed his skill by touching down gently despite an extremely strong crosswind. Stepping out of the aircraft, I had my first taste of the Falklands wind, and was glad not to be wearing my official uniform. The plumed hat would have disappeared upwards like Dorothy. The piercing wind went right through me and I was relieved to be ushered into the red London taxi that passed as the Governor's official car. Its driver, Don Bonner, was from a family of four generations in the Falkland Islands. Like many other Islanders, he had gone to sea on whalers in South Georgia, minesweepers in the Royal Navy and various smaller vessels of dubious seaworthiness before settling down on one of the sheep farms in the Falklands and siring a family of seven. Now he was not only the Governor's chauffeur, but also valet, steward, major-domo and general factotum at Government House. He was to become my fishing mentor, snooker opponent and lasting friend.

Driving the four miles into Stanley from the airport, Don kept up an enthralling commentary until we reached Government House, where the rest of the staff were

Sir Rex Hunt returns to Government House in Stanley.

waiting to greet my wife and me. We both fell in love with our new home, which had great character and charm and yet remained homely and comfortable to live in. On that first day, however, I had little time to appreciate my surroundings because I had to change quickly into uniform and go to the Town Hall for the formal swearing-in ceremony. For the first of many times, Don took us on the two-minute drive from Government House to the Town Hall, where I inspected the guard of honour of Royal Marines and the Falkland Islands Defence Force before going inside. In a welcoming speech, the Chief Secretary said that I could expect a 'tranquil but absorbing way of life' in the Islands. That was the first of many memorable occasions in the Town Hall over the next six years.

The Town Hall was the hub of Stanley. Legislative Council met there, criminal and civil courts were held there, dances, May Queen Balls, darts matches, horticultural shows, wedding parties, amateur dramatics and public meetings all took place there. In my memory, two occasions stand out above all others.

The first was on 2 April 1982. To explain the circumstances, I have to go back a day to 3.30pm local (Stanley) time, when I received the following telegram from the Foreign and Commonwealth Office:

We have apparently reliable evidence that an Argentine Task Force will gather off Cape Pembroke [the entrance to Stanley's outer harbour] *early tomorrow morning, 2 April. You will wish to make your dispositions accordingly.*

With 69 Royal Marines, 10 Royal Navy hydrographers and the local Falkland Islands Defence Force, we made our dispositions accordingly. Government House was the obvious target. It was the seat of Government and I decided that it was where I had to stay. Like many another that night, I found myself reflecting on my life. It had been hugely enjoyable and I was relieved to find that I could face the prospect of death with equanimity. I was desperately concerned, however, about the Royal Marines and FIDF members. Many of them were not much older than my own son, on the threshold of life and with everything ahead of them. The thought that a decision of mine could cut off their young lives was to be my main anxiety until the final outcome.

The Argentines launched their assault on Government House just after 6am and a fierce firefight ensued. The firing petered out as dawn broke about half an hour later. We had repulsed their first attack. By that time we had heard that armoured personnel carriers were trundling into Stanley. To avoid unnecessary casualties, I decided to call for a ceasefire.

The Admiral in charge of the Task Force came to me at Government House. He explained that the Military Governor, a General Garcia, would be arriving to take over command at 10.30am. I expected him to come to Government House but, to my surprise, he went to the Town Hall and sent his emissary to escort me there. I told the emissary to tell his General that I would see him here, at Government House. This went on with rising acrimony until after midday, when I finally agreed to go under threat of being frog-marched if I refused. I was thus considerably angry as I entered the Town Hall. My anger knew no bounds when I surveyed the sight in front of me. The room was full of Argentine soldiers, pressmen and cameras. There was even a battery of studio lighting that they must have flown in for the occasion. A sallow little man with General's epaulettes came towards me, with his arm outstretched and a fixed, sickly smile on his face. Cameras whirred. I could imagine the rejoicing Argentine public back home. I put my hands pointedly behind my back. The cameras stopped. The smile disappeared. I looked directly at the General and said: 'You have landed unlawfully on British territory and I order you to remove yourself and your troops forthwith.' Whereupon Garcia retorted angrily, raising his voice: 'We have taken back what is rightfully ours and we shall stay FOR EVER.' Thanks to Margaret Thatcher, 'FOR EVER' became 74 days.

The second outstanding occasion at the Town Hall could not have been more different. It was on 10 January 1983, now celebrated annually in the Falkland Islands as 'Margaret Thatcher Day'. That was the day when the Freedom of the Falkland Islands was bestowed upon her, in recognition and appreciation of her saving the Islands from Argentine rule. It is a unique honour. There are a few recipients of the Freedom of Stanley, but Margaret Thatcher is the only person who has been given the Freedom of the Falkland Islands.

Monday 10 January 1983 was a busy day, spent jumping in and out of helicopters (a tiring business) and visiting six settlements, where Margaret Thatcher gave speeches to the troops and to the Islanders, many of whom had come in from outlying farms. She also spoke to many of them individually. She had brought some beautiful wreaths from England, which she laid at Blue Beach cemetery and on the individual graves of Lieutenant Nick Taylor RN at Goose Green and Captain Hamilton of the Green Howards at Port Howard. Having been told that the approach to the cemetery at Port Howard was very muddy, I went across to the Prime Minister in the helicopter with a pair of Wellingtons and suggested she might wish to put them on. 'Certainly not,' she replied indignantly, 'I am not wearing Wellingtons to Captain Hamilton's grave.' And she splashed through the mud in her smartest shoes.

We arrived back at Government House with just half an hour to change and get to the public reception at the Town Hall. On the short drive between the two, the Prime Minister expressed the hope that we should not be there for too long. I had to tell her that the Councillors had a surprise in store. They had decided to confer upon her the Freedom of the Falkland Islands. Harold Rowlands, the Financial Secretary and most senior Islander in the Falkland Islands Government, had been chosen to present the scroll. I would introduce him and we would both speak for no more than two minutes. She would be expected to say a few words in reply, but that was all.

The Town Hall was packed, the atmosphere electric, and as soon as the Prime Minister entered she was engulfed in a sea of grateful well-wishers. It took the best part of an hour to guide her through the crowd to the stage at the other end of the hall. I introduced Harold and stuck to my allotted two minutes. Harold was equally brief. Describing the occasion as the greatest moment in his life, he said that he was echoing the sentiments of all Falkland Islanders in expressing his pleasure at being able to thank Mrs Thatcher in person for their liberation. He pledged Islanders to build a better future to ensure that the war had been worthwhile and that British lives had not been lost in vain. He read out the formal proclamation, presented the scroll to the Prime Minister and then brought the house down by taking her in his arms and giving her a big kiss. Clearly elated, Margaret Thatcher spoke brilliantly for 20 minutes, without notes, and struck exactly the right chord. Not normally demonstrative, the Islanders gave her the most enthusiastic reception ever witnessed in the Falkland Islands. The biggest cheer came when she said: 'Today again the Union Jack flies over Stanley, and may it ever fly there.' I rather wished that General Garcia had been present.

Sir Rex Hunt's memoirs, My Falkland Days*, are published in paperback by Politico's Publishing*

The British Cemetery at San Carlos Bay.

GORDON SMITH

Author

'Gotcha,' said the *Sun* in its usual elegant and loving style. 'Will we be called up to fight?' asked some of the middle-aged men in the mental-health centre I was running at the time. Those are my immediate memories of the Falklands War. The only other one was the query 'Why hadn't we fired the torpedoes just to damage the *Belgrano?*', which seemed a stupid question bearing in mind what submarine warfare is all about, and especially in near-wintry southern seas. Apart from those recollections, little else stuck. I had other things to occupy me. Only a year before, I had walked out of a very secure, over-paid but basically boring management job in a then nationalised industry and, after a few months watching the grass grow, had taken a job with a charity. Then the war came to a successful end – as I believe the British Ambassador said to an Argentine official at the time, 'Britain doesn't lose many wars', and that was it.

Two or so years later, now trying to make the grass grow, I came to the conclusion that it was time to find out why my father was killed in 1943. Not the details, which I knew, but the overall picture that placed him and his ship in the wrong time and place, making them the target of two German torpedoes off the French coast. I therefore decided to explore the whole war at sea month by month across all theatres and sent the idea to a publisher; they liked it, and I had a book contract. I struggled to meet their deadline, but at last it was finished. A further meeting took place and, much to my surprise, I was commissioned to write a battlefield atlas of the Falklands War. But I'm not interested in the Falklands War, and knew nothing about it. Pride comes before a fall: I was obviously on my way to becoming an established author. I had to say yes.

Going through that modern disease of divorce at the time, this project was even more of a struggle. But eventually, and with a lot of support from family and friends, I collected together each and every (mainly British) published resource I could find and completed the atlas – 40 maps, thousands of facts, checked and double-checked. Note that I had never visited the Falklands or Argentina, and had exchanged not one word with a Falklands veteran. But then, you don't visit the site of the Battle of Jutland or talk to Royal Navy veterans of the time to write about that incredibly complex event!

The book was published in 1989, and received some gratifying reviews – my most low-key but professionally treasured being: 'may prove to be a most useful source . . . maps are well presented . . . [there are no] inconsistencies between text and maps – additional corroboration of the general accuracy and thoroughness of the author's research and collation . . . . So far as the Official Secrets Act permits, the detail is remarkably accurate' (Commander James McCoy RN, *Naval Review*). And a little later: 'contributed tremendously to my knowledge of the war' (Francois Heisbourg, Director of the International Institute for Strategic Studies, London).

The book sold fairly well but I discovered I would never make a living out of writing and went back to work in time for our last major economic recession. Redundancy! I started playing around with personal computers and the new Internet, and eventually decided to upload – as the experts say – my two published books and a lot of unpublished Naval material on to the Internet. The books have been even better received on the web, and the compliments even more satisfying – from a British-born journalist/researcher/writer in Argentina: 'Since 1982, I have visited the Falkland Islands over 15 times and on every occasion your book has been in my rucksack and has become something of my bible on the war. Over the years of research, I have also had numerous opportunities to cross-check the information there contained against the Argentine versions of the same events and have usually found that it stands up as a fair appraisal of the war even 17 years later.' And then, in April 2000, the Argentine Army Journal *Soldados* listed the book at No. 1 of recommended English-language books on the Falklands War.

If much of this is about me so far, then please forgive me. I come from a Naval family – grandfather sunk twice in the First World War and awarded the DSM for fighting the Bolsheviks; my father survived the Malta convoys and was sunk off the French coast in a mess of an operation (Tunnel); half of my aunts and uncles served in the RN or WRNS. All I wanted to do was join the Navy, didn't, pursued a successful but totally unfulfilling career apart from learning to be a decent analyst of complex systems, to end up writing on things Naval and maritime. Now just turned 60 and really enjoying my 'work' for the first time, I'm afraid I tend to wallow in any professional Naval or military compliment.

So what's this all got to do with the Falklands War, the men who fought there, died and were wounded, sometimes horrifically, the ships sunk and aircraft shot down? Especially in an article written by an armchair amateur. Well, I can only give you my reactions and impressions after having to dig deep into the published information on and accounts of what, in terms of British history, will be little more than a footnote in a few hundred years from now.

First, the Argentines – on balance, they have quite a case historically for claiming the Malvinas, but perhaps not much more than Rome's case for taking back Britannia. Even so, their invasion was immoral and illegal and, on at least two counts, plain stupid – they have set back Argentine/Falkland Islands relations by at least 100 years, and

Britain knows how to fight wars, especially when the Prime Minister happens to be a fan of Winston Churchill, and our Navy has 300 years' experience of carrying hastily assembled forces thousands of miles, landing them on hostile shores and beating the hell out of the enemy. Having said that, the Argentine forces appear competently to have carried out a largely unopposed landing, and the country's air forces fought a brave and potentially war-winning campaign. If all their iron bombs had exploded, we might not have had enough warships left afloat to complete the recapture. But this should not have been a surprise. South America is not all Amazon rivers and undiscovered tribes, but largely southern European-type societies, quite capable of fighting modern wars. And as one commentator put it, any country that can produce a racing driver like Juan Fangio is going to field some pretty hotshot fighter-bomber pilots. The Argentine Navy wasn't prepared to lose its few modern and very expensive warships, and the Army seems to have had a Maginot Line complex. Sit in your bunkers and wait for the enemy to come to you. Not that a more offensive approach would have had much effect on the outcome. To pit mainly conscripts against Britain's Royal Marines, Paras, Guards and Gurkhas is the stuff of nightmares.

As for Britain, most of it has just been said in the context of Argentina. What else can be added? Compared with the two World Wars, in the Falklands we had, on balance, better equipment than the opposition. But in the end, it was the older virtues that prevailed. Centuries of diplomatic and often underhand manoeuvring (we do not always play cricket) meant that Britain was soon able to isolate Argentina in the world, even in South America. Our muddling through, together with the usual happenstance, such as the Royal Navy having warships on exercise near Gibraltar and access to Ascension as a base halfway to the Falklands, enabled us to assemble a Task Force in double-quick time. That our men are trained to think and act independently meant the recapture of South Georgia as another base much sooner than one could have expected. The logistics of getting just one obsolescent bomber at a time over Stanley smacks of the same sort of thinking and planning that went into such wartime projects as Enigma. Our Second World War lessons in combined operations remained with us to an admirable degree: one country was fighting, not three or more services individually – at least most of the time, I imagine, although I'm sure there were occasional comments about the Navy, brown jobs, Brylcreem boys, etc, or whatever the modern equivalents are.

When it came to fighting, the Navy got up to its old hit-and-run tactics, so the Argentines never knew where and when they would turn up. It launched successful carrier strikes against a range of land targets, as it did with the biggest ever British Pacific Fleet off Okinawa and Japan in 1945. The SAS, with their Pebble Island raid, delighted in a rerun of their air-base attacks against Rommel in North Africa. When all but one of the Chinook helicopters were lost, the Marines and Paras did what the 'Forgotten Army' had to do in Burma – 'yomp' and 'tab' across East Falkland with 100lb packs, and fight battles on the way. And when they did fight, it was with rifle and bayonet, machine-gun and grenade, with all the blood and pain and death and fear and noise and hellish chaos known by foot soldiers throughout history.

However, we are now told that with the coming of new-fangled asymmetric warfare, with its threefold tasks of diplomacy, humanitarian aid and military intervention (what's changed for Britain's services?), and of course with the advent of smart munitions (to misquote the *Sun*), wars will no longer be the same. Yet the last news I heard before writing this piece was of British SAS troops fighting their way into Afghanistan caves to winkle out Taliban fighters (as they would have done with Argentine, or Korean, or German, or Turkish, or Napoleonic, or . . .)

Goose Green, the East Falkland Settlement recaptured by British Forces on May 27 1982.

ERIC GOSS

Falkland Islander

From my memory, supported by my diary, on 1 April 1982, I recall an interruption to the evening radio programme as broadcast from Stanley Studio, with a live broadcast from Governor Rex Hunt warning of a possible invasion by Argentine Naval forces.

That evening, at 1830 local time, the population was urged to listen at 1915 to an important message from the Governor. I deduced something serious was on as we sat down to our evening meal – the Governor Rex Hunt announced that an invasion by the Argentines was imminent and that he had only received this information himself at 3pm that afternoon. Why he kept the population in the dark for four and a half hours remains a mystery. At our table, chewing slowed up and then stopped as the message sunk in. This scene of stunned silence was probably repeated in every home and bar throughout the Falklands. As far as I remember, there were very few telephone calls or exchanges on the 2-metre band that evening.

I was awake most of that night listening to radio bulletins that were keeping us up to date with developments in the invasion. A state of emergency was declared at 0325: the invasion fleet was first sighted from Cape Pembroke lighthouse and, one hour later, it could be seen from the high ground in Stanley.

My wife, Shirley, made contact on the land-line telephone with her sister Norma in Stanley to discuss the predicament we were in. Brother-in-law Willie Bowles was persuaded to bring out his family and our son Morgan to Goose Green, away from the risk of bullets and shellfire.

They closed up house and departed Stanley in the dark, in Willie's Series 3 Land Rover, with wife Norma, daughter Hayley and her boyfriend Graham, son Troyd and our son Morgan as passengers. They drove around Sappers Hill heading west on the gravel track. Unbeknown to them, they had crossed the front line of the Argentine Buzo Tactico Marines advancing on Moody Brook barracks and Government House.

Next day (and for many more days), Eileen Vidal, the Government radio operator, kept us all informed on the situation in Stanley. Dr Alison Bleaney, the Chief Medical Officer, gave comfort and support to those living in isolated places.

On Saturday 3 April, I despatched six Land Rovers to the end of the road (at that time, it ended about halfway between Rolon Cove and Bluff Cove, with another stretch coming east from Elephant Canyon). Their purpose was to pick up children evacuated from Stanley, bound for Walker Creek, North Arm and Port Howard.

As anticipated, once the invaders had consolidated their position in Stanley, the next move would be to take control of the two larger settlements in the camp.

On Sunday 4 April, Yona Davis on Lively Island reported two ships passing, one up Choiseul Sound heading for Goose Green and the other to south of Lively Island, no doubt bound for Fox Bay on West Falkland. The first ship was identified as the Argentine transport *Isla de los Estados* – no stranger to Goose Green, as she had berthed at the jetty on 2 April 1981 to load 1,500 mutton wethers from North Arm bound for Ushuaia.

The ship was sighted nearing the narrows at 1145 hours and anchored in Goose Green basin midway between the narrows and the jetty at 1240 hours. A white Sea King helicopter from Stanley circled overhead, obviously checking for troops or defence systems on the ground. Shortly after, the *Isla de los Estados* came alongside the jetty and disembarked around 70 Argentine armed infantry.

The soldiers assembled at the jetty head and a small detachment approached the nearest house, which was depicted on the old settlement plan as the manager's house. The house was now occupied by the storekeeper Keith Baillie, who was driving one of the Land Rovers in the convoy to collect the children coming out of Stanley. Friends of the Baillies, Ray Robson and his wife, had come over from Seal Bay, the lonely shepherd's house on the north coast, belonging to Port Louis. They had arrived on a white Suzuki TS250 motorcycle, hoping that here would be a peaceful location in which to sit out the invasion. He was ordered by the Argentine lieutenant to bring Brook Hardcastle, the General Manager of Falkland Islands Company farms, to the jetty head. I can still visualise Brook riding behind Ray along the Darwin track: I bet he had not ridden pillion for many years.

The residents of Goose Green were told to meet up near the Centre Shed at the jetty head and bring along their firearms and any bullets, to hand them over to the troops for safe keeping! Soon after this gathering, more demands were made, this time for accommodation. Thinking quickly, I pointed them in the direction of Darwin Boarding School, a large building used to house camp children and teachers, now used only as a day school for the children of Goose Green and Darwin. My decision isolated the invaders, freeing the people of both Darwin and Goose Green from having armed men living in their midst. The day school was relocated to the Recreation Hall.

On Monday 5 April, the Argentine Commando party carried out a house-to-house search, recording the occupants in each dwelling, and taking details of passports held, vehicles owned and transceiver radio equipment. I was obliged to escort the invaders around the settlement by Sub Teniente (2nd Lieutenant) Juan Jose Gomez Centurion, who assured us that we would come to no harm and could continue with our normal routine farm work. The local radio station was taken over by LRA 60 Malvinas Radio Station. The first notice issued was to drive on the right-hand side of the road.

By Tuesday 6 April, the Argentines were short of rations and demanded provisions from the farm store. I accompanied storekeeper Keith Baillie to the farm store, who recorded 12 items issued off the shelves, signed for by Gomez Centurion. Business was conducted in a polite and cordial manner by both sides, but what option has one got when the customer is armed with a sub-machine Colt 45 pistol and has a variety of hand grenades pinned on his tunic? Behind his back, we referred to him as the walking bomb. Were the grenades he wore armed?

More edicts came over the radio imposing restrictions on travel and radio communication, by amateur operators overseas or local calls on the 2-metre band.

Each day brought something new to contend with. Life went on in spite of the restraints imposed. I maintained a close watch on all incoming movement, by ship, helicopter or other aircraft, recording the numbers that landed and deducting those who left. This information was most useful to the British forces when arranging the surrender.

On 22 April, I observed a party land by helicopter near Darwin School. These visitors seemed to create much excited activity, revolving around someone dressed in a white uniform and wearing lots of scrambled egg (gold braid) on his cap, shoulders and chest. After the war, I learnt it was General Leopoldo Galtieri.

Moving my story on to 1 May 1982, at about 0715 local time I was outside emptying the sitting-room ashpan when all hell erupted. Screaming jet aircraft and loud explosions were accompanied by erratic 7.62 FN gunfire, disturbing the peace and tranquillity of a bright, quiet morning.

In the sky above, I saw three Sea Harriers climb steeply over my house and fan out in a formation resembling the Prince of Wales's feathers. The concussion of exploding ordnance took my breath away; my chest felt squeezed flat. The stench of cordite and jet fumes was heavy on the air. My house is only about 450 yards from the airstrip where the bombs landed, scoring hits on Pucara aircraft and an accommodation tent where fitters and pilots slept. Explosions on the airstrip continued for some time, and thick black smoke billowed up in the clear sky.

When the dust had settled and the noise subsided, soldiers arrived at the office door of my house, ordering everyone out. I refused to move and was taken down the steps with a double-edged blade of six or seven inches under my jaw, by a nasty-natured oriental-featured individual who piloted a Chinook helicopter, which at night he parked between my house and the blacksmith shed. I was instructed to knock on every door to tell the inhabitants to assemble with haste at the Recreation Hall for a meeting. Residents of Darwin settlement joined us later, not knowing that this was the beginning of the confinement of the entire civilian population of both settlements. We were now incarcerated.

Returning briefly to the Chinook pilot, I believe that he flew his craft from Goose Green at dusk, after landing more troops to reinforce the Argentine defence against the

Rear-Admiral Sandy Woodward as he arrives aboard HMS *Hermes* in the mid-Atlantic
to assume command of the Task Force.

2 Para Brigade in attack, then west to refuel on Weddell Island and onwards to the nearest mainland base in Argentina. I never did see his face among the prisoners in the woolshed.

Life in the Recreation Hall is a long story. The first night was spent on the bare floor with only a meagre snack that I had managed to get from the farm store by the grace of an elderly FAA senior aircraft fitter, whose attention I attracted when he was passing the hall at dusk. He said he was at risk by allowing this to happen. Only two people, the storekeeper and I, could go to the store to collect basic essential food and beverages under guard – but strictly no lights were to be shown in the store or warehouse. Fortunately, Baillie knew where his stock was placed. We loaded up what we could carry and much more. The kindly officer shared out the rifles, releasing hands of conscripts to carry our much-needed provisions.

On 4 May, I was out of the hall tending the water supply. As usual, I was returned to the hall by my guards at about 12 noon. Stewart (Tooty) Morrison and I witnessed from the porch window the shooting down of the Sea Harrier flown by Lt Nick Taylor. During the day, Ray Robson and Bob McLeod salvaged an old radio receiver from a waste trap under the bar floor. They assembled a receiver; a test with Dolly Jaffray's torch battery proved it worked. That night, at 2300, groups of three were detailed to chatter at the windows of the teenagers' bar to blot out emissions from the BBC World Service. We were depressed by the news; the shooting down of the Sea Harrier was old hat, but we were shocked to hear about the Exocet missile strike on HMS *Sheffield*.

Skipping the events over many days, I pick up the story on Thursday 27 May. It was a busy day, tending to the wants of our people in the hall, getting stores for those now back in their homes and fuelling and tending the water pump. During the day, sirens warned of air attacks. I was out and about, at times taking cover under banks to evade rifle fire or cluster-bomb drops. At one point, I saw smoke from a Harrier. I saw what I thought to be an ejector seat tumbling to the ground north-west of my house. Loud cheering from the garrison marked this spectacle. I assumed from their joy that they had clobbered a Harrier. I recorded in my diary: 'I hope the brave lad landed safely and is cared for.' It was later confirmed that the pilot was Squadron Leader R. D. (Bob) Iveson, who came down near the only camp house I had provisioned for emergency evacuation of Goose Green. He later apologised for eating a can of Heinz Baked Beans from our cache while he watched the battle from an upstairs window in Paragon House.

On Friday 28 May, I recorded a mild, clear evening, followed by moderate rain at first, becoming heavy, making a cold, wet night for all concerned. Morning brought driving drizzle on a fresh, chilling wind from the north-west. A noisy battle raged all night to the north of Darwin and Goose Green. There was lots of shelling from ships in Grantham Sound – star shells and parachute flares lit up the sky and camp as bright as day. These illuminations were always followed by heavy gun, mortar and small-arms fire. This pattern of action continued all night.

I had a ringside seat as I watched the battle progress from the upstairs window above the sitting room. My wife and sons moved downstairs at 0400 hours. I moved down to the sitting room at 0430, then into the passage, before eventually taking shelter under the medical-room floor, through traps previously cut so we could lie at ground level, hopefully protected from incoming rubbish by the cement foundation wall.

Observing the progress of the battle from both sides, I saw the retreat of Argentine troops and some forward sorties along the beach towards the school. These were lead by Gomez Centurion, and I saw the last one as darkness fell.

I had had traps cut in the floors of houses occupied by civilians and for those still incarcerated in the Recreation Hall, allowing them to get below ground level should the going get tough.

In my house, all except Nanny McCullum (82 years of age) took refuge under the floor. At 0730, we had to strengthen the inside barricade, covering the hole in the cement foundation wall which had been made some days before to serve as an escape route should the house catch fire. The frightened and desperate conscripts sheltering around the house had tried to gain entry.

During the noise of the battle, a hungry Argentine soldier broke the scullery window and got in. Graham Morrison went above floor to check on Nan McCullum and fetch a jug of fresh water. He quickly returned to tell me that someone was in the pantry. I went up to investigate and found a dirty, dishevelled conscript spooning Fil-mil powdered milk into his mouth like there was no tomorrow. By sign language, he indicated his hunger, mollifying me by pointing to his FN rifle outside the back door by the broken window. I took him to the garage behind the house: a scraggy sheep carcass to feed my dog hung there. The starving lad cut off some chunks to eat, braising them over a field cooker. I found a piece of plywood and some nails to cover the broken window-pane and left this scared young man in the shelter of his new-found kitchen.

With the patch nailed in place over the broken window, I checked on Nan McCullum, under her covering of blankets and mattress to protect her from flying splinters. Then I joined the other nine below the floor.

At about 2200 hours, there was knocking on my office door. Turning out the lights, I opened the door and three Argentine soldiers bustled in. Once the door was shut, the lights were put on to reveal three dirty, worn men, who announced that the purpose of their call was to take me to the headquarters for a meeting. Willie Bowles recognised the Captain, who explained that his clay-dusty uniform was a result of crawling along the track from Darwin Hill back to Goose Green. With his command of Spanish, Willie insisted that the Captain stay to keep out others in my absence. This agreed, I left with my escorts. The Captain accepted a chair and a cup of coffee, and shortly fell into a deep sleep.

At Baillie's house, I was escorted into the dining room and seated at the large table. I was soon joined by Vice-Commodore Wilson Dosio Pedroza, his subordinate Vice-Commodore Oscar Varra, Lieutenant–Colonel Italo Angelo (Kojak) Piaggi, the Argentine Naval Lieutenant (call me George) Canevari Copevich and other senior ranks, making a total of 11 in all. Pedroza opened the meeting by asking how we could evacuate the civilian population out of the area of conflict. He then requested my help in making contact with the British troops nearby. I enquired: 'How close?'

'Very close,' he replied.

I suggested Darwin Boarding School. He said: 'Yes, but the school is no more, it has burnt down.'

I thought to myself: 'In that case, the front line must be only 400 metres away.'

After suggesting that they break into the field radio frequency, or go out and shout across the void ground, I directed my next idea to the Naval guy. I said that they should call on the international distress frequency from *Monsunen*. He responded quickly by saying that the bad British Harriers had shot up the radio system. (After the surrender, we found this not to be so. The radio was still operational.)

I then suggested that they return my 2-metre transceiver, although it would take some time to rig up an antenna. But because of earlier edicts on the dismantling of all antennas, it was unlikely that anyone would be on the air. Pedroza said they had a 2-metre on line upstairs. We all went up and there was Baillie's Yeasua on 147.000. I told them I would have to shift channel to the local call band 145.000. It was agreed that I do so. I opened by saying: 'This is Eric Goss calling from Goose Green – is there anyone listening out there?' To my surprise, Allan Miller, at Port San Carlos, came on enquiring how I was. I told him I was in the presence of all the foreign top brass who wished to make contact with the British forces nearby. To my question 'Is there any British officer there?', Alan asked: 'Do you have many little men in green jackets there?' I replied: 'By the present company I am in, it would be a military indiscretion to tell you.' Taking advantage of the circumstances, surrounded by very tired combatants, I speeded up my reply by saying: 'In excess of a grand.' This went unchallenged; Alan came back to say: 'Thanks. We got that in one, I now hand you over to the senior officer.' I never did find out to whom I spoke that night.

I stated that the Argentine officers in Goose Green wished to arrange a meeting with the British forces the next morning. Then came long periods of silence while a communication link was set up between Port San Carlos, British headquarters in San Carlos (probably a ship) and into Darwin Hill. The triangular link was slow. I was escorted back home but, every hour or two throughout the night, I was taken back to the radio room to confirm that the meeting in the morning was still on. It was a long night, with plenty coffee and little sleep.

At 0700 hours, I was once again escorted back from my home to the radio room to make sure that the meeting was still on. It was agreed that the officers of the two opposing units would meet at the airstrip flagpole at 0900 local time. I accompanied the three senior officers on a route south of the houses to a point past my house, where I paused to hand Pedroza a note I had written during a lull in communications, while my armed guard, Premier Teniente Kishomotto, a swarthy Japanese-like character who was built like a sumo wrestler, was asleep in his chair. I guess the battle wore heavy on him.

My note was addressed to Vice-Commodore Wilson Pedroza and Lieutenant-Colonel Piaggi. It was dated 29 May 1982.

'With the concern you show over the safety of civilians, can I now ask you to take this a step further and in view of the brave and courageous way your soldiers fought;

in the interest of saving the lives of such valiant soldiers on both sides – will you consider an honourable surrender? Britain and Argentina need these young men.'

This note was written on a page of Amateur Radio logbook paper at 0710 local time in indelible pencil, while I waited for Brigade headquarters to confirm that the meeting was still on schedule.

Halfway between my house and the iron gate off the green into the paddock known as the Near Race, I handed my note to Vice-Commodore Pedroza. He read it, then passed it to Lieutenant-Colonel Italo Piaggi, who, after reading it, passed it to Lieutenant Copevich, who took it upon himself to interpret it to the other officers. (Both of them had equal or as good a command of English as he did.) Copevich said it was none of my business and ordered me to go no further. They proceeded towards the airstrip hut to meet the two Argentine NCOs who had been sent forward from the British front line on Darwin Hill carrying a message in Spanish for them to agree a face-to-face meeting with the British officers.

The two POWs returned to Darwin gorse wall. At this time, I spotted two 'sneaky beakies' peering over the hedge at the three Argentine officers waiting by the flagpole.

Time passed, and then a group made their way down from the Darwin sod wall to the flagpole. Surrender was agreed. The opposing sides returned to their lines. Some hours passed while the various units assembled for the formal surrender, laying down their arms in the Near Race paddock, north-west of the farm garage.

I photographed the surrendering troops as they assembled and marched past. Piaggi had drunk too much gin and threw up as he passed me. Seeing my camera, he shouted: 'No photographs!' My retort was: 'You are not in charge now.' Another of his group shook his fist at me, shouting: 'We will be back!'

The first two in British camouflage whom I met and welcomed were the BBC reporter Robert Fox and David Norris from the *Daily Mail*.

The pace of life went into high gear. I was busy getting all Paras and 105 Gunners under cover. Major Neame and his group of seven set up HQ in my office. I came across Sergeant Alan Bullock throwing the contents out of the head shepherd's motorcycle garage. I asked him what he was up to. Making space to sleep under cover was his reply. With that, I showed him my conservatory, to provide shelter and warmth from the Rayburn that was plumbed in to heat the seedbeds. He soon had other Gunners sharing the floor space.

Major Chris Keeble, Major Roger Miller and the radio operator with all his field communication kit were accommodated in the house where Dave Smith, Nora and children had lived until being evicted on 1 May. That evening, Dave came to request permission to take some vegetables from his garden. Keeble told him to go ahead. Dave, ashen-faced, rushed back in saying that there were three bodies under the tree in his garden. Keeble, irritated by the interruption, retorted: 'I know, I had them put there – they are dead and won't hurt you. Go and get your swedes.'

Over the next few days, I checked out foxholes and trenches for dead bodies in the company of Reverend Peter Hudson, who flew in daily from HMS *Fearless* in bomb

alley. My 13-year-old son Morgan came with us in the farm Land Rover. The only Para we saw was on his back at the head of Fish Creek, near the milking shed. Morgan was shocked, and shouted: 'Look, Dad, there's one of ours.' Two Argentine dead lay close by, but he made no comment about them.

Meanwhile, Michael Minnell drove the tractor and trailer (known as the death cart), with Kevin Browning riding in support. A party of conscripts, escorted by Paratroopers, lifted the bodies on to the trailer and they were taken behind the gorse hedge near my house. Dave Smith and the mechanic Albert McLeod corrected the knobbling that had been done to our best tractor to put it out of order for use by the invading forces. When it was up and running, Dave drove the machine to Darwin Horse Park valley, where he excavated a trench in which to bury the 39 Argentine bodies collected from the battlefields. He also dug trenches for defence positions for the Parachute Regiment and the 1/7th Gurkha Rifles.

The involvement of MV *Monsunen* (the Falkland Islands Company coastal supply ship) began late afternoon on Sunday 23 May when, under Argentine command, she tied up at Goose Green jetty, where she remained until the push forward to take Stanley had begun. Lt-Col David de P Morgan, in command of 1/7th Duke of Edinburgh's Own Gurkha Rifle Company, approached me about the means of transport that were available. This drew my attention to the vessel at the jetty. Knowing that I had capable seamen on hand and an ex-engineer of the little ship (Mike Robson), I ran the idea first past Finlay Ferguson, our local skipper, and then past Mike Robson, who said that he could easily fire her up but that, before he went below deck, we should have the Explosive Ordnance party check her out for booby-traps.

Safety checks done, Bob and Janet McLeod in the sub-aqua kit cleared the rope fouling the propeller. Taking a full load of Gurkhas, they left at nightfall, bound for Fitzroy. Other members of the crew were Martin Ridge, Steve Ball, Gavin Browning and the engine-room assistant Brian Jaffray. At Fitzroy, Lt Ian McClaren RN and three ratings joined the ship. The voyages to Fitzroy carried JP1 fuel decanted from Argentine pillow tanks into 45-gallon steel drums, which were shipped to fuel British helicopters operating behind the forward lines, corralling the Argentine forces into Stanley.

On request from Brigadier Tony Wilson, an LCU Foxtrot 4 came from HMS *Fearless* to pick up some Land Rovers that were arriving in Goose Green on 8 June. When the vehicles were loaded, the coxswain ordered cast-off. Finlay suggested that he wait till dark, making passage in the company of the *Monsunen* to Fitzroy, but his orders did not permit delay. At midnight, the *Monsunen* came upon the drifting hulk of LCU *Foxtrot 4*, with one dead body aboard. After this incident, the Royal Navy commanders decided to put the 'kelper' crew ashore, sparing them from enemy attack.

I never once doubted that Prime Minister Margaret Thatcher would pussyfoot around sending a Task Force to repulse an invasion of British territory. My affectionate name for the Right Honourable Lady is 'Mother Falklands'. Not since Boadicea has Britain had such a fighting lady. My most humble and grateful thanks to her, all who supported the cause and those who sailed, fought and died for our freedom.

JIM DAVIDSON

Comedian

My first sight of the Falkland Islands was through the Pilot's window of a C130 Aircraft (Hercules) after an epic 13-hour flight from Ascension Island. We'd been refuelled mid-air by a VC10 tanker, which in itself was incredible. The pilot explained to me the way that they received the fuel. You see, a C130 is the old troop transporter known affectionately by all the troops in the RAF as "Fat Albert". She has 4 Turbo pop engines and a top speed of just over 20mph, or it seems like that when you're travelling to the Falklands! However, the fuel was on board a VC10 tanker. Now – work this one out! The fastest speed of a C130 is still slower than the slowest speed of a VC10 tanker. I said to the pilot "Well how do we get the fuel? Is he going to throw it back in bags?" He said "No, here's what we do: We climb to 28,000 ft – both aircraft – and then go into a shallow dive where the Victor tanker goes as slow as it can with all its airbrakes on and the C130 goes flat out to catch up. This lasts about 20 minutes as the pilot puts the probe of his fuelling tank into the basket of the VC10." It's quite an incredible thing to see, and set us up for our six hour journey onto Port Stanley.

I was very moved by the Falklands War. I suffered what was probably the same as everyone else – outrage at the fact that a British dependency had been conquered by a foreign country and the fact that on the news there were civilians from Port Stanley saying, "Would someone please come and help us?" and Margaret Thatcher's speech in the House of Commons that Saturday, saying a large task force would set sail, was both worrying and yet again sort of jingoistically marvellous really. The fact that we could still wave a big stick and say "How dare you pick on us!" made me feel part of Great Britain. "How dare you mess around with us! Go and pick on some weenie country like America or Russia but don't mess around with the Brits!".

I was moved beyond belief when HMS *Sheffield* was sunk on 4 May 1982. I was at a football match (as a Director of Bournemouth Football Club) and we were playing away at Wigan that day. At the time Wigan was under the chairmanship of Ken Bates, now with Chelsea. At half time Mr McDonald came on television and said that HMS *Sheffield* had been hit by an Argentine missile. I couldn't believe it. Just 2 days later we sunk the Argy Battlecruiser, the *Belgrano*. That dreadful headline in the *Sun* "Gotcha!", despite being in bad taste, I couldn't help thinking "yeah gotcha!" Ironically the *Belgrano* was one of the only ships that survived the raid on Pearl Harbour where she was called the USS *Phoenix* and of course being born from the ashes of her former self changed her name to *Belgrano* only to be sunk by HMS *Conqueror*.

Anyway, the war ended and that is history, even though the conflict has not ended really, with the boys still on patrol there, ever watchful for Argentinian movements. To go down there a year on was marvellous for me As the plane touched down I just felt exhilarated. I remember leaping with joy that I was actually standing on Port Stanley airstrip, and my mind was spread on, "Oh look at that aircraft and "oh look at those Phantom jets and "I'd like to see the bloody Argies try it now!"

We were met at Government House by General Keith Spacey, an ex-Para – a little wiry, heat-seeking whippet looking man, fit as a fiddle and his lovely wife. All very colonial and wonderful. Then I met someone who's remained a friend to this day, Sir Rex Hunt. What a marvellous chap he is and his lovely wife, Lady Mavis. They gave us a tour of Government House and showed us what was going on during the invasion. It was wonderful. Then for the first time I also got to meet the Falkland Islanders. I met Don Bonner, Sir Rex Hunt's marvellous chauffeur. When the Argentinian fleet was parked a mile off the shore and the Amtrax (that is the floating track vehicles, armoured personnel carriers) bringing the Argentinians ashore, Don Bonner ran into Sir Rex with his 12-bore shotgun and Sir Rex asked, "What are you going to do with that Don? He said, "I'm gonna sit by the flagpole and the first bastard that takes our flag down is gonna get it!" The great spirit of the Falkland Islanders.

I just adore the place, the wonderful fresh air. It was cold, in June 1983, when I went. I journeyed down to Goose Green and I walked the battlefield from the bottom of the Sussex Mountains all the way through to Darwin, and then into Goose Green where I did a show in a tiny assembly hall – like a town hall in many ways, where 128 of the locals were rounded up and captured by the Argentinians and made to stay there for a month, with one toilet. I met some wonderful people including Eric and Shirley Goss. Eric was the Settlement Manager during the war and has now moved down to Northarm. I just got to love these people. Nothing seemed to move them, nothing seemed to make them flap. A little corner of my heart is set aside for people from the Falkland Islands. In fact, I'm going back there this year, as Chairman of the British Forces Foundation, to make a little film for the BBC. In November I hope to accompany 300 veterans back there for the 20th anniversary of the conflict.

I don't quite know why the Falklands means so much to me. I think it's because I feel proud of being British and of our lads' achievements. I was so pleased to have met the Islanders and seen what it was all about. The right for them to choose their own democracy and choose who they're going to be governed by. It's a wonderful place and I'm looking forward to going back.

DAVID HART DYKE

Captain, HMS *Coventry*

The Falklands conflict showed that, as always in war, the critical factor is morale. High morale is the quality which makes men endure and show courage in times of fatigue and danger. It is this quality, not so much the advantage in numbers of men and weapons, that counts. And the cultivation of morale depends on good leadership, discipline, comradeship and devotion to a just cause.

The British Task Force had all those ingredients off the Falklands in 1982, and the enemy did not. We had confidence and the enemy did not. Our men never doubted that they would win and they could not wait to start the battle and then to get home after the victory. That is what made the Falklands such a total triumph.

First, let me go back to the beginning. Oddly, the most testing and frightening time for me was the period before the conflict started, as we sped south and prepared for war. It was a time of sobering self-examination and adjustment. Somehow you do have to remove yourself from the safe and familiar world of peace and come to terms with the largely unknown existence of real danger and violence. I found this far from easy.

The days of not knowing whether we had to fight or not – of listening to the BBC giving the latest reports on the chances of successful negotiations – were unnerving, mentally exhausting and for most people extremely hard to take. I suppose it was because we feared to go to war and to leave our safe and friendly world – maybe for ever.

These days were hard for me because I had to remain outwardly unafraid and cheerful in order to provide that much-needed strength of leadership for my ship's company. My men began to watch me more closely and listen to every word I uttered, such that any chink revealed in my armour would have considerably increased their anxiety and even, perhaps, reduced their will to fight. Their lives were in my hands and I could feel it. As the chances of a political settlement slipped away and war seemed a real possibility, we became somewhat concerned. A mood of anxiety pervaded the ship.

There was also the traumatic experience for many of preparing the ship for war;

HMS *Antelope* explodes in San Carlos Bay. A Bomb disposal man was attempting to defuse an Argentine bomb lodged in the ship's engine room when it exploded.

securing for action, for real. The issue of morphine, lifejackets and identity discs to wear around the neck, together with the removal of pictures, trophies and soft furnishings made a dramatic impact. Letters from home, thoughts of family and friends, heartfelt messages and telegrams wishing us good luck and a safe return all added to the tension and highlighted the risks ahead.

After three weeks of worry and uncertainty, it finally came as a great relief when it became clear that there was no option left but to fight. Our anger mounted against this harsh and unpredictable enemy, morale rose and we became united to a man in our purpose. The faint-hearted became strong, the ship's company as a whole stiffened to the tasks and we went headlong into battle, confident, and, outwardly at least, cheerful.

For myself, I was particularly thankful that I had a long experience at sea in destroyers and frigates. I was confident and did not find it difficult to go to war. I was surprised how very quickly I discarded all peacetime inhibitions and thinking. Many rules and regulations became irrelevant. My life suddenly became very straightforward and my aims crystal clear: they were aimed solely at getting at the enemy and surviving; and that concentrates your mind on essentials.

One essential to grasp very early on is that you are on your own. It is no use worrying the flagship with your problems or expecting a spare part to appear out of the sky to overcome this or that defect. You have to fix things yourself. We somehow fixed our long range radar in the middle of an air raid by nursing the elements of a toaster from the junior ratings' dining room. We used the steel legs of swivel chairs bolted to the floor of the helicopter to provide revolving machine gun mountings.

As we approached the war zone, the dangers and the challenges seemed to produce a step-up in ability overnight in most people. Young sub-lieutenants found themselves conning the ship while refuelling alongside a darkened tanker in the blackest of nights and in the dirtiest of weather, and they did it magnificently. The First Lieutenant often took command of the ship for a few hours in the night so that I could get some sleep.

This was a new experience for us all and until the first disaster occurred we could not begin to imagine what the horror of war was really like. Besides, there is always the hope that "it will never happen to you". Hopes such as this, however fragile in reality, are very strong in war; they actually keep you going, however dangerous the fighting might be, and they prevent you from anticipating or imagining what disasters could befall you, or indeed what the real risks are. This is a perilous state of mind which I suspect prevails among all but the really war-hardened.

The first few days of war were nervously exciting and cheers erupted throughout the ship when enemy aircraft were shot down. But we had not yet seen real war, we were naïve and far from being battle-hardy.

The real conflict started when we began to suffer losses ourselves. Attitudes then changed and our excitements and reactions became more measured and mature. We were quite close to HMS *Sheffield* when she was hit and the effect on my ship's company was devastating. Hardly a word was spoken for nearly 24 hours and people had to struggle to overcome their fears and emotions. At the end of that day my Petty

Officer Steward came into my cabin and with noticeable emotion remarked: "It has been a bad day today, sir." I replied: "Yes, it has been a bad day." That is all we could say and that was difficult enough. It was hard to talk without giving away one's fears, and our minds were too occupied. We were stunned.

This incident shocked us into reality and made us all realise how difficult it was going to be to bring our ships close to the enemy air force and land the army with all its equipment safely on the beaches of the Falkland Islands.

This was, after all, the only way to win the war. We were now rapidly becoming battle-hardened. Twenty four hours after that first tragedy, we were no longer gloomy, morale returned to a high point and we became even more determined to hit back at the enemy just as soon as we could.

Thoughts of getting home to a hero's welcome were highly motivating, and I became acutely aware that nearly 300 people were depending on me to get them home safely. I told them that my holiday was booked from 4 August and so we could have to be back by then; out of this statement arose an almost mystical belief that no matter what happened, we would get back by this time – because the Captain had said so.

After HMS *Sheffield* was sunk and HMS *Glasgow* put out of action, we shouldered more of the hazardous tasks. We were frequently deployed to the front line against the enemy air force and to protect the vital amphibious shipping in San Carlos Water. Our task was to control the Sea Harriers [carrier jet fighters] so as to get them poised in the right place to meet the incoming air raids and to use our Sea Dart missiles. It was clear that we had to draw the enemy fire away from our troops and to be sacrificed if necessary.

We only saw our friendly forces to the east of the Falklands when we refuelled or re-ammunitioned in the middle of the night. We always felt safe among the familiar dark silhouettes of the Task Force on these occasions and when we came to leave to return to our solitary post, we had to steel ourselves to do so and hide the fear at what the next day's battle might bring. When we had survived, the daytime darkness came to give us some measure of protection. I used to sit down in my cabin with a glass of port, a King Edward cigar and a Mozart symphony. That was sheer heaven!

During these last few hectic days we all knew the odds were against us emerging unscathed. We always knew that we might be hit from the air; it was just a question of where and how many casualties we would sustain. After all, several other ships already had been damaged. I frequently thought along these lines and I am sure most of my sailors did, but we never admitted it openly. That would have been demoralising. Conversations were brave and cheerful, and invariably confident that we would all get home safely. We were all strengthened by such reassuring talk, however much we inwardly believed that some of us might never get back.

I was shocked when a day or two before the end my First Lieutenant came into my cabin and with hesitation said: "You know, sir, some of us are not going to get back to Portsmouth." Although it disturbed me to hear him say that, it was very brave to admit to his captain what he really felt, and we now no longer had to pretend to each other about the risks we were taking. He included himself among those that would not return and in his last letter home he told his wife so. She received the letter just after she heard news of his death.

These were difficult days indeed, and I found it demoralising to wake each morning to beautiful, clear and sunny weather which favoured the enemy airforce and illuminated us sharply against the calm blue sea. I waited on the bridge, heavily clothed for protection against fire, life jacket and survival suit around my waist, ready for the next air warning signal. I then went down to the operations room to prepare to counter the threat. I then went down to the operations room to prepare to counter the threat. These moments demand considerable nerve and a brave face as men silently watch you go below wondering whether they would see you again.

Tuesday 25 May was one of those days. We had survived two air raids and shot down three aircraft with missiles. I responded to the next inevitable air raid warning nand went below with more feeling of fear than before. I paused momentarily at the top of the hatch and talked to the officer responsible for the missile system. I never saw him again. At 6pm precisely I pressed the action station alarm from the command position in the operations room.

We listened to the air battle and tried desperately hard to avoid losing the fast and low-flying enemy aircraft on radar and to predict where they were going next, so as to guide the Sea Harriers to the right place. It was like a fast-moving computer game, full of tension, all eyes strained and almost impossible to win. We knew we would lose if we could not keep up with the quickening pace. The pale and anxious faces told the whole story. I looked at the clock – it was nearly 6.15pm – and prayed that it would go faster to see out this last air raid of the day and bring on the night. The light was already beginning to fade as another brilliant sunset developed.

At 6.15pm we came up against a very brave and determined attack by four aircraft. We engaged with everything we had, from Sea Dart missiles to machine guns, and even rifles, but one of the aircraft got through, delivering three 1,000 pound bombs, which exploded deep down inside the ship. The severe damage caused immediate flooding and fire, and all power and communications were lost.

Within about 20 minutes the ship was upside down, her keel horizontal, a few feet above sea level. Later she sank. It is still remarkable to me that, but for the 19 men tragically killed by the blast of the bombs, some 280 of us got out of the ship – much of which was devastated inside and filled with thick suffocating smoke. I can only put that down to training, good discipline and high morale.

It was about 6.20pm when my world stopped. I was aware of a flash, heat and the crackling of the radar set in front of my face as it disintegrated. As I came to my senses nothing could be seen, except for people on fire, through the dense black smoke but I could sense the total devastation of the compartment. Those who were able took charge calmly and effectively. It seemed like an age, but when you are fighting for your life, the brain speeds up and time slows down, your actions and thoughts are very narrowly focused, enabling a precise concentration on the right priorities for survival.

At times like this pain, injury and freezing seas are not even distractions; they do not enter into your calculations or decision-making. There are more important matters to think about.

I could see no way out and was suffocating in the smoke. Ladders were gone and doors blocked by fire. I was calm, rational in my thoughts and quite prepared to die: there seemed no alternative. Then I suddenly found myself in clearer air and began my escape up twisted ladders, through heat and thickening smoke. When I eventually got to the upper deck, as the ship was beginning to roll over, I saw the ship's company abandoning ship. It was quite remarkably orderly and calm, looking just like another peacetime exercise. I am still trying to discover who gave the order to abandon ship! Perhaps no one did. People just very sensibly got on and did it. It was the only thing to do. When I had watched everyone jump into the sea and get into their liferafts, I walked down the ship's side, jumped the last two feet into the water and swam to the liferaft. My war was over.

When we were fighting for our lives and being rescued from the water, there were many brave deeds done by many of my sailors. A young officer directing the close range guns from the very exposed position of the bridge wings did not take cover when the enemy aircraft were closing at eye level and strafing the ship with cannon fire. He stood there for all to see and ordered the gun crews to stay at their posts and engage the enemy until he gave the order to stop. This order was not questioned by the very young sailors manning the guns, and they kept firing despite their totally exposed position. They remained at their posts, even though the ship was burning badly and listing steeply, in case of another attack. Eventually they were ordered to join the rest of the ship's company in abandoning ship.

Between decks, two Chief Petty Officers, separately and on their own initiative, revisited smoke-filled compartments when everyone else was on the upper deck and the ship listing dangerously to port; they ensured everyone still alive was got out of the ship. One found a senior rating unconscious, his clothes on fire and slumped over a hatch above the engine room. He got him to the upper deck and saved his life.

The other Chief Petty Officer managed to get two very frightened young sailors, trapped in a compartment, to climb past a large hole in the deck through which intense heat and flame was flaring. He saw them safely to the upper deck and saved their lives. This Chief Petty Officer then continued his search, totally alone, and by wriggling on his stomach to keep below the layers of suffocating smoke, looked into several spaces for survivors before saving himself and swimming to a liferaft.

It is, of course, terrible to lose a ship and some of your people, but it is made easier to bear when you have seen your officers and men, regardless of the dangers, being cheerful, fearless and totally dedicated to the ship and the cause for which they were fighting. It was an unforgettable privilege to have led such professional and brave men in action.

Since that fateful day I can say that I have learned a great deal about the effects of shock. The most immediate is that your are unable to appreciate what has really happened and you are therefore largely unaware of the horrific experience you have been through. This is nature's way of shielding you from the awful reality and protecting you until you are ready to know the full scope of the tragedy.

It is a process which takes considerable time and cannot be easily speeded up. It is like entering a narrow tunnel whose limited and close horizons can be seen and coped with, and which gradually widens as progress is made through it, until emerging at the other end with full consciousness and a normal appreciation of events in the real world. The tunnel was very narrow when I started the journey of rehabilitations on the night of 25 May and I finally came out at the other end.

It is only now, looking back, that I can fully realise what a traumatic and frightening experience I had been through. At the time you are so completely wound up and braced for war that everything is taken in your stride; fear and even disaster can be faced with not too much difficulty. Times of great stress that call for the hardest test of leadership are also comparatively easily coped with in the heat of war. But when it is suddenly all over, then it is impossible to adjust to an environment where there is no war and no requirement for decisions or leadership.

The City of Coventry presented my ship, when she was first commissioned, with a cross made from three large medieval nails from timbers of the roof of the Coventry Cathedral, which was destroyed by German bombers in 1941. When it came to preparing the ship for action, all such trophies were taken down and secured in a safe place. However, at the particular request of a young and rather frightened petty officer, I let this cross remain defiantly where it was. It had, I think, become a symbol of hope and survival for him, no doubt to many others as well at this time. Tragically, like the medieval cathedral our cross did not survive that day; but very many of us did.

ROGER EDWARD

Lt Cdr, Royal Navy & D Squadron, 22 SAS

In 1982 I had been appointed by CNOCS (Captain, Naval Operational Command Systems) to work on the EHI01 (the Merlin) Type 23 Frigate Computer Interface and as part of that brief I was attending a computer course at the Royal Naval Airship Station Cranwell, now claimed by the RAF as their College.

At this time my wife Norma and I, along with our two daughters Emma and Rebecca, were living in Dorset and so rather than drive all the way down to Dorset for the last weekend of the course I decide to visit Noleen and Alistair Sloggie in Lavenham. This was the weekend of 27/28 March. The Sloggies had been in the Falkland Islands when I had visited in the early 1970s aboard HMS *Endurance*. Alistair was the overall manager of the Falkland Islands Company which in those days owned about one third of the farming land, ran the only shipping line into and out of the islands and owned about 90% of the retail outlets in Stanley. One the Saturday evening Noleen had invited a few friends to dinner where Alistair stated he thought the scrap metal fiasco in South Georgia could well be the prelude to the Argentines invading the Falkland Islands. "What rubbish!" I declared. "It is just another cry wolf, just like the many before."

The following Friday afternoon (2 April) the course finished and I left RAF Cranwell to travel back home to West Dorset. I was staggered to hear on the radio that reports were coming in of an Argentine invasion of the Falkland Islands. At this stage the Foreign Office were still denying that any such thing had happened. When I eventually arrived home I found my wife in a very distressed state, worrying about her family still living in the islands. I resolved to clarify the situation and rang around a few naval colleagues and sure enough I discovered the Argentines had indeed invaded and a Task Force was at that very moment being assembled to sail to the South Atlantic.

I had only just left a flying post as Flight Commander, HMS *Argonaut*, with (then Captain) Kit Layman, at the end of December 1981, so I asked my old Squadron boss David Yates at Yeovilton and asked if there was any chance in getting involved with the

Captain Nicholas Barker, HMS *Endurance*, pictured in 1982.

Task Force. The thought of sitting behind a desk at Portsmouth when all my friends and colleagues went off to war was too much to handle. "No", he said, "we have 5 Lynx and their crews flying out tomorrow morning (Saturday 3 April) as far as Ascension Island, to back up the Spring Train fleet, and I can put you down as a first reserve". It was very late when I went to bed only to get a telephone call just after 3am in the morning asking me to come into Yeovilton there and then with all my kit. It appeared that one of the Lynx crew's family had problems and I was wanted to take his place. I explained that all my kit was at Portsmouth. "Don't worry", I was told, "come into Yeovilton as you are and we will arrange to collect your kit".

I disappeared into the loft to get what gear I had at home. The noise had woken the two girls who got up see what all the fuss was about. They arrived on the landing in time to see Daddy's Green Beret come floating down, followed by a naked Daddy. "What is Daddy doing?" asked Emma. "Going to war, I think", said Mummy. "Not like that, surely", said Emma.

We all set off to Yeovilton where we were all amazed to see every hangar and store open and Fleet Air Arm personnel rushing to and fro with armfuls of stores. Normally three chits and five signatures were required for a new pencil, now everything was open and it was almost Help Yourself.

I reported to the Squadron as briefed only to be told that a Wessex V was waiting at the base of the Control Tower to take me to collect my kit from HMS *Dryad* (home of the headquarters for the D Day landings). There were many surprised Officers at *Dryad* to be woken at some unearthly hour by a huge noisy lumbering helicopter landing on the lawn outside the Wardroom. It took only a few minutes to collect my gear and once more was airborne back to Yeovilton.

Back at Yeovilton I was instructed to draw a personal weapon from the Armoury and be in the Squadron by 0945. At 1000 I boarded an RAF Hercules and started the journey south.

Less than seven days from telling Alistair Sloggie he was well mistaken, I was on an a plane flying off to war in the Falkland Islands.

Our first stop was Gibraltar where we had to collect various stores etc. and then took off again for Ascension Island. As can be imagined we were all fairly excited and a little fearful as we climbed up to a cruising attitude of about 25,000 feet. Suddenly there was quite a loud bang followed by a rattle of 'machine gun fire' and the Hercules nosed down and plummeted towards the Atlantic Ocean. Adrenalin and fear was replaced with the realisation that the pressurisation valve in the fuselage had gone. The 'bang' was the loss of pressure and the 'machine gun fire' was the packets of crisps in our lunchboxes expanding and bursting. Not having oxygen masks for all the passengers like civilian airliners the aircraft had to descend to an altitude that was safe for us to breathe – i.e. below 8,000 feet. What excitement in the first few hours of setting off to war.

We returned to Gibraltar to effect repairs before continuing our journey South to Ascension.

We had a few days on Ascension Island putting the Lynx helicopters back together, test flying and sorting a mountain of kit before our first ship, Fort Austin, was due to arrive.

While there we first met up with some of the SAS who were due to join the force nominated to retake South Georgia. I and another Lynx crew had each served for two years on HMS *Endurance* and during this time had spent several months surveying in and around this glaciated island. (South Georgia is only as far south as Carlisle is north, but, being south of the Antarctic Convergence is two thirds covered with snow and ice the year round). Together we were able to put a little brief together explaining the climate was not at all like Norway where most of us had done our Arctic training, but much more violent and unpredictable, with very rapidly changing weather. This point was to be brought home to us in the not too distant future.

Eventually the RFA *Fort Austin* arrived and we embarked. Our first task was to rendezvous with the first of the ex Spring Train ships to resupply and store them prior to their proceeding south to the Falklands and South Georgia. Unfortunately one of the ship's Lynx helicopters had a major defect so the aircraft I had been allocated was transferred to this ship and we flew the broken one back to the RFA. I now had no helicopter.

Later we were to meet up with HMS *Endurance* and I asked if it would be possible to transfer ships as I might be of some use to them. I was told no.

We all know now of the story of the SAS sorties into South Georgia and the tragedy of the loss of two Wessex V helicopters and the superb efforts by Lt Cdr Ian Stanley which saved the lives of both the SAS troops and the crews of the two helicopters in the most appalling weather.

We were next to meet up with HMS *Brilliant* (Capt John Coward) who had two Lynx helicopters embarked and was being diverted to South Georgia to provide backup to the force after the loss of the two helicopters. When I asked Captain Coward if I could join him on *Brilliant* he agreed straight away. I transferred to a ship going to war from one that at that time we thought was going round and round in circles half way between Ascension Island and the Falklands.

As we approached South Georgia signals were picked up indicating that an Argentine Submarine was in the area and needed dealing with most urgently. The Type 22 Frigate, which *Brilliant* was the second class of, is an Anti Submarine frigate with superb systems and sonars, but surrounded by icebergs and bits of ice meant that the capability of the ship was somewhat limited.

At first light helicopter patrols were launched to search for this submarine. Once again Ian Stanley came to the fore, when, armed with old Second World War depth charges, he first spotted the submarine on the surface leaving Cumberland Bay. Ian carefully positioned himself behind the submarine and ignoring the small arms fire from the Conning Tower flew up the wake and dropped the two charges straddling the hull at amidships position. The two depth charges exploded under the stern of the *Santa Fe*, lifting the propellers clear of the water. The submarine turned about and returned to the jetty at

King Edward Point. Other attacks were subsequently launched against the *Santa Fe* but the damage had already been done and the threat had been eliminated.

Later, Captain Coward, a submariner, was to move the *Santa Fe* from King Edward Point Jetty to the disused jetty at Grytviken whaling station. During this move an incident occurred where a crewman of the *Santa Fe* was shot dead by a Royal Marine.

With the threat of the submarine out of the way it was decided to immediately launch the attack on the Argentine forces occupying King Edward Point and Grytviken. I acted as a crewman in one of Brilliant's Lynx helicopters and so am able to claim to have helped in the retaking of South Georgia. In fact the ships had put down such a barrage to cover the helicopter landing assault that by the time the first troops were on the ground white flags were already showing.

After South Georgia I was invited to join D Squadron, 22 SAS, as a liaison officer and to brief them on my knowledge of the Falkland Islands. My wife and I had travelled extensively all over the islands while I served on Endurance. The first job that arose was on Pebble Island.

By now we had transferred to HMS *Hermes* and some of the Sea Harriers flying 'recon' over the islands had reported being illuminated by radar while flying near Pebble Island. If indeed the Argentines had installed a radar site on Pebble they would have excellent coverage to the whole of the north of the islands, so it was essential that it was taken out.

A four man patrol was inserted into Pebble Island but instead of finding a radar installation, they discovered 11 Argentine aircraft occupying the island's airstrip. Quickly, a force was mobilised to take on this newfound threat and having briefed them as well as I could on the layout of the island and settlement I asked if I could land with them. Thankfully I was accepted so I blacked up my face and dripping with bombs and bullets waited for the helicopters that would take is from Hermes to Pebble. We boarded the helos and waited, only to be told a few minutes later that we were to disembark. We waited, feeling rather dejected, in the crew briefing room for news of when we would go. We were all smoking and drinking coffee when a young naval doctor popped in and told me smoking was bad for my health! I burst out laughing. Here we were, faces blacked, dripping with explosives and bullets all ready to land in the middle of the night on an island with several hundred well-armed enemy and he tells me smoking is bad for me.

Eventually *Hermes* had closed the Island, for we had been too far away for the helicopters, and were able to launch. After a flight of an hour or so we landed at Philips Cove on the South East side of Pebble Island. Instead of the planned six hours or so on the island we now had only about two as we had to get back to the *Hermes* for her to clear to the East, out of range of the Argentine bombers and fighters. With a destroyer standing offshore we dashed past the settlement onto the airstrip, placing our demolition charges on the 11 aircraft, the fuel dumps and stocks of ammunition.

We then beat a hasty retreat back towards the helicopter pick up point while the destroyer put down a barrage on to First Mountain. Looking back over our shoulders was a dramatic scene of shells bursting over the mountain and huge fires where there had once been aircraft, fuel and ammunition. It had been a total success, with no casualties on our side whatsoever. We landed back on *Hermes* just in time for breakfast.

Our next task was to cover the landings at San Carlos. It was decided that we should carry out a diversionary raid on the Argentine forces at Goose Green/Darwin. First we had to tranship for the *Intrepid*. I went across first to find accommodation etc for the following members of D Squadron. During the afternoon and evening men and stores steadily trickled into the ship. The last load of the day consisting mainly of men who had been loading the helicopters aboard *Hermes* crashed into the sea with the loss of 22 men. It was thought an engine failure due to bird strike was the cause.

We were landed to the East of Mount Usborne carrying huge weights of ammunition just after dark on the night of 20/21 May. After struggling down the mountain side we were spread out and given the tasks to open up at likely enemy positions surrounding Goose Green/Darwin. It was quite a racket and must have kept a lot of Argentines awake. Later it was reported the Argentines thought they were under attack by a full Battalion of troops. Having completed this task we set off to walk back up the west side of Mount Usborne and then on to the Sussex Mountains to join up with the Paras who were landing on 21 May.

About two hours after daybreak we were buzzed by an Argentine Pucara, which then pulled around as if to attack. Luckily we were carrying some Stinger missiles and the first missile fired tracked the aircraft and blew it out of the sky. We did not see the pilot escape, but later learned that he did eject and made his way safely back to his unit. Later in the day we were again buzzed by Pucaras and fired two further Stingers without luck. They in turn did not fire on us so we thought it a draw. We joined up with the Paras at about teatime and I don't mind admitting I was absolutely shattered.

D Squadron then established a base in one of the LSLs now occupying San Carlos Water. Two bombs, neither of which had exploded, had struck this one but it was not going anywhere. The purser used to turn up during air raids with two respirator bags, one with his respirator (gas mask), the other full of the ship's money. After one particularly hairy air raid he declared that the ship's freezers had some wonderful food in them and as the ship had been lucky twice he believed it would not be so lucky the third time so we should eat all the food. It was very strange sitting in the middle of a war dining on some of the very best food prepared and served by the excellent Chinese crew of the LSL. It was rumoured that at least one of the SAS patrols cut was cut short due to Fillet Steak being on the dinner menu.

As the troops pushed further towards Stanley our final task was to occupy Beagle Ridge, high ground to the North of Stanley searching out Targets of Opportunity by day and then calling down fire from ships that would move into Berkeley Sound by night. We established a camp only a mile or so from Argentine positions but when we moved in to attack them they had gone leaving lots of ration packs and other stores behind. It was here I discovered that Argentine soldiers got very inferior ration packs compared to their officers. I had only found soldiers' rations packs, but some of the troopers were dining in luxury from the officers' packs. From here a raid was under-taken on the north side of Navy Point in an attempt to ease the pressure on the troops fighting on Wireless Ridge. The SBS boats were illuminated by an Argentine Red Cross ship in Port William and it all turned into a can of worms, but fortunately only two of our men were wounded, neither very severely.

It was on Beagle Ridge that we learnt of the surrender of the occupying Argentine forces and we had an excellent vantage point to watch the British troops move forward into Stanley and watch the defeated Argentines stream out of Stanley towards the airport.

Several days later I managed to cadge a lift with a few D Squadron lads out to Saunders Island where my wife's Uncle was the farm manager. Through a friend of his in the UK, a keen radio Ham, we were all able to either speak directly to our wives or pass a message to them. While there we shot several Upland geese, and, flying back to the LSL via Fox Bay, we were able to liberate a case of good Argentine wine and half a case of Bols Geneve from an Argentine supply vessel strafed while alongside the jetty. We had a victory dinner that night to be proud of.

I arrived back in the UK about a week after the Argentine forces had surrendered, arriving at RAF Lyneham at 3am. It was wonderful to see my family again but I was about to lose my new SAS family and return to the drudgery of computers and office life.

CHARLES LAURENCE

Journalist

The sign of the Upland Goose is swinging in the stiff South Atlantic wind, just as it always did. The old shipwrecks - and here at Port Stanley on that faraway stage of British adventure, the Falkland Islands, they still have wooden hulks in their harbour poke their ribs from the water – and the Giant Petrels wheel and turn as if far out to sea without a thought for human colony.

It will be 20 years on June 14th since I last stepped up the short path to the plain wooden door of the Goose, and pushed it open in search of a room. That was the day the Argentinian army of occupation bolted their bunkers and raised the white flag. A military junta, 'Stick It Up Your Junta', in the tabloid language of the day had decided to solve an old sovereignty dispute by liberating their Islas Malvinas from the yoke of British colonial rule. But we were back. We had won.

To look up and down Ross Road on the harbour front, to count the sea-beaten old cottages standing between the water and the rolling wilderness of peat-bog and crag beyond, to take the measure of commerce, government and population, is to chuckle all over again at the evident absurdity of the war fought here.

But it is equally to open the door to a cascade of memories and meanings, histories both national and personal, that are sure to visit anyone who was here back in 1982, whether warrior, local Kelper or just one of the small party of British hacks who had sailed from Southampton three months earlier to find themselves, well, here.

In the coming months as anniversary celebrations from Royal visits to sentimental medal tours of aging sailors, soldiers and Royal Marine Commandos unfold, strange thoughts and reckonings will be back in British living rooms too. The war in the Falklands saved a small and exceptionally remote settlement from hi-jacking by the force of Argentine arms. It also restored a large measure of national self-confidence at home. Mrs Thatcher and her government were charged by victory to full reforming power strikers and socialists of all stripes walloped by the Falklands Spirit and the conflict has even been credited with sounding the starting gun to British recovery.

That is the macro view, but in the doorway of the Goose it is inescapably micro. I ding the brass bell for service, and cannot miss the same old smell of chip-pan oil. There is still the bizarre sensation of travelling 8,000 miles only to land at a B & B in the Scottish moors. This time, there is electric light and central heating. Candles and peat-fired stoves were all that were left functioning at the end of the battle for Stanley but it is the same narrow, creaking staircase with the 'mind your head' sign leading to the bedrooms in the tin-roofed eaves. I unfurl an old, cracked map and pin it to the wardrobe.

Lines of black ink mark the route of the yomp, the forced march I followed over soggy bog and ankle-turning tussock and which prompted a dispatch which put a word into the dictionary. Yomping, they call it in the Royal Marine Commandos, I had written, and it turns out to be the secret weapon of the Falklands war. True: yomping remains the best measure of the power of the individual commando and paratrooper, the training, strength and sheer guts which did more than anything to win a land battle against the odds.

I peer out of the window, past the memorial made of the mizzen mast of Brunel's SS *Great Britain*, brew a cuppa, and lean back to savour the place names on my map: Ajax Bay, Red Beach at San Carlos where 45 Commando, my Yompers, had stormed ashore as if in a scene from Normandy; Douglas Settlement, Teal Inlet, Top Malo, Estancia House, Mount Kent close to Stanley now Two Sisters, Sapper Hill and, finally, the road from Moody Brook past the racecourse to the Upland Goose. Where, I wonder, are Pat Chapman, Ian Gardiner, Diesel Bill Bailey and all, commandos to whom I owe favours of survival I can never repay? It is so very strange to be back. Twenty years matches the time span between 1945 and 1965, from VE Day to Swinging London, and the changes wrought since 1982 have been at least as great. But battle-fields hold their ghosts.

The ghosts, indeed, turn out to have San Carlos pretty much to themselves. This is the place where the Brits landed, and where our spindly post-imperial Armada came close to being shot out of the water by the Argentine airforce. The details belong to the military historians. Think of the haunting photograph of the frigate Antelope sinking into the sound below its plume of acrid smoke but it turned out to be the crucial battle of the war, our survival in itself the turning point.

It was also the place where we discovered that the Falklands can look stunningly beautiful on a clear day, but then turn in a just a few moments to the blasted heath of Shakespeare's darkest imagination. The wind howls and the sky falls. The locals, knowing that a future under the Union flag must depend on the sentiment of voters back home, have become terribly sensitive to the cliched description of their islands, a total land mass about the size of Wales, as bleak and desolate. But as anyone who has bivouaced under those Southern constellations will attest, they can be truly, truly bleak and desolate, and very close to barren, too.

The British dead outnumber the living islanders at San Carlos now because it is here that we built our cemetery for the two-dozen bodies left behind. They include the

A street in Stanley pictured in June 1982. The road surface had suffered due to
heavy military traffic.

Parachute Regiments Col. H Jones who commanded the attack on Goose Green, the first big land battle, and was awarded a posthumous V.C. for personally, and probably foolishly, storming an enemy trench. He and his troop of seaman and soldiers and helicopter pilots will command the hillside at San Carlos for as long as the War Graves Commission continues to draw a budget. But the Falkland Islanders who rose from their beds to greet us – 'We knew someone would turn up sooner or later', they had said – have mostly gone.

This is where the changes start: there is no need to yomp from San Carlos now, because there is a road. It is a dirt road, and it involves a lot of leaping in and out to open and close gates, but it is road that will bear a wheeled vehicle. This is as revolutionary to the Falklands as it would have been to lonely spots of Europe reached by the Romans. And the roads came with another revolution: land reform. The Task Force sailed to islands where the farms would better have been described as estates, most of them owned by absentee shareholders wholly dedicated to raising wool for export. All areas outside Stanley are still known as camp, for Campos, a revealing term with its echos of great South American feudal estates. The manager controlled all, and nobody owned their own home. The place was run by the sheepocracy: I was amazed to discover that Alastair Cameron, the last squire of Port San Carlos who had died in a post-war car accident, had narrowly missed coinciding with the Prince of Wales at Cheam, and had gone on to Eton.

The farms, and the total flock of 700,000 sheep, have been broken up as the government buys-out absentees: there are now 86 farms, where once there were 43. But the price of wool has collapsed, and the roads have been used mostly for one-way trips to Stanley. The islands have turned into a classic example of urban drift: in 1982, the population was divided roughly in half between town and camp: now, there are 340 in camp and 2,380 in town, not including the 530 civilians imported to run the military's new barracks at the Mount Pleasant airfield.

'It's all changed, that's sure', says Ben Minnell, who is 67 and living, retired but still helping out when needed, in a farm cottage at San Carlos. The roads are good, but they have spoiled things. His wife, Hazel, puts on the kettle for tea and produces home-made chocolate cup-cakes. Later, I find a Falklands Wool sweater in a gift shop in Stanley with a label reading: 'Hand Knit by Hazel Minnell'. It seems a bit odd to hear a kettle whistle without a smell of peat burning in the stove: even out here, the old ways of cutting peat has been replaced by oil.

The same gift shop – souvenirs, in Stanley! – produced a copy of 'Cooking the Falkland Island Way', a compilation by Tim Simpson, a post-war émigré, of domestic history and pioneer recipes involving Upland geese, penguin eggs and mutton. Local cooking has become a heritage cuisine, and there could be no clearer proof that while the Queen may still be sovereign, the old island way has gone forever.

'Used to be the best thing about life out here was the Farm Get Togethers', Minnell goes on. 'Because it would be a day's ride on horseback to anywhere, the dances and sports would go on all weekend. And even with the Land Rovers, when they came, getting bogged and rescued was part of the fun. You never had such a time in your life as back then'. He takes a long pull from a can of beer. I have noticed a large pile of them in the back yard, by the old outhouse and the new plastic oil drum. You cannot burn beer cans or feed them to the chickens, and so far at least, there is no round of bin men with recycling bags.

Camp is dying, but Stanley is booming. You can tell that right away by the Land Rovers. They are everywhere. Old patched-up farm vehicles, customised jobs with double back wheels for the peat bogs, brand new Defenders and spanking Range Rovers, they have, somehow, become the yardstick of unlikely prosperity. There is an old Morris Minor still puttering about, and the occasional wife in a Suzuki, but the Land Rover is the vehicle of choice and the measure of status. There are, I am told, 1,100 in the population of less than 3,000, a concentration to make the Cotswolds look cheap..

They drive past such novel signs as SLOW! MINEFIELD, spitting stones from the dirt road at each others' windscreens. Rough-country pioneering and the military necessity of the 2,500 strong garrison at the pre-fab city of Mount Pleasant have created a quirky Falklands Chic of wind-burn, camo-jackets, and Defenders.

There are no mobile phones, at least not yet, but direct dialling to London has replaced the old one-crank-for-the-next-farm-down-the-wire system of 1982 and not far from the souvenir shop is the Hard Disk Café where, for a price, a customer can plug into the Internet and the world.

When change comes so fast, there can be a disconnect in the mind: islander after islander tells me at the bar of the Goose that a top reason to be here is to see their children run safely through the streets, free to enjoy a childhood. But 100 yards down the road Mr Justice Wood, flown in from London in the old colonial way, is sitting in scarlet robes to sentence Kenneth William Duval, 22, to five years in jail for raping a child, buggery and forced oral sex. He turns out to have been the home-grown paedophile, taking children off the streets as they walked to and from school.' At least we have lanced the boil', says John Fowler, once the primary school teacher and now the tourism manager. A few years ago, it would have been swept under the carpet. Duval, a dim looking young man with a silver earring, uncomfortable in his Sunday-best and still denying everything, was led over the street to the Victorian jailblock the size of a garage.

'The important point is that these islands are very different from 1982', says Donald Lamont, the Governor. 'When the Argentinians felt they could invade, there was economic decline and a dwindling population. Now, we are prosperous and forward looking'. Lamont, who moves on next autumn, was met with some suspicion by the islanders. All representatives of the Foreign Office are considered dubious. The FCO was accused of trying to give the Falklands away before the Argentine Junta made the mistake of grabbing them without permission but Lamont, islanders noticed, can speak Spanish. Who, they wonder, has he been talking to in that foreign tongue? From the Whitehall point of view, managing the legacy of the Task Force's victory has been like riding a wobbly bicycle, simply because Argentina continues to claim the islands, and

Britain continues to struggle to find a reason to keep them.

'Have you noticed', Lamont asks, 'how people here refer to our country?' Now that he mentions it, I have. It might boggle the imagination, but with the islands running a subsidy-free economy apart, of course, from the defence budget the locals seem to be thinking of themselves as in some way independent. Richard Cockwell, for instance, a powerhouse councillor and former farm manager, talks of the need to get out from under the shoulder of the Foreign Office. 'We run our own lives now', he says.

Off-shore oil has been found, but not yet exploited. The source of all the prosperity is fishing: after 1982, someone had the bright idea of using the presence of the Royal Navy to declare territorial waters for 200 miles around the islands, and then start selling fishing licences. That brings in a handy £29 million a year. The islanders are famously frugal, and their pot is big enough to have built a new school and a new hospital, and to fund mainland education for any child bright enough for A-levels and university. There is no unemployment, and more than 40 per cent are on the public payroll. All the old sheepocracy, local lore insists, have become millionaires.

It is the islands' own navy which may be pointing the way to the future, at least in dreams. If you are going to live on fishing licences, you must be able to enforce them, and that is what Cockwell, head of the fishery department, decided to do. He bought a boat, the Dorada, and fitted it with a 20mm Bofors gun. It has been fired in anger twice, and a Chilean boat rests among the wrecks in Stanley harbour as a warning to all. 'The gun boat flies our flag, and there was a huge rumpus about it', says Cockwell. 'But I could see it was the only solution.'

'Argies beware: Falkland Islanders never, never will be slaves. Fillaballoo!' says Don Bonner, in his 70s now and famed thoughout the island as the Governor's butler and chauffeur for 20 years. It was he who drove Sir Rex Hunt to exile, in his London taxi and fully decked out in plumed hat, and who then drove him back again. I have met him in the graveyard; he is now guiding my quest for the oldest headstones, and we have found one commemorating the deaths of all five of a pioneering couple's infant sons.

'Fillaballoo! What does it mean?' he goes on. 'It's a word my father used; it means putting your head in the ground and breaking wind, loudly! And that is what you have been listening to, my boy!' Bonner is a Falkland Islander of a slightly different hue. His name goes back to the first British settlements in the early 19th century. Basically, he says, they were a bunch of pirates, seamen who jumped ship for a girl and who, like Cornish Wreckers, lived off bonanzas limping into harbour from the storms of The Horn. He points to the wreck of the iron-hulled *Elizabeth*, beached in the sound, and tells me that all the wood for the cottages of Stanley came from her holds.

When the Argentinians ran up their flag at Government House, Bonner the butler took up his twelve bore and tried to shoot it down again. But in his heart, he thinks all this talk of sovereignty and independence and co-relationships is fillaballoo because life on an archipelago of wild islands, as close to the South Pole as the Hebrides are to the North, is simply about survival. 'Know what? If those Argies had just sent in a couple of boat loads of pretty girls and handsome fellers, they'd have these bloody island by now!'

This thought horrifies Patrick Watts, a man with buccaneering blood in his veins too, and of whom Bonner has warned me that he was a dirty football player aggressive, like. He is better known as the one-man radio station awarded an MBE and a place in broadcasting history as the fellow who would not stop until an Argie had a gun in his back. Anyone who seriously doubts the British nature of the islands should read the transcript of Watts' last broadcast: 'Do you want to speak with the people?' he asks of an invading Capitaine. 'Tell them to wait alongside their receivers. In some minutes the chief is going to communicate them what we want for the population', replies the captain. There is a great deal of shouting in the background: the captain screams at his men: 'Senors! Senors! Un minuto, un minuto!'

And then Watts' voice comes back: 'Well, if you take the gun out of my back, then I will transmit your messages, if you take the gun away. But I am not speaking with a gun at my back.' He goes on to feed a telephone call from the Governor directly into the microphone for broadcast to the islanders, while the Argentines retreated to the corridor to decide, Ealing Comedy style, whether they should shoot him.

They did not, and now I find Watts living in the new Stanley in one of the imported kit houses that have almost doubled the housing stock and made parts of the village look a bit like Essex. He has retired from the radio station to a civil service pension, and is picking up cash as a knowledgeable guide for tourists.

We decide to go yomping over the battlefields of Mount Longdon and Two Sisters, and in search of a site on Mount Kent, the Commandos assault base for Stanley and the destination of our 65 mile slog through the bogs and stone-runs and sudden, brief blizzards of a South Atlantic winter. Time unravels. It is astonishing to find Argentine boots simply left in their trenches, rusting ammunition boxes, the bones of sheep stolen and slaughtered for rations, and even the soggy remains of sleeping bags abandoned below the shelter of rocks twenty years ago. On top of Longdon the British have installed a stainless steel cross and a marble slab on the spot where Sgt Ian McKay secured the second VC of the campaign. Looking at the site in cold day light, you wonder where the man got the energy to rush the rocky crag protecting a machine gun nest, let alone the courage to brave the fire. It seems more sad than glorious.

'You know we all feel guilty, don't you?' muses Watts. 'I don't think people understand how guilty we feel that you lost husbands and brothers and fathers and sons, just for us'. And he is angry too, angry at what the islanders see as a brutish and simply stupid Argentine adventure. They believe that they lost a good part of an aging generation to the stress and despair of invasion. One old lady never left her cottage again. Watts' own mother, who had made tea for Jeremy Moore, the British commanding officer, and given him aspirin for his cold on the victory night in Stanley, is believed to have died ten years before her time. 'We will have nothing to do with Argentina again while we live', he says, and it as simple as that.

But is it? Before I leave the Falklands, I decide that I simply must see a penguin. If anyone had heard of the islands before the war, it was for the penguins, and yet throughout the conflict I had caught not so much as a glimpse. So Watts drives me to the far end of a dirt track, and for miles across the turf to a lonely beach with a single shepherd's cottage at Volunteer Point. It is the top destination for adventure tours and every year, a few hundred make the trek to a legendary penguin breeding ground. Kings and Gentoos and Magellanics, birds who burrow to make nests, all live in dense colonies side by side, fussing about the beaches like bathers at Blackpool in a comedy of nature. It is enchanting.

It is only as I am leaving the islands that I bump into a young researcher who tells me that in the twenty years since the war the penguin population has plunged by as much as 80 per cent. It is a shocking figure: breeding grounds have been lost to mine fields and the rambling feet of cruise ship passengers, and perhaps to the warming Antarctic climate too. But the biologists suspect that there is one reason above all others: the fishing bonanza has left them hungry. The young researcher added another detail, quietly, so as not to be overheard: he is on a counting mission, and is finding some of his birds turning-up on the coast of Argentina. Traitors!

Prince Andrew ashore in Stanley at the end of the war.

TAM DALYELL

Labour Member of Parliament, 1962–

I firstly became deeply interested in the Falklands on a balmy evening in 1976, when, as leader of the Inter Parliamentary Union to Brazil, I sat next to the then Governor of Rio de Janeiro. His name was Admiral Faria Lima. He said quietly and sincerely to me: "I really have no taste for the military government of Argentina, some of whose members I know personally. But, you on the British delegation ought to realise that we in Brazil think that the Malvinas have far more to do with South America than with a European country 8,000 miles away. When you go back to Parliament in London, tell them that unless changes are made in the Malvinas situation, there will be unwelcome trouble." Faria Lima registered with me when James Callaghan, as Foreign Secretary, asked me to sit in for him on Foreign Office talks with the islanders. I was chairman of the Parliamentary Labour Party Foreign Affairs Group at the time. I was appalled. Here were islanders, having hired Leolin Price QC to help them, lambasting the Argentines. Yet many of them owned land in Patagonia, had been educated at schools of the 100,000 strong Anglo-Argentine community, received their healthcare in Buenos Aires, and were largely victualled from the South American mainland. Why the vitriol? In the Christmas holiday before he tragically died, Foreign Secretary Tony Crosland, according to his widow and biographer Susan Barnes, had been determined to reach a settlement with Argentina. Subsequently, Nicholas Ridley, then one of Margaret Thatcher's Foreign office Ministers, had been disgracefully mauled by the Opposition Front Bench, Peter Shore in particular, and some of his colleagues, Bernard Braine to the fore, when he tried to reach a constructive solution. Rancour and ignorance prevailed. Against this background, on 3 April 1982, as Labour Party Science spokesman, I hastened in the early morning to see Michael Foot, the Leader of the Opposition, before the fateful Saturday morning debate. "Michael," I said, "I know more about South America than you do. Michael, I know more about military technology than you do. There are huge dangers in giving the Labour Party's imprimatur to military action!"

"Tam," Michael replied, "I know more about fascism than you do!"

For Michael Foot, Leopoldo Galtieri was Benito Mussolini incarnate.

I had no more success with Margaret Thatcher. On 20 April, Roy Jenkins, recently returned by Glasgow Hillhead, asked her: "In view of the string all-party support that the Government have rightly received during the past two and a half weeks, will the Prime Minister bear in mind that she will be expected to take future, I hope and believe, un-rushed decisions in an equally non-party way? Does she agree that that demands more than merely asking the right hon Gentleman, the Paymaster General, as chairman of the Conservative Party, to a meeting of senior ministers last night?"

The Prime Minister replied: "If the right hon Gentleman wishes to see me – I am sure the same applies to my right hon Friend the Foreign Secretary – about this matter I am always available to see hon Members on these important issues."

On the strength of what she said, I, to the subsequent annoyance of my front bench colleagues, asked to see her. To her credit, she saw me with the late and much missed Ian Gow, in her room at 9.30pm on 21st April. The conversation went like this…

"Margaret, it is good of you to see me!"

"Tam, I always have time for the awkward squad!"

"My concern stems from the despair of my mother in childhood when friends of her on HMS *Prince of Wales* and HMS *Repulse* went down. Capital ships against land-based aircraft."

"I know. One of my chief advisers is Admiral of the Fleet, Sir Henry Leach, the son of Captain Leach, who went down on the *Prince of Wales*."

Then she became very vehement. So much so, that I went back to my sceptical colleagues and said: "That lady does not want to be deprived of battle. What she is about now is military victory!"

Subsequently I discovered I was not wrong. Cecil Parkinson had the same impression on 18 April. Sara Keays writes in her memoirs, "A Question of Judgement":

> On Sunday 18 April, Cecil came to see me very late and rather angry. It was the only time I heard him make a serious criticism of the Prime Minister, for whom he had great admiration, being deeply impressed by her courage and determination. He was infuriated by an exchange he had had with her at a meeting of the Inner Cabinet with the Chiefs of Staff. When he had expressed his concern about the risks attendant on a particular course of action, one of several under consideration, she had rounded on him with words to the effect that there was no room for faint-hearts in the Inner Cabinet. I thought it a very telling incident. If the Prime Minister's closest colleagues could not feel free to express their opinions to her absolutely frankly, they could be of no use to her at all. When I next saw Cecil, he had put the incident behind him. The rift with the Prime Minister had been only temporary and eventually he became her close confidant.

For Margaret Thatcher, the Falklands was more about her survival as Prime Minister in particular, and British politics in general, rather than the problems of the South Atlantic.

Though day in day out I opposed the despatch of the Task Force, I did not complain about the sinking of the Belgrano until 7 July 1982, when the submarine *Conqueror* returned and the Captain revealed that he had sunk the Argentine cruiser on orders from Northwood. This was a different story than that given in early May to Parliament, Press and People. The precise untruth that Mrs Thatcher told was that she did not know about the Peruvian peace proposals until after orders had been given for the sinking of the Belgrano. By that time, it was clear that she did not want to be deprived of battle and military victory for domestic political reasons.

Argentine troops who died during the battle for Goose Green.

T O N Y   M cN A L L Y

Royal Artillery

I was looking forward to going on Easter leave, when it came on the news that Argentina had invaded an island off the coast of Scotland – or at least, that's where we all thought the Falklands must be. I was a 19-year-old Gunner with T Battery 12th Air Defence Regt Royal Artillery and I was going 8,000 miles to war.

On Saturday 3 April 1982, we set off from our sleepy village base of Kirton Lindsey on the long 16-hour drive aboard shagged-out white army buses to the docks in Plymouth. We all felt like heroes already as the public beeped their car horns and waved Union Jacks at us. We now knew where the Falklands were on the map and we were going to kick some Spick arses. The only trouble was, they would be flying American, French, Italian and even British aircraft, which we had spent years learning as the good guys in aircraft recognition. In 1982, the Soviet Union was very much the enemy we were trained to face.

We loaded all our Rapier missiles and equipment and, of course, ourselves on to an old flat-bottomed troop ship called RFA *Sir Geraint*. We seemed to load more cases of beer than anything else – well, after all, it promised to be a long voyage. We were kept very busy on board ship learning Argentine aircraft, A4 Skyhawks, Mirages, Pucara and Aeromachi MB 339. We were part of 3 Commando Brigade and 79 Commando Battery were on board. They lovingly referred to us as 'crap hats' because we never had a green or red beret; they were simply 'cabbage heads' to us, in reference to their green berets. The 'cabbage heads' taught us a great deal about surviving in arctic conditions, how to build snow holes and what to look out for with hypothermia, as well as how to drink more beer than us and sing louder Regimental songs.

We were happy to get into more tropical waters after a bout of extremely bad sea sickness in the Bay of Biscay, where most of us had to have injections to stop us throwing up. We would be amazed watching the dolphins and flying fish in the clear blue ocean. Sunbathing was all the rage. Just one minor problem: who would have packed sunscreen to go to the frozen Falklands?

Survivors come ashore at Bluff Cove after two British landing ships, *Sir Tristram* and *Sir Galahad*, suffered air attacks.

Our bodies belonged to the Army and we were in trouble if we damaged them. Several Gunners were fined a day's pay for being sunburnt. As a deterrent, they made us do PT and leapfrog over each other's blistered backs.

After stopping off at Ascension, being at sea during the sinking of the Argentine cruiser *Belgrano* with the deaths of 350 sailors and then the loss of HMS *Sheffield* by an Exocet missile built in my home town of Barrow, I was glad to get to our destination, Port San Carlos, and the start of 'Operation Corporate' and the liberation of the Falkland Islands.

The first action I witnessed on D-Day was a lone Pucara strafing our ships before being shot down. Then we lost two helicopters, shot down by Argentine machine-gun fire. One of the Gazelles crashed into the sea and the pilots were machine-gunned in the water. The second Gazelle was hit and exploded into the San Carlos hillside with the loss of the crew.

At end of the first day, we had brought 3,000 men ashore, practically unopposed, as the Argentines had expected us to land at Port Stanley.

After our detachment had landed, we got into action as soon as possible to give our troops air-defence cover. Our radios soon blared out: 'Air Raid Warning – Red eight bogies coming west through the Sound.'

The first warning of an imminent attack was the enormous sound of all the anti-aircraft guns on the ships opening up. I was sat in the tracker seat sweating – even though it was freezing cold – through my bone dome (helmet). I got the alarm signal and went through my drill that I had simulated many times in Germany: 'ALARM NARROW TARGET TRACKING HOSTILE INCOVER.' Out of the seven or so enemy aircraft, I picked out one and had my cross-hairs lined up on the Mirage fuselage.

Bob, my Sergeant, ordered 'ENGAGE', and I pressed the fire button with my left-hand index finger. There was a loud bang as the missile left its beam only to go wildly out of control and explode into the ground. The second and third missiles were 'rogue' (faulty) as well. I acquired another target – a bright white Naval A4 Skyhawk – and engaged. This missile gathered correctly and hit the Skyhawk head on, exploding it spectacularly in a huge ball of flame. At this moment, you don't think of the pilot sitting in the cockpit; the aircraft is just a weapons platform and it is trying to kill you and your mates. Several Royal Marines nearby cheered and threw their berets in the air in celebration.

This was the routine that went on for days. Dozens of enemy sorties attacked the shipping in the Sound, with some success, until the Argentines were simply running out of aircraft. As well as us shooting them down, they had to fight it out with our RAF Harriers with their newly acquired 'sidewinder missiles'. The Skyhawks and Mirages were no match for them.

I was lucky also to shoot down a Mirage at San Carlos, but then we developed a fault with the tracker. If our Rapier had been working better, we would surely have had more kills. The long sea journey and the battering it suffered in the hold of the ship had taken their toll. T Battery was credited with more than 20 kills after the war.

On the night of 7 June, we were tasked to travel with the Welsh Guards on board the troop ship *Sir Galahad* to a place called Bluff Cove. The next morning, we arrived at Port Pleasant, of all places, and weighed anchor. Having seen the devastation caused by enemy aircraft at San Carlos, I wasn't too happy to be bobbing around in broad daylight like a sitting duck. After a very unnecessary delay while the CO of the Guards argued that he wasn't getting off there as it was not his destination, we finally started to get the men and ammunition ashore. We landed among the 'Maroon machine' of 2 Para and ran around like ants on LSD to get the Rapier up and running. In record time, we were operational and looking for targets; we didn't have long to wait.

Once or twice, I got the system-fault tone in my helmet, which didn't fill me with confidence. I was sitting in the tracker seat looking through the optics out to sea when my heart skipped a beat and I could clearly see several enemy aircraft heading towards us at very low level and high speed; we hadn't received any radio warning this time.

'ALARM NARROW TARGET TRACKING HOSTILE INCOVER.'

Bob screamed: 'ENGAGE.'

I pressed the fire button but nothing happened. I had to sit there and watch the *Sir Galahad* explode like watching a movie. It was the most sickening moment in my life. The equipment was useless and I felt sure that we were all going to die. We were defenceless against enemy air attack. I jumped into a nearby trench and waited for them to come back and finish us off. By this time, the casualties were coming ashore, horrifically burnt, some with limbs missing, and I felt so guilty that my missile hadn't fired.

The whole attack was over in seconds; 50 men were killed, and hundreds were mutilated and burnt beyond belief.

But it wasn't over. We could hear the horrible sound of jet engines again. One of the other lads, Ricky, jumped into the tracker seat and bravely went through the drills. We were all lying on our backs firing our rifles up at the Skyhawk, the Paras were standing firing GPMGs [general purpose machine-guns]. The Skyhawk was so low that you could clearly make out the pilot inside, and I have since discovered that this aircraft was making a reconnaissance flight to photo the damage. Suddenly there was a bang, as one of our missiles left the beam, streaking up towards the Skyhawk; it veered left and right and then, with a quick angled turn, hit its target. The enormous ball of fire that followed led us to believe that the aircraft may have been carrying napalm.

It started to snow and we were told that a white flag was flying over Port Stanley; we had just fought our last major action of the war and survived. We were transported to Stanley by Chinook helicopter, and I fell into the sleep of the dead with the warmth of the chopper. Port Stanley had been totally trashed by the Argentines, and they had used the place as one big toilet. And guess who had to clean it? After coming down with dysentery, we were moved on board ship, and then finally, after the Battery Sergeant-Major told us 'The holiday's over, gentlemen', we flew home to RAF Waddington. Unbelievably, we had all survived the Falklands War. Even our Battery Commander Major Smith wrote in a post-Falklands report: 'Given the vulnerability of the Rapier crews, particularly the operators, we were constantly amazed that we suffered no casualties. There were a few attacks on FUs [Fire Units], and one was splattered by shrapnel from a bomb, but our luck held.'

It's 20 years since the Falklands War and I remember it as if it were yesterday. I believe that it will go down in history as the last great colonial war Britain fought. When the politicians run out of hot air, war is a continuation of politics through other means. A world without war would be paradise. I believe this war was just, but I will take the psychological scars to my grave.

Details of Tony McNally's book, Cloudpuncher*, can be found at www.britains-smallwars.com*

Welsh Guards pause for a meal outside the Fitzroy settlement while waiting for helicopter lifts to more forward positions.

ALAN CLARK

Conservative MP, 1974–92 and 1997–99

I had hardly got home last night when I realised that the House would be so crowded that I would have to be there to book my place before 8am. So I rose early – it was another glorious day with a thick heat haze – and took the 6.17am train. By 8.30am, the Chamber was a snowstorm of cards, like Budget Day.

I had spent the previous evening trying to convene a joint meeting of the Defence and Foreign Affairs Committee to discuss the question. For reasons of protocol, I had advised Bob Boscawen [Conservative MP and whip] and he, predictably, tried to talk me out of it, said it would be better to have a meeting 'after Margaret had sat down'. I knew very well what this meant. It was an attempt to shift all the most pugnacious Tory MPs out of the Chamber up into Room 10.

I would have none of it. [Sir Anthony] Buck was unobtainable, presumably out drinking somewhere. Little Winston [Churchill], following his new appointment of what must be the tiniest job in the whole Government – that of 'presenting' Government defence policy under the aegis of Central Office – was somewhat spaced out in his response. However, I managed to get hold of a few like-minded colleagues and we had agreed to assemble in Committee Room 10 at 10.15am.

Later, Bob Boscawen had rung back and said that he had arranged for Victor Goodhew (an old whip and 'very reliable' in crises) to chair the meeting. In fact, when I got up to Committee Room 10 this morning, I was gratified to find it extremely full, and the panic that my moves had set in train was reflected in the fact that no lesser than the Chief Whip had been brought in to 'listen'. Michael Jopling [Conservative Chief Whip] led off by making a soft-cell appeal for (need one say) loyalty, absence of recrimination and so forth. This did not go down very well. Speaker after speaker expressed their indignation at the way the Foreign Office had handled things. Many were critical of John Nott. Much the best speech, and the only one that elicited the banging of desks, was by Robert Cranborne. Expressionless, Michael Jopling took notes. Then, fortified by our mutual expressions of empathy, we trooped down to the Chamber for prayers.

The place was absolutely packed. Julian Amery, who very seldom puts a card in, had to sit on the stairs in the gangway between the Government bench and the lower block.

First, Humphrey Atkins made a clear, short, but unsatisfactory statement explaining why he had misled (unintentionally, of course) the House about the timing of various announcements yesterday. This certainly did not make the Lady's task any easier, as it set the tone, giving further corroboration, as it were, to the general impression of almost total Government incompetence which was to pervade the debate.

The Lady led off. At first she spoke very slowly but didactically, not really saying much. But then, when she got to a passage, 'we sent a telegram . . .', the whole Opposition started laughing and sneering. She changed gear and gabbled. Far too fast she rattled off what was clearly a Foreign Office brief, without any reclamatory or even punitive action.

This was depressing for the Conservative benches who were already in a grump and apprehensive mood. Michael Foot followed with an excellent performance. Fortunately, for those of us who wish to thump the Argentines, the fact that they are a fascist junta makes it very much easier to get Labour support – and my God we are going to need this over the ensuing weeks as, apparently, it will take 21 days for the flotilla to arrive on station.

I was tense and had written an excellent speech, provocative and moving. But as the debate wore on, I realised that it might, curiously, have been inappropriate and was glad not to have been called. Although I did intervene when provoked beyond endurance by Ray Whitney's toadying defence of the Foreign Office, the weasel words in which he still and most ill-judgedly plugged the sell-out argument which we used to hear all the time from Ridley.

The debate wore on with Bernard Braine turning in a robustious performance. One of his great ham displays of indignation. So splutteringly bombastic that, in a curious kind of way, he makes the House, that most cynical of audiences, pay attention.

Poor old Notters, on the other hand, was a disaster. He stammered and stuttered and gabbled. He faltered and fluttered and fumbled. He refused to give way; he gave way; he changed his mind; he stood up again; he sat down again. All this against a constant roaring of disapproval and contempt. I have seen the House do this so often in the past. Like the pack that they are, they always smell the blood of a wounded animal and turn on it. I saw them last do this to Nicky Fairbairn in January, and once this mood is aboard it requires a superhuman display of courage and fortitude to overcome it.

The *coup de grace* was delivered by David Owen, who had spoken earlier. He forced Nott to give way and he told him that if he could not appreciate the need to back negotiations with force he did not deserve to remain one minute as Secretary of State.

After the debate, we all trailed, yet again, up to Committee Room 10. This time Carrington and Nott were both present. Thirty-three Members asked questions and, with the exception of three heavy-weight duds (Patten, Kershaw and van Straubenzee), every single person was critical. I asked a long, sneering question about

Foreign Secretary Lord Carrington pictured at a Foreign Office press conference in early April 1982.

the failure of our intelligence. I made a point of addressing it to Peter Carrington whom, with my very long memory, I had not forgiven for snubbing me at a meeting on Afghanistan in December 1980, in the Grand Committee Room. As my irony developed, people in the Committee Room started sniggering, but poor Notters was still so rattled and blubbery that he leant across and answered it, while Carrington was staring at me in haughty silence.

This meeting finally broke up before 4pm. I still had had no early morning tea, no breakfast, no coffee and no lunch, but felt wonderful, full of adrenalin. What an exciting and historic day. I could not go home as I was booked to appear on *Newsnight* at 10pm. Ravenously hungry, I went to the curry restaurant, but it was closed. I was lucky to find a plastic carton on the back seat of the Chevrolet in which there were some old sand-wiches and an orange that Jane had given me for a train journey to Plymouth. I drove into St James's Park and ate them and fell asleep.[2]

SIR HENRY LEACH

Chief of Naval Staff and First Sea Lord, 1979-82

One of my main memories of the Falklands War was my first meeting with the Prime Minister and the Defence Secretary in the PM's room in the House of Commons on the evening of 31 March – two days before the invasion. Because I had been on a visit earlier in the day, I was not wearing uniform and encountered some difficulty getting past the House of Commons's rather zealous security officials. Eventually I was asked to go up.

'Good evening, Prime Minister,' I said on entering. 'Is there anything I can do to help?' She was her usual charming, purposeful self. 'Come in, Admiral,' she said. 'You are very timely. We are of course discussing the Falklands situation and what we should do about it.'

Present also were the Defence Secretary and the Permanent Secretaries from the Ministry of Defence and Foreign and Commonwealth Office, Ministers and officials from the FCO, and the Prime Minister's Private Secretary. Discussion was fairly general, with the FCO pressing for the despatch of a third SSN and the Defence Secretary reluctant to initiate any further action. The reality or otherwise of the threat, the importance of not prejudicing the forthcoming talks with Argentina, and the courses of diplomatic action open to us predominated. In due course, I had my chance.

'Admiral, what do you think?'

'On the basis of the latest intelligence,' I replied, 'I think we must assume that the Falkland Islands will be invaded and that this will happen in the next few days. If it does, there is no way the garrison can put up an effective defence against the amphibious force known to be embarked in the Argentine Fleet. Nor, now, is there any effective deterrence that we could apply in time. Therefore the Islands will be captured. Whether we take action to recover them or not is not for me to say, but I would strongly advise that we do. To do so would require a very considerable Naval Task Force with strong amphibious elements. I believe we should assemble such a force now, without further delay. To be seen to be doing so in sufficient strength might conceivably cause the Argentines to hold off from landing, though I doubt it. Arguably such a move would be too late to provoke them into doing something on which they already seem bent.'

'The Task Force. That would be *Invincible*, *Fearless* and some frigates?'

'Yes. It would also include *Hermes*, *Intrepid* (which is currently being pit into reserve), a substantial proportion of the operational destroyers/frigates, very considerable afloat support from the Royal Fleet Auxiliaries and the taking up from trade of a number of merchant ships. The whole of 3 Commando Brigade Royal Marines would be required, supplemented by at least one additional Army Unit.'

'What about the third nuclear submarine?'

'Contrary to the advice I gave my Secretary of State yesterday when I opposed this suggestion, in the light of today's information I think we should sail a third SSN as soon as practicable. For other operational reasons, this would not be for a few days, but I don't think that would matter.'

'You talk of *Invincible* and *Hermes*; what about *Ark Royal*?'

'The old or the new? The old is in the throes of being scrapped. The new, regrettably, will not complete building for another three years or so.'

'Shall we have enough air cover?'

'We shall be entirely dependent on the Sea Harriers embarked in *Invincible* and *Hermes*. No, we have not really got enough Sea Harriers. But the Sea Harrier is a highly capable aircraft and I believe it to be more than a match for anything the Argentines could put up. Provided we deploy every single aircraft that can be made operational, including those normally used for training, we should be able to inflict sufficient attrition on arrival in the area to achieve at least local air superiority before the landing. I won't pretend that it will not be an operation involving considerable risk; but in my judgement it is, on balance, an acceptable risk – and anyway, there is no better alternative.'

'You keep on about Sea Harriers. What about the Buccaneers and the Phantoms?'

'They were all transferred to the RAF when the old *Ark Royal* was paid off. They cannot be operated from *Invincible* or *Hermes* and they cannot get there on their own.'

'How long would it take to assemble such a Task Force?'

'Apart from the merchant ships, which would be subject to an Order in Council to equip them, and *Intrepid* whose precise state I would need to check – 48 hours.'

'And how long would it take to get to the Falkland Islands?'

'About three weeks.'

'Three weeks, you mean three days?'

'No, I mean three weeks. The distance is 8,000 nautical miles.'

'Could the preparations be carried out without it becoming generally known?'

'No. Something on this scale would be bound to get out fairly quickly.'

'Could we really recapture the Islands if they were invaded?'

'Yes, we *could*, and in my judgement, though it is not my business to say so, we *should*.'

'Why do you say that?' snapped the Prime Minister.

'Because if we do not, or if we pussyfoot in our actions and do not achieve complete success, in another few months we shall be living in a different country whose word counts for little.'

The Prime Minister looked relieved and nodded.

Discussion then turned to other aspects: a telephone call to Al Haig, the American Secretary of State, in Washington; the drafting of a personal message from the Prime Minister to President Ronald Reagan; messages to our Ambassadors to the United States and Argentina, and to the Governor of the Falkland Islands. All this lasted well into the night.

When the meeting finally broke up, I left with full authority to sail a third nuclear submarine when current tasks permitted, and to assemble and prepare further instructions. One thing was certain: faced with a crisis, we had a Prime Minister of courage, decision and action to meet it.

A further meeting was held the following evening at No. 10 Downing Street. Yet again, all possible options were reviewed, but no panacea other than continuing high-pressure diplomacy was identified. There was considerable debate over what instructions should be sent to the Governor of the Falkland Islands. A message of confidence? Of exhortation to fight to the last? Of restraint on such heroics to reduce bloodshed? After a period of heavy drafting, a message was shaped up along the lines of: 'complete confidence in your ability to handle the situation . . . realise you may be faced with impossible odds . . . know you will exercise your judgement in avoiding needless loss of life . . . our thoughts are with you at this critical time.' To me, it seemed at worst back-seat driving and at best a package of platitudes. Evidently I displayed my distaste, for the Prime Minister spotted it.

'You're shaking your head, Admiral. You don't agree?'

'Prime Minister, I can only say what I, as an operational commander, would do, were I on the receiving end of such a message.'

'What?'

'Put it straight in the wastepaper bin and lose any remaining confidence in Whitehall.'

'What would *you* say, then?'

'Nothing. At this late stage, I should leave it to the man on the spot.' And so it was.

During these long night sessions, the Prime Minister was at her very best, exhibiting no sign of the gruelling 16-hour day that normally preceded them. Indeed, such were her stamina and resolve in a crisis that I believe she rather enjoyed it. At one stage, she rounded on me sharply: 'Admiral, supposing we did send the Task Force: what would you do if you were C-in-C of the Argentine Navy?'

'I should return to harbour, Prime Minister, and stay there,' I replied.

'Why?'

'Because I should appreciate that, although I could take out some of the British ships, they would sink my entire Navy. It would take years to recover, if indeed it were practicable to do so.'

At dawn on 2 April, the Argentine invasion force landed, and by 0830 the Governor of the Falkland Islands had surrendered. Another chapter in maritime history had been opened.

Nine years later, by courtesy of the Admiralty Board who generously sponsored my trip, I paid a brief visit to the Falklands for the first time. Seen from the air, the Islands looked very much as expected: barren, craggy, undulating peatland from which rose steep mountain peaks, water everywhere in myriad inlets, rivers and lakes – not unlike the Outer Hebrides or the remoter parts of Sutherland – and with that rugged beauty associated with wild places. A haven of quiet peace on a still evening when the sunset flames; a challenge for survival only a few hours later when storm-force winds sweep the treeless wastes, horizontal rain lashes the quartzite outcrops and thick cloud blankets the uplands.

After so many hours spent poring over maps and charts during the war itself, I had imagined that I knew the various scenes of action fairly well. What I did not realise was the steepness of the mountain crests, the size of the boulders in the outcrops and the jaggedness of their edges, and the general difficulty of making any kind of fast progress. Add to this winter bogginess, darkness, landmines and being under fire from a well-concealed enemy on the crest, and a rather more realistic understanding of what our assault troops achieved begins to dawn. I can only reiterate what I often thought in the Second World War: thank God I am a sailor. [3]

LORD BRAMALL

Chief of the General Staff, 1979-82

The Falklands Campaign Through the Eyes of the Chiefs of Staff

When the Argentines invaded the Falklands, the First Sea Lord was the only Chief of Staff of the Armed Forces available in Whitehall. The Chief of the Defence Staff, Admiral of the Fleet Sir Terence Lewin, was on the point of arriving in New Zealand and I, as Chief of the General Staff (CGS), was in Northern Ireland on one of my regular visits.

Fortuitously, Admiral Sir Henry Leach, who had already taken certain anticipatory action, was able to assure the Prime Minister, against Civil Service and political advice, that he could send a powerful Naval Task Force to the South Atlantic within a matter of days. This was a formidable achievement and provided exactly the sort of encouragement the Prime Minister needed. Because, without this projection of power to the area, there was no way that pressure could be brought to bear on the Argentines to withdraw or, if they refused, conditions could be created in which a landing to recapture the Islands might then become possible.

With the country, as well as Parliament, soon demanding Government action to restore the honour, credibility and future status of the country, the Chiefs of Staff collectively were soon charged with producing a practicable plan to bring this about. This was no easy task when the Task Force would have to operate some 8,000 miles from home in very unfavourable weather and within 150 miles of Argentine air bases. The risks would have to be assessed accurately if humiliating mistakes were to be avoided.

We met once, sometimes twice, daily under the Chief of Defence Staff (CDS) Lewin, who had returned post-haste from New Zealand. The discussions and arguments ranged forcibly and comprehensively over every aspect of the crisis and demonstrated, I think, that four minds covering the whole spectrum of professional competence and military judgement were better than one, when properly led and directed as they certainly were by the CDS.

Cheerful waves from Scots Guards as they embark on the *QE2* at Southampton.
Three thousand troops sailed to the Falklands aboard the liner.

Once decisions had been taken on the composition of the Task Force, which had to include enough ground troops to retake the Falklands if negotiations failed, the next major issue discussed was the chain of command. As the initial phases of the operation were likely to be almost entirely Naval, command and detailed planning were entrusted to Sir John Fieldhouse, C-in-C Fleet, at his joint maritime headquarters at Northwood, where air advice was available through the integrated 18 Group Royal Air Force, and Army advice could be provided from headquarters UK Land Forces. Fieldhouse was to exercise command, other than over the submarines that remained directly under him, through the Task Force Commander, Rear-Admiral Sandy Woodward, flying his flag in the carrier *Hermes*. If a landing had to be made, Fieldhouse would also have a Land Force Commander reporting to him – Major General Jeremy Moore, Royal Marines. Upwards, Fieldhouse reported to the CDS who, having discussed key issues with the service Chiefs of Staff and been given their views on broad strategy and on the implications affecting their own services, tendered his own advice to the Defence Committee Falklands – in effect a War Cabinet, and often described as such. This consisted of the Prime Minister, the Lord President of the Council (William Whitelaw), the Foreign Secretary (Francis Pym), the Defence Secretary (John Nott) and the Chancellor of the Duchy of Lancaster (Cecil Parkinson), with the CDS always in attendance. It became a model of its kind for crisis management, and it enabled Lewin to give Fieldhouse his general directions, aims and objectives, and leave him free to plan in detail and execute the sea and air battles that could lead to the repossession of the Islands.

With Fieldhouse now responsible for the detailed planning, the next issue the Chiefs of Staff had to establish with the War Cabinet was the extent to which Britain was to be considered actually at war with Argentina, and hence the rules of engagement and restraints that needed to apply. Clear definition was needed to establish early psychological superiority and to seize the initiative, which was all-important to success. Although the junta had committed a clear act of aggression, it had achieved its aim without inflicting a single British casualty. As long as there was any hope of international political or British military pressure persuading the Argentines to withdraw, the British Government was naturally reluctant to start hostilities or to use any more force, under Article 51 of the United Nations Charter, than was absolutely necessary. Taking action in self-defence was perfectly legal under international law, but in the missile era, when stand-off weapons could inflict crippling damage from considerable distances, it was not easy to find what exactly constituted 'imminent hostile intent' against which pre-emptive action would be legal in the sense of defence.

The reconciliation of these conflicting factors led to some arguments between the Chiefs of Staff, but an agreed formula was soon found that led to a maritime exclusion zone with a 200-mile radius being declared around the Islands. This was to be effective from 12 April. Later, on 30 April, as the Task Force came within range of the Islands, the zone would become a total exclusion zone (TEZ) for aircraft as well as ships and would be patrolled by Harriers from the Task Force.

Once the rules for engagement for operation inside and outside the exclusion zone had been established, it was up to Lewin, Fieldhouse and Woodward to ensure that no Captain had any doubt about what was expected of him in any situation. The rules, as modified from time to time, on the authority of the War Cabinet, were strictly observed throughout the campaign. Indeed, the strategy that the Chiefs developed struck a well-judged balance between giving the Task Force protection and not escalating the conflict during the international toing and froing to find a possible solution to the crisis; and it seized the initiative in a subtle way. The Argentines could either run the risk, while trying to resupply their garrison, of being attacked by powerful British nuclear submarines, to which they had no counter and whose numbers they could not accurately assess; or they could accept the terms of the exclusion zone and be seen to be driven from the seas around the very islands whose sovereignty they were claiming. They chose the latter, with the loss of face, prestige and initiative that it entailed.

Perhaps the most important issue that the Chiefs had to settle was the concept of operations for the period immediately after the Task Force reached the South Atlantic. What additional Land Forces would be needed if diplomatic pressures and the show of force did not persuade the junta to withdraw, and instead it ordered the troops on the Islands to offer spirited resistance, fully supported by their Navy and Land Force? On the other hand, if the risks of undertaking an opposed landing were assessed as too great, what alternatives such as blockade were available? There was one thing that the Chiefs and the War Cabinet were very clear about: it would be disastrous for Britain's future status in the world to do a 'Grand Old Duke of York', sailing the Task Force 8,000 miles south and then back again, without restoring a Government at Port Stanley of the Islanders' own choice.

The first military moves of the campaign took place in a phased approach, allowing ample time for political negotiations. These were: Phase I, the sailing south; Phase II, the retaking of South Georgia; Phase III, establishing the TEZ and bombing Port Stanley airfield; and Phase IV, positioning the Task Force within striking range of the TEZ and the Falklands but out of effective range of most of the Argentine Air Force. These moves had all been predictable, the risks calculated and success as certain as anything can be certain in war. The military risks were, however, becoming greater every day, with fewer than 40 Harriers to give air cover from the tossing decks of *Hermes* and *Invincible* in the foulest weather of the South Atlantic, whereas the Argentine Air Force and Navy had some 200 aircraft with secure and stable land bases only 350 miles away. Moreover, any doubts as to whether the two sides were in earnest and whether lives would have to be lost before an equitable political solution could be found were quickly dispelled by the closely linked sinkings of the *Belgrano* and HMS *Sheffield*.

The Prime Minister and the British people, however, were in no mood for a sell-out, nor was General Galtieri, and when the end of the political road was reached with Peru's failure to find a peaceful way out of the crisis, the War Cabinet had no option but to plan to retake the Islands by force. Fieldhouse had in fact done much of the outline planning with his commanders at a meeting held on board *Hermes* on 18 April. It was only necessary to make final amendments based on the most up-to-date reconnaissance information and intelligence to get his plan approved by the War Cabinet. The arguments and counter-arguments about operational policy surrounding the plan were then thoroughly debated by the Chiefs, who would be required to support it, and this helped when the balance of advantage and disadvantage was a fine one and open to differing interpretations. Although Lewin was the only Chief who attended the War Cabinet regularly, and held the ultimate responsibility for military advice, the other Chiefs met the Prime Minister frequently and at all critical times, either at No. 10, in her room at the House of Commons or at Chequers. This enabled Lewin to produce dynamic solutions, having tested them for realism and practicability in the Chiefs of Staff meetings and seen that all loose ends across all three services were tied up.

At one of the Chequers meetings, I remember so well saying to Margaret Thatcher in front of the representatives of the Foreign Office, who, for totally spurious reasons, had wanted to keep the Gurkhas out of the campaign: 'Prime Minister, you do realise that we are sending a Gurkha Battalion with the Task Force?' After only a short pause, she exclaimed: 'What! Only one?!'

Fieldhouse's plan, approved by the Chiefs, was designed to make best use of the physical and electronic shelter of San Carlos Bay on the west side of East Falkland to reduce to the minimum the risks from weather, from sea-skimming missiles and from submarine attack. The Special Air Service and the Special Boat Service were to pinpoint the Argentine positions and carry out raids on vulnerable targets, and behind them the Commando Brigades, three Commandos reinforced by two Parachute Battalions, would seize a bridgehead at San Carlos Bay. Once enough troops, equipment and supplies were ashore, they would advance across the island to attack the main Argentine forces holding Port Stanley. For this, however, Fieldhouse needed a reserve brigade that could be used for a variety of tasks, such as taking over the beachhead to enable the Commandos to develop their operations across the island or reinforce their assault. Thus 5 Brigade was despatched to the South Atlantic in the only way possible in the time available, on the SS *Queen Elizabeth*, especially taken up from trade for this purpose.

With the Task Force now poised to repossess the Islands and with negotiations accepted by HMG as having broken down, the War Cabinet had a final meeting to decide whether to give the go-ahead. On 15 May, it met with the Chiefs in attendance in the Cabinet Room of Downing Street and each Chief was required to back his own judgement and say how the landing would turn out, and whether it should be attempted. All felt that, despite the undoubted risks, which had been reduced as fast as possible by the operational plan, we now had no option but to carry out a landing with a view to repossession; and that given an element of good fortune – which we would need – the operation, which would be pushed through with the greatest resolution, courage and skill, would be successful. Some ships would be lost in the early stages, but once the troops were ashore the risks would diminish significantly. It was also stressed that the assaulting troops should not remain too long on the bridgehead, but should get out to threaten the main Argentine positions just as soon as possible.

Presented with this united front, the Prime Minister, who had shown herself to be the ideal war leader – robust, quick, thoroughly well informed and decisive – gave the order to go ahead.

The landings and the subsequent land operation at Goose Green and against the mountainous area immediately west of Stanley were, in the event, completely successful, despite the setback of the bombing of the *Sir Galahad* with Welsh Guards on board. Great credit goes to Admiral Woodward, who handled the Task Force with consummate skill, and to Brigadier Thompson and General Moore, whose Commandos and Parachutists, Guardsmen and Gurkhas overcame long distances, arduous climatic conditions and an enemy superior in numbers to win victories at Goose Green and in the mountains west of Stanley, bringing about the Argentine surrender within a fortnight of the landing.

It was a remarkable feat of arms; and perhaps the best epitaph for this small epic of British history might be Churchill's words – that 'all great battles in history have been won by superior willpower wresting victory in the face of odds or upon the narrowest of margins'.

The campaign also reaffirmed the soundness of the Chiefs of Staff system, which allowed a nice balance to be struck between the needs of detailed examination of all possible courses of action and complete decisiveness down the chain of command through the CDS Lewin and the Commander-in-Chief Fieldhouse to the Task Force and the Land Force Commanders. How different from the start of the Norwegian campaign in 1940!

But of course the greatest single factor in the South Atlantic victory was the way in which all ranks of all three services showed the will to take risks; the will to overcome obstacles and setbacks; the will to face dangers; the will, if need be, to make the final sacrifice; the will to decide and the will to win – the true and indomitable spirit of the warrior, fully supported by the same spirit in the Prime Minister.

SIR ANTONY ACLAND

Permanent Secretary, FCO, 1982–86

I took up my appointment as Permanent Under-Secretary at the Foreign Office and Head of the Diplomatic Service six days after the Argentines attacked the Falklands and three days after Lord Carrington and the three other Foreign Office Ministers resigned together. Thus I found myself in a post for which I wasn't sure that I was well suited (I hadn't been on my own list of those who might have succeeded my predecessor, Sir Michael Palliser, so I was more than surprised to find myself as Permanent Under-Secretary at this crucial time). There were four new Ministers to deal with, and probably an impending war; and there was some tension, to put it mildly, across Downing Street, between No. 10 and the Foreign Office. It was something of a baptism of fire.

Because Lord Carrington and Michael Palliser were both abroad at the time, Richard Luce and I attended, from the Foreign Office, the meeting in the Prime Minister's room in the House of Commons on 2 April, to be told of the Argentines' occupation of South Georgia and the impending invasion of the Falklands. As has been described in several accounts, it was a gloomy affair, until Admiral Sir Henry Leach erupted into the room, angry at being delayed by House of Commons security. He told the Prime Minister that, if she gave the order, he would put together a Task Force to recapture the Islands. This transformed the atmosphere, and so began the days and weeks of planning.

I was a member of the inner group of Ministers, Heads of the Armed Services and Senior Officials whose task it was to manage the military, political and diplomatic aspects of what was recognised by all to be a hazardous enterprise. My view throughout was that, if an honourable settlement could be found which safeguarded the interests of the Falkland Islanders, then conflict should be avoided. This seemed unlikely, however, and the emphasis was rightly on preparing for battle. I was involved in the negotiations with the US Secretary of State, General Al Haig, which nearly brought off a deal, though whether it would have been wholly satisfactory in the long run was questionable.

These were weeks of hard work, anxiety, admiration, sadness and exhilaration: anxiety that the aircraft carriers *Hermes* and *Invincible* and the supply ship *Atlantic Conveyor* might be hit and sunk on their way southwards by Exocet missiles; anxiety that the uncamouflaged *Canberra*, carrying the troops and so vulnerable in the moonlight in Goose Bay, might be destroyed before being unloaded; admiration at the skill and courage of our Armed Forces; and deep sadness at the sinking of HMS *Sheffield* and the other casualties. News of these disasters came as body blows in the Cabinet Room at No. 10 and were felt intensely by all present.

But, after anxious days, the tide turned. On the evening of the surrender, I was dining at the Spanish Embassy – paradoxically in honour of Lord Carrington, who in the light of the subsequent report by Lord Franks need not, on the merits of the case, have resigned. I knew that the Argentines were giving up, and halfway through the meal I was told that, unusually, the Prime Minister was going to make a statement in the House of Commons at 10pm and wanted me to be there. My official car wasn't due back until 10.45, and with difficulty I found a taxi, which got me to the House as the Prime Minister was entering the Chamber. I slipped into the Officials' box with Robert Armstrong and Admiral Lewin, and heard Mrs Thatcher's memorable statement that the white flags were going up over Port Stanley. Later we drank the Prime Minister's health in her room in the House. It was an emotional moment, with tears of relief not far away that the burden had been finally uplifted and that the operation had been brought to a splendid and successful conclusion.

As a postscript, some weeks later, I was asked to see Robert Armstrong, the Secretary of the Cabinet, to be told that the Prime Minister and Denis Thatcher were going to fly to the Falklands and that knowledge of this was to be kept on the very strictest 'need-to-know' basis. Having learnt that the restored Governor was being told of this with a message hand-delivered by one of the pilots of the regular supply flights, I pondered the instruction and decided that no one needed to know in advance. So I told no one. Some time later, when challenged by the Prime Minister on whether secrets could be kept about another operation, I told her this – and she nodded approvingly.

It was a great privilege to be involved in this historic enterprise.

Major Jeremy Moore, who commanded the British Land Forces
during the Falklands War.

CECIL PARKINSON

Chairman of the Conservative Party, 1981-83

On Friday 1 April 1982, I was due to speak at a party meeting in Cambridge followed by a fund-raising lunch at the Jockey Club at Newmarket. I left home very early in the morning feeling rather pleased. In a poll published the day before, the Conservative Party had taken a lead over Labour and the Liberals. Over a six-month period, we had moved from being bottom of the polls to top. You can, therefore, imagine my horror when I heard on the BBC that the Argentines had invaded and captured the Falkland Islands. When I arrived at Cambridge, I was told that a Cabinet meeting had been called, but of course it was too late for me to get back to London for it. I therefore decided to carry out my programme. The morning meeting went quite well, because there was no real news from the Falklands and thus there was much speculation, but no anger.

On my way to Newmarket, I heard a recording of a message from a radio ham in the Falklands, who was saying that Argentine troop carriers full of Argentine soldiers were rumbling past his door. This was followed by a live broadcast from the House of Commons, in which the number two at the Foreign Office, Humphrey Atkins, reported that the Foreign Office had no news from the Falklands and could not confirm or deny the invasion. The Foreign Office was apparently waiting for a message from Sir Rex Hunt, who was already a captive of the Argentines and in no position to pass on any messages. The Government seemed incredibly feeble and powerless. When I arrived at Newmarket, I was told that another Cabinet meeting had been called for six o'clock that evening and I therefore had to abandon a speaking engagement in Hertfordshire. My wife took my place, and the following year I received a letter from the Chairman of the same dining club inviting me to speak, but adding that if I was not available they would be very happy to listen to my wife again – the only light memory of a difficult day.

The Cabinet was very tense, and all but one member thought we should despatch the Fleet. On the following day, the Saturday, we had a debate in the House of Commons. It was by no means a complete success and, as the debate ended, Margaret Thatcher asked Willie Whitelaw, Francis Pym and myself to join her in her office at the House. Ian Gow, her PPS, went off to a meeting of the 1922 Committee, where John Nott and Peter Carrington spoke: again, this was only moderately successful, and Peter Carrington had a particularly hostile reception from a group of members who were known to Ministers in the Commons, but not to him as a member of the Lords, as fully paid-up trouble-makers. He and John Nott subsequently joined us in the Prime Minister's room. The next day, I heard nothing until early evening, when Margaret Thatcher telephoned me saying that Peter Carrington felt he should resign and that she and Willie Whitelaw had tried to persuade him not to. He had apparently agreed to postpone any decision until he saw the following day's newspapers, in particular the *Times*. She asked me for my view. I knew how much she valued Peter's experience and straightforwardness. Although I had been in the Cabinet only a short time, I too had developed an enormous respect for the contributions he made. Looked at objectively, however, as Party Chairman, it seemed clear to me that as long as he was in the Foreign Office and unable to defend himself in the Commons, the debate would be dominated by the past. The question of how we got into the situation we were in, rather than of how we were to get out of it, would be the one exercising people's minds. It was with enormous reluctance that I advised Margaret that, if Peter insisted on going, she should accept his resignation. That was one of my most unhappy memories of the Falklands War.

On the other hand, the finale to the Falklands crisis – the dinner in No. 10 at which for the first time people like Sandy Woodward and Brigadier Thompson became persons rather than names, was one of the happiest moments. At the end of the dinner, attended by all the leading figures and followed by a reception for the wives, Margaret Thatcher and Terry Lewin made brief but memorable speeches, at the conclusion of which Mrs Thatcher, the only lady present, stood up and said, 'Gentlemen, shall we join the ladies?', to an outburst of loud laughter.

Postscript

It is an interesting thought that, had the Falklands War taken place a year later, it would have had a totally different cast of characters. We would have had a different Defence Secretary; a different Chief of the Defence Staff; a different head of the Navy; a different head of the Army; a different head of the Air Force; a different Ambassador in Washington and a different Ambassador to the United Nations. Britain was incredibly lucky that such a gifted group of people were available to serve their country at such a critical time.

DR RICK JOLLY

Surgeon Commander, Falklands Field Hospital

An Airborne Tribute

Scene One:

On the morning after, we paused and took stock. All the 64 wounded in the fight for Goose Green had survived and were now in the hospital ship *Uganda*. It was all down to their basic fitness, plus the wonderful work done by the Regimental Medical Officer of 2 Para, Captain Steve Hughes, and his battlefield medic teams. What a tiger that young doctor had been. 2 Para's brother unit, 3 Para, were halfway across East Falkland on their long tab between Port San Carlos and Teal Inlet. No doubt their time would also come, but now they would be sweating from their heavy loads, as well as worrying about the butcher's bill that has had to be paid by their friends in this first real test of 3 Commando Brigade's mission to regain the Islands.

The rumours concerning the numbers killed varied widely. All we knew for certain was that the Commanding Officer had died at the head of his Battalion.

Scene Two:

A Naval helicopter arrived and settled gently on the grass. The aircrewman beckoned me forward, a look of real pain and resignation on his tired face. He was sharing the cabin with British dead – Paratroopers from Goose Green. The bodies had been loaded in on top and alongside each other, their limbs frozen in rigor mortis, and each man's combat smock or poncho cape pulled up over his face. Silently, sadly, we unloaded the bodies, placing each corpse on its own stretcher at the side of the Ajax Bay main building. The RSM of 2 Para, Mr Malcolm Simpson, and a lightly injured Company Commander, Major Roger Jenner, helped us in this task. The two men then stood back, quietly, near to tears, watching us.

My little team of volunteer Royal Marines and I prepared the bodies, one by one, for burial. A journalist hovered in the background, obviously thinking about a photograph. Our thunderous looks indicated that the production of a camera would result in him joining our waiting customers. I told one of the boys to keep him – and any other outsiders – well away.

The cold, wet clothing was deftly cut off. The pockets were examined, and a few personal possessions sorted, logged and put in a plastic bag. With the body stripped naked in the freezing air, I carefully examined each man to confirm his identity, and certified both death and its primary cause. They had died in a fight to uphold Her Majesty's Sovereignty. They had also died on British soil, and British law applied. To save the need for any later examination of the bodies by a Coroner, I had to do the job properly now. Those names were burned into our memories: Dent, Bingley, Cork, Hardman, Melia, Illingsworth, Mechan, Wood, Findlay, Barry, Dixon, Fletcher, Prior, Smith, Sullivan, Holman-Smith and, finally, 'H' himself. That same shy, almost quizzical smile lay on his face as easily in death as it did in life.

Like his men, the late Commanding Officer of the 2nd Battalion was lifted up carefully and then placed into an opaque, loose shroud. Gently and reverently, his body was then placed in the outer layer, a thick grey PVC body bag, with a heavy zip and six carrying loops. Chief Petty Officer Scouse Davies wrote each name on the outside using a broad felt-tip pen, the big black capitals contrasting sharply with the shiny grey of the bag.

We straightened up, our backs aching from an hour's crouching and our bloodied fingers stiff with cold. The RSM looked me in the eye and saluted. It had not been a pleasant task by any means, but it had been an honour for us to undertake. We felt satisfied and glad that some sort of dignity had been restored to these brave men.

Scene Three:

The funeral itself was a fierce event. Goose Green had to be defended against counter-attack, and there were friends back there who could not be spared from duty for this service. On their behalf, nearly 200 men stood in silence around the edge of the mass grave, heads uncovered, the majority with hands clasped loosely in prayer. Officers mixed with soldiers, Paras with Royal Marines. Above us was the dome of a perfectly blue sky, while in the distance snow gleamed on the summit of Mount Simon. San Carlos Water was a flat calm, the Fleet lying still as the helicopters moved busily from ship to ship with their loads, like bees in some distant English flowerbed on a summer's day. The snarl of their engines and clatter of rotor blades carried for miles in the crisp cold air.

It was a beautiful spot, this carefully chosen, silent hillside.

One by one, the bodies were carried down into the grave. Eleven of the 17 being buried today were officers or NCOs, showing exactly what Airborne Forces and Commandos meant by the word 'leadership'. Each body bag had six canvas handles, so the burial party consisted of six men of similar rank to the deceased, plus one more senior escort. Major Chris Keeble, acting CO of 2 Para, preceded the four dead officers; RSM Simpson acted for the NCOs and private soldiers. A Sapper Major led the group bearing Corporal Melia; Major Peter Cameron and six brother Royal Marine pilots carried Lieutenant Dick Nunn to his place of rest. Each body bag was covered by the Union Flag, which was removed when the precious load was in position.

When everything was finally in place, the 2nd Battalion Padre, David Cooper, began the service. As his firm voice rolled through the now-familiar words, the emotional pressure wound up to a crescendo. Eyes that were red with tiredness and strain now brimmed over with silent tears that splashed down on to the soggy earth.

'Ashes to ashes, dust unto dust . . . '

The sound of handfuls of earth cast by the RSM on to taut body bags echoed like thunder around the grave. Led by Major-General Moore, we saluted our friends and colleagues in a final, reluctant farewell – then we turned, and walked away . . .

Surgeon Commander Rick Jolly was the Senior Medical Officer of the Royal Marines 3 Commando Brigade and also ran the Field Hospital at Ajax Bay, where nearly 800 British sick and injured were treated during the land battles of the 1982 campaign. Despite the dust, dirt and danger (there were two unexploded bombs in the building), only four of those wounded in action subsequently died of those wounds. He was appointed OBE in the South Atlantic Honours List; the Argentine Government added the Orden de Majo 17 years later, when they discovered that more than 200 Argentine casualties had also passed through his hands. It is a unique achievement to be decorated by both sides in the same war. Now retired, Rick Jolly is Chairman of the South Atlantic Medal Association (1982), details of which can be found at www.sama82.org.uk, and he has recently revised and republished the story of Ajax Bay as The Red and Green Life Machine

HEW PIKE

Commanding Officer, 3 Para, 1980-83

For all of us in 3 Para, the Falklands campaign was an extraordinary chapter in our lives. For many of us, it was also the professional high point of our military careers. So I thought I would offer four snapshots, to try to recapture the atmosphere and uncertainties that prevailed, as well as the conditions under which we fought. Imagine, therefore, that you are a young, 18-year-old soldier in the Battalion, suddenly caught up in a great military enterprise. Initially, you experience six weeks of life at sea, undergoing intensive preparations for what is to come. Then you land on East Falkland Island.

Landing
The Battalion Log for the 21 May reads: 'After several changes in timings, 3 Para went to action stations on HMS *Intrepid* at 0130 hours Zulu.'

D-Day, San Carlos Water. Forty-eight hours earlier, after a change of plan at the dead of night, the Battalion has hurriedly cross-decked itself, with all its ammunition, from a spacious cruise liner, SS *Canberra*, in which its outloading drills had been endlessly rehearsed, to an overcrowded assault ship, HMS *Intrepid*, a rabbit warren in which even a Section Commander has difficulty in accounting for his little flock. Then the Battalion's landing at Port San Carlos is endlessly delayed while the darkness so badly needed gives way to a calm, clear dawn – perfect conditions for enemy pilots. At last the landing craft manoeuvre back into *Intrepid*'s flooded dock, we load up and are under way, less one company for which we can't risk a further wait. Everything seems to be taking so much longer than we expected and hoped. The bigger landing craft, with more displacement, hit the sea bed well out from the beach – and it's too deep to wade. So the smaller craft, having emptied B Company ashore, must manoeuvre alongside for another unscheduled cross-decking. It's just as well that we are unopposed – or are we? As we advance towards the settlement, a Sea King and two Gazelle helicopters – 'What are they doing here anyway?' we are asking ourselves – take avoiding action ahead of

A Company's leading elements. Both Gazelles are hit by enemy small-arms fire and crash, one into the water, one into the hillside. Three of the four crewmen die. As we move up to try to establish what has happened and why, an enemy Pucara ground-attack aircraft whines slowly over the scattered houses of the settlement, machine-gunning indiscriminately as it goes.

Emerging from behind a protective pile of drying peat, just as the body of one of the Gazelle pilots is being loaded into a local farm Land Rover, the realities of our situation begin to press upon us.

Just before we left the *Canberra*, the CO had quoted Brigadier S J L Hill, Commander of the 3rd Parachute Brigade on D-Day 1944, to the Battalion. 'Gentlemen, despite your excellent training and briefing, do not be daunted if chaos reigns. It undoubtedly will.'

Battle Procedure – The Reality

The Battalion Log reads: '26 May, 2100 hours. CO received warning order for future tasks. There would be a Battalion raid by 2 Para . . . 45 Commando would advance to Douglas settlement and 3 Para would move through them to secure Teal Inlet.'

After five days of constant interference from enemy air attack with logistic unloading into the bridgehead – the essential pre-requisite for a general advance – the *Atlantic Conveyor* is hit by an Exocet. Only one Chinook escapes. 'No move from the bridge-head can be contemplated for some days,' is the steer from the Brigade Commander. But late that night comes a warning order to advance east as soon as possible after first light. We are wrong-footed, and many of us are already tired after intensive patrolling in awful weather. Another upheaval at the dead of night, another test for the flexibility of our battle procedure. There is a need to challenge the Brigade plan for the Battalion to advance via Douglas settlement, yet our own plans must be made, orders issued and the show got on the road with everyone briefed, equipped and bombed up for a journey of unknown duration. As we stumble eastwards the following night in driving rain and sleet, over rock, bog and tussock, the thumps and flashes of violence intermittently reach us across the night sky, from 2 Para's first action at Camilla Creek. We are all conscious of how reliant we are upon the cohesion of each fire team of four, each section of eight, and especially upon our leaders – tough, determined, confident, youthful corporals.

'The first quality of the soldier is fortitude in resisting hardship and fatigue,' wrote Napoleon, 'bravery but the second.' This first quality was severely tested on that long haul from Port San Carlos to Teal Inlet, and on again to Estancia House. To add to our discomfort, intelligence was little better than guesswork. We knew very little of what the enemy might do, where and in what strength. Hardship, fatigue, uncertainty – these were our constant companions.

Battle

The Battalion Log reads: '10 June, 1630 hours, CO attended Brigade Orders. 1930 hours, CO held his Orders in the Regimental Aid Post at Estancia House. Before

British paratroopers carry out emergency medical treatment whilst under fire on Mount Longdon.

giving them, he stressed that 3 Para were to move as far east as possible towards Stanley, having captured Mount Longdon – we were to exploit to the full our opportunities.'

After our Orders, for the Battalion's greatest endeavour in a generation or more, we feel elated, excited and optimistic. We see the Battalion exploiting as the Brigade Commander hopes beyond Mount Longdon and across Wireless Ridge.

How different it all is, as we crouch behind an enormous granite outcrop on that mountain. Alongside us, in the dim moonlight, lie a collection of Argentine corpses; there are several snipers moving among the rocks ahead, causing considerable trouble. We have just crawled forward past two wounded men – Sergeant Gray and Private Barrett, lying under blankets muttering encouragement to each other. Worse than the snipers, a number of heavy machine-guns will not be silenced by our own firepower – not GPMGs, not MILAN missiles, not mortars, not guns. Worst of all is the accuracy and persistence of the Argentine artillery, clinging uncannily to the Battalion's dogged progress. Behind us, a huge explosion that we think at first is a mortar engagement of great accuracy is identified as a 105mm recoilless rifle engaging Corporal McCarthy's MILAN team to deadly effect as they try to establish a better position – three are killed by a single shell. Attempts to outmanoeuvre these strong positions by moving round the northern shoulders of the mountain are not succeeding. Meanwhile, on the lower ground north of the mountain, A Company cannot move forward either. Dominated by machine-gun fire from other positions ahead of us, they already have two dead and others wounded. Too little is known about Wireless Ridge – its wire, mines and positions – to launch C Company on a wider outflanking movement, especially as our artillery can't reach east of Mount Longdon from their present positions, and can't be flown forward until daylight. And HMS *Avenger*, our fire support frigate, must move back from its station well before first light for fear of Exocet attack.

We seem to be out of options. It is a black moment in a long, dreadful night – and a commonplace of battle. To win, we must persist, sustaining pressure through fire and relentless assault on one position after another until the enemy's will is broken, his courage killed.

The Aftermath of Battle
From the Battalion Log, 12 June: 'CO sent message back to Brigade "Mount Longdon under continual heavy shellfire and we are sustaining further casualties".'

From the Battalion Log, 13 June: 'At first light, the removal of 3 Para dead continued. Stretcher-bearers assisted, moving up from the Regimental Aid Post at the foot of the western reverse slope. The dead were then flown back to Teal Inlet. Another task is clearing the position of enemy dead. Pits were dug and a large number were buried. However, our positions came under such intense fire that this activity had to be abandoned.'

So after that awful night, what then? Relief that we had done it, yes – but little elation. There was shock at lost comrades and friends, and in realising how many were badly wounded as the list was compiled. Can 'Doc' Murdoch, one of the great characters of the Battalion, and big Stewart MacLaughlin, who had fought like a lion, really be dead? Was it worth such sacrifice, this pile of rock? Even to ask the question seems to insult their memory. The misty scene as dawn broke will perhaps be the most haunting image of this place. The debris of battle was scattered along the length of the mountain, encountered around every turn in the rocks, in every gully.

Weapons, clothing, rations, blankets, boots, tents, ammunition, sleeping bags, blood-soaked medical dressing, web equipment, packs – all abandoned along with the 105mm recoilless rifles, heavy mortars and .50mm Browning machine-guns that had given us so much trouble during darkness. The enemy dead lay everywhere, victims of shell, bullet and bayonet. The sour odour of death lingered in the nostrils long after many of these corpses had been buried, for it was a slow job, and eventually the task was abandoned when their artillery and mortars started again – the latter especially lethal, without the warning whistle of artillery shellfire. The enemy bunkers provided an Aladdin's cave of Camel cigarettes, bottles of brandy, huge cakes of solid cheese, letters from home and family snapshots. Standing among the shell holes and shambles of battle, and watching the determined, triumphant but shocked and saddened faces of those who had lost their friends on this mountain, the Iron Duke's comment was never more apt: 'There is nothing half so melancholy as a battle won, unless it be a battle lost.'

The Demands of War

What do we conclude? That war piles adversity upon misfortune, and misfortune upon adversity, for winners and losers alike. The conditions are timeless and universal – the circumstances of the moment always unique. We should therefore continue to seek in our soldiers the qualities once described by Gibbon of Alaric, King of the Goths. Alaric possessed, he wrote, 'that invincible temper of mind that rises superior to every misfortune, and derives resources from adversity'. This is the clue, surely, to the qualities required of those who will succeed in war. The atmosphere is always chaotic, always uncertain, often depressing. Those who fall prey to these timeless realities will always struggle against defeat, those who can exploit them may well prevail. 3 Para prevailed and, 20 years on, it makes us all grateful to have been with a band of brothers who served their country and the cause of freedom well.

CAROL THATCHER

Journalist and author

On the evening of Friday 2 April 1982, my father was downing a gin and mixer in the drawing room of the flat at No. 10, when a message was delivered by a member of the Prime Minister's staff. Argentina had invaded the Falklands. Now, Denis prides himself on his geography, but this caught him out. 'I remember looking at the *Times Atlas of the World* to find out where the bloody hell they were – and I wasn't the only one.' Denis was already in fighting mood. 'As an ex-soldier I thought: how the hell are we going to get a force 8,000 miles away? I looked at the distances and it was a logistical nightmare – but I had no doubt that we had to do something.'

An emergency session of the House of Commons was called and the Prime Minister's own survival was in doubt. I had never seen my mother on her feet in the House of Commons as Prime Minister and it occurred to me that, if things were as bad as they appeared, this might be my last opportunity. I slung on some clothes, caught the Underground to Westminster and joined the queue for the public gallery.

My mother later described the mood of the House as 'the most difficult I ever had to face'. She began solemnly, but then her voice took on a harder edge. 'It is the Government's objective to see that the Islands are freed from occupation and returned to British administration at the earliest possible moment.'

There were several interjections, including one by Edward Rowlands, Labour MP for Merthyr Tydfil, who blanched at the PM's reference to Southern Thule, which was occupied in 1976 when a Labour Government was in power. He said it consisted of 'a piece of rock in the most southerly part of the Dependencies which is completely uninhabited and which smells of large accumulations of penguin and other bird droppings'.

As I left the public gallery, my mind was filled with farcical images of bird shit and scrap-metal dealers. It made the cries of shame seem rather over the top.

Back at No. 10, I gently opened the door of the sitting room, not quite knowing what to expect. I genuinely feared that my parents might be moving out of No. 10

within days. A few months earlier, my mother had gone round the flat with little sticky dots marking anything that was ours as opposed to HM Government's. The idea was that, if we had to move in a hurry, the removal men would find their job easier.

'Hello,' I said cautiously. She was sitting on a gold-coloured velvet sofa. There was no sign of doubt; this was Britain's first female Prime Minister auditioning for the part of war leader. 'Are you OK?'

'Fine,' she said, stuffing her hands into the pockets of her dress. 'We're down but not for long. I've just been downstairs and told Peter [Carrington] and John [Nott] that we're going to fight back.'

By the following morning, her resolve had hardened even further. Having been to the local church near Chequers, she marched purposefully across the Great Hall and announced: 'I'm going back to London. I know we can win. I know we can get them back if only I had six strong men and true. And I don't know if I've got them.'

During the first few days of the crisis, my father saw very little of Margaret. She didn't need reassurance – at least, not from her husband, who shared her views entirely. If it had been down to Denis, he would have dispensed with the diplomatic foreplay and evicted the 'Argies' at the first opportunity. 'From the word go, I said: "Get them off!" I never had any doubts that we were going to win but it was such an enormous operation.'

I was working for the *Daily Telegraph* at the time and would drop into No. 10 occasionally to pick up mail and hopefully see my mother. She was rarely home, but one weekend I found her sitting on the floor in the drawing room surrounded by peace plans – one brought back by Francis Pym, the new Foreign Secretary, another from Al Haig; there was even a proposal from Chile. They all had a conciliatory tone, suggesting things like 'interim administrations' and 'mutual withdrawals'. The Prime Minister wasn't prepared to 'bargain away the freedom' of the Falklanders and insisted: 'I'm not agreeing with anything until they get off.'

And get off they did. On a Monday night two months later, I was driving down Ebury Street when I heard my mother's voice on the car radio. 'There are reports of white flags flying over Port Stanley,' she said, and I took my hands off the wheel and cheered. Slamming on the brakes and parking, I listened to the rest of the speech, feeling absolutely elated.

My main emotion was relief for my mother. Although I had seen very little of her, images of her leaving No. 10 dressed in black, on her way to give bad news to the House, showed the strain she was under.

Denis wasn't in the gallery for that statement. Instead, he waited in the Prime Minister's room and they went back to Downing Street together, saying goodnight to the policemen on the door of No. 10. 'We went inside, and as we walked past the famous bulldog-pose portrait of Winston Churchill by Salisbury, hanging in the anteroom to the Cabinet room, I swear the great man bowed and said "Well done, girl".' [4]

CHRIS PURCELL

HMS *Sheffield*

I was an Able Seaman (missile man) on board HMS *Sheffield* during the Falklands War. The following is my most-thought-about moment of that time.

We had gone on watch around 12 o'clock; I was on the gun direction platform acting as one of the lookouts. I was one of a few people dressed in our action working dress. On top of that, I had a thermal suit, but could still feel the cold. At about 13.30, I was asked, because I knew the chefs, to go and make a brew for the lads up top. When I got down to the galley, I asked one of the leading chefs (his name was Tony) if I could make a brew for the lads. He said yes, but we had no hot water so I would have to put the copper on. This would take some time to boil, so I took the opportunity to talk to the chefs and the master-at-arms, Brian Welsh. After about 20 minutes, I said to the chefs that I had better get back up top, because I didn't want to abuse the privilege of being in the warm.

So I asked them to give me a shout, or get a message to me, when the water had boiled. Back on the gun direction platform, I made my way to the starboard side, where everyone was asking where the tea was. I said I would go back in 15 minutes. This was at about 1400 hours. I was now positioned on the starboard-side bridge wing talking to the helicopter pilot. The next thing I remember is hearing a broadcast just as the pilot said 'Exocet'. At that, I took cover behind a large ammunition storage box. The missile then impacted 12ft below where we stood. After the impact, I looked to my friend Johnny Trousdale, who was in the Local Aiming Sight (LASSIGHT) but had been blown out, but I didn't realise the impact of the blast. I remember laughing when I saw him trying to relay messages to the Missile Gun Director (Blind) in the ops room, to no avail. Apparently my laughter was shock, but I suddenly grasped the reality when some of the lads came running through the cross passage from the port side (one of whom was really panicking, asking to get off the ship). This made me realise the whole picture of the impact. Not a day goes by when I do not think about that day. And if I had gone back to that galley, I would not be here now.

Members of 'A' Company, Royal Marine Commandos keeping in trim on the deck of the carrier
HMS *Hermes* as she heads south with the Task Force.

DAVID STEEL

Leader of the Liberal Party, 1977-88

In 1981-82, the Liberal-SDP Alliance was winning every by-election in sight, culminating in the hard-fought campaign by Roy Jenkins at Glasgow Hillhead in March.

A week later, the political momentum of the Alliance was stopped dead in its tracks by an event over which we had no control. Argentine forces invaded the Falkland Islands. Fate dealt us a cruel blow. With the sending of the Task Force, British domestic politics were virtually swept aside. We had to back our boys and our Maggie, leader of the War Cabinet. Thus in May, both in the local elections and in the next by-election at Beaconsfield, where Paul Tyler had had high hopes of returning to Parliament, we advanced only marginally. These and two other by-elections in June, at Mitcham and Coatbridge, became almost khaki elections, with Paul Tyler complaining that the Tories were 'hiding behind the Marines'.

The Falklands War was to alter the entire political scene and crucially affect the general election a year later. There was an emergency debate, of which David Owen claims: 'the occasion gave me a tremendous, unexpected public role which I could not have foreseen'. That is not quite the full picture. The Speaker always gave me priority as leader of the third party in the House, but I decided that this made no sense for this occasion.

After all, David Owen had not only been Foreign Secretary, but had actually dealt with a previous Argentine threat to these islands. If I used my position, he would be called well down the list. Consistent with my view of the Alliance, I decided we should play our best card. He should speak up front with Russell Johnston, our foreign affairs spokesman, adding a Liberal voice later in the debate. David appreciated the gesture at the time. He is a better speaker in the House than on the public platform, and he was right to be pleased with his impact. He had a natural authority on the subject which paid us – but especially him – well. My critics say that it was yet another example of my deference to the SDP leaders. I would say that it was fully justified from an Alliance point of view.

The episode deservedly enhanced David's reputation in the eyes of the press and public, and of his own party. He had a good war. The result was that the July leadership election in the SDP was not the walkover for Roy Jenkins that had been previously expected. He won by a respectable margin of 26,000 votes to David Owen's 20,000.

Throughout the war, David Owen and I together accepted private briefings on Privy Council terms from Margaret Thatcher, Francis Pym, the new Foreign Secretary, and John Nott, the Defence Secretary, on the conduct of the war (an offer refused by Michael Foot as Leader of the Opposition), but in the main I was happy for David to lead in public on this issue.

The war ended in the summer, but the political repercussions persisted through the by-elections later that year in Gower, Peckham, Northfield and Queen's Park, where we made further but unspectacular progress in adding to our votes. By the time of our autumn assembly, the Alliance was smothered by the external effect of the Falklands War and internal difficulties over seat allocation.

In my speech, I criticised the post-Falklands outlook of the Prime Minister.

> *Whilst I realise that it does not do to be too fastidious in politics, I have to confess to a real sense of repugnance at the way the Prime Minister has tried to use the heroism of British servicemen in the Falkland Islands campaign to the greater glory of herself and her party. As one Tory MP wrote candidly on Sunday: 'The party is high on the Falklands factor, the gift of courage and skill of our servicemen, which has served to mask for a time the realities of politics.'*
>
> *But that is not enough for the Prime Minister. She has presided over a shambles of incompetence in her conduct of foreign policy and defence. Yet she has set out, quite deliberately, to cover up her administration's nakedness by wrapping herself in the Falklands bunting, by belligerence of language, by a simplistic invocation of the Falklands spirit in the totally different sphere of industrial relations, and by a wish to turn a service of remembrance into a glorification of war. As she plans her parade she should learn there is a difference between patriotism and jingoism.*

I had particularly objected to the way in which all the intelligence warnings prior to the Falklands invasion had been ignored, especially with the announcement of the withdrawal of HMS *Endurance*. She also had declared – ridiculously – that the wishes of the Islanders would be paramount, a view that has resulted in the expenditure of £2.7 billion and a freezing of non-diplomatic relations with Argentina.

The Franks Report of inquiry was in fact highly critical of long-term Government policy, but was packaged and presented in such a way that only the absence of specific blame for invasion that day was highlighted.

In 1980, Mrs Thatcher's Government had been contemplating handing over the Islands on a leaseback arrangement to the military junta; yet Britain had failed to capitalise on one of the major benefits of the war – the collapse of that junta and the return to democracy. In 1985, I met President Raul Alfonsin in the Argentine Ambassador's house in Madrid, just across the road from our own Ambassador's residence, which I used as my base. We were both in Spain for the Liberal International Congress. We drew up a joint agreement that could fully restore relations and safeguard the interests of the Islanders. The wishes of the British Parliament were paramount on the issue, but personal obstinacy on Mrs Thatcher's part prevented a sensible settlement even being considered.

Shortly after the war, I attended the state funeral in Moscow of President Brezhnev together with Margaret Thatcher and Michael Foot – on such occasions, the Liberal leader was always dragged along with the PM and Opposition leader to display our pluralist democracy. It was about this time that my staff shamefacedly admitted to a classic office 'cock-up'. Before the coming of the word processor, the only way we could cope with the volume of correspondence, especially on controversial issues that generated even greater postbags, was by having a standard letter for general issues, which I would 'top and tail' to instruction. I had come in for some criticism for attending the funeral of the Soviet leader Brezhnev, who very much symbolised the old-style and repressive Soviet system. In response to those critics, I had a standard letter. In the aftermath of the Falklands War, also during 1982, I came under fire for not attending the Falklands Victory Parade through the City of London. While I meant no disrespect to our Armed Forces (and had attended a Thanksgiving Service in St Paul's Cathedral), I found the triumphalism of the parade unappealing. After all, the services had had to clear up the mess left by the politicians and did so with great professionalism. But the loss of lives on both sides, and the huge waste of resources involved as a result of political bungling, were not, in my view, cause for particular celebration. And so I again had a standard letter explaining my position. I am afraid that an irate retired Colonel in Surrey, loudly protesting at my absence from the parade, mistakenly got the Soviet funeral standard letter instead. With mounting apoplexy, the Colonel would have read that my attendance did not 'imply approval', that I found the whole affair 'macabre and grisly', but that I took advantage of the occasion to 'renew my personal contact with those from foreign capitals who were also in attendance'.

RODNEY HUTCHINGS

Falkland Islander

After the events of April 2 1982, the Falkland Islands would never be the same again, and this certainly applied to Teal Inlet. Two years earlier, with my wife, Janet, and seven-year-old son Gavin, I had travelled from Northamptonshire with all our possessions to this sheep-farming settlement to begin a new life of tranquillity, and to indulge our love of islands and wildlife.

Now, living in this isolated community of 23 kelpers set in 100,000 acres with 25,000 sheep, we were told that we were extremely unlikely to see any Argentine personnel. Indeed, except for a heavy flow of cargo aircraft and helicopters, and being occasionally 'buzzed' by Pucara and Skyhawk fighters, it was more than two weeks before we saw any ground troops. Then, one morning, two helicopters flew low into Teal Inlet and unloaded Argentine troops, who surrounded and searched each house. An officer informed us that, as the 'English family', we were no longer welcome in the Falklands, and we would be sent back to Britain. Happily for us, the British exclusion zone around the Falklands put a stop to their plans.

Winter was approaching, and the soldiers who were left to occupy our settlement had no food and were poorly clad. For warmth, they lived in the cows' hay barn and visited our houses to demand food. A curfew and blackout were imposed on us, all radios were confiscated, and we were cut off from news of the outside world. We knew that a Task Force was approaching Ascension Island, and our farm manager was not at all happy because he felt that any fighting around Teal Inlet could destroy his farm. We were told that he did not want to get involved with the Task Force should it arrive!

Within days of the invasion, families had left Stanley for the safety of the settlements, but they soon returned when they learnt that Argentines were occupying their houses. Many schoolchildren were evacuated to camp and we received children aged from five to 15 years. With soldiers patrolling our settlement and children wandering around, we felt it would be better if they were safely occupied. I approached our manager who grudgingly gave me permission to continue the children's education in the school room, provided that I fitted the lessons around my own job as handyman.

May 28 was a cold, damp day, with sleet driving across as dusk fell. At 11pm, we went to bed by candlelight after marking school homework. We were soon startled by a banging on the house door. We were concerned that it was the Argentines and so didn't answer the door. But the knocking persisted. I opened our bedroom window to hear the words: 'Well, chaps, obviously no one here, we must try the next house.' I called out 'Are you British troops?', and the reply came: 'We are indeed, sir, men of the 3rd Battalion, the Parachute Regiment.' We rushed downstairs and opened the door to five weary and dirty men in camouflaged uniforms, whom we were astonished but delighted to see. We welcomed Graham Heaton, John Ross, Ian McKay, Stewart McLaughlin and Mark Cox into our home, and as my wife, Jan, prepared the starving Paras a meal, they brought us up to date with the developments around us. We heard of the extraordinary walk they had completed across dreadful countryside from San Carlos to reach us, and for two days they had neither eaten nor had any clean water to drink.

I suddenly exclaimed: 'Do you mean that just the five of you have walked all that distance?!' Someone said: 'Good grief, we are supposed to take you to our Commanding Officer who is waiting on the steps of your school house.' (British Special Forces had been observing our settlement for two weeks and knew where we lived and worked.) I asked: 'How many men are there outside?' I was told that there were between 600 and 700 Paras! Outside in the freezing, sleeting night, Major Martin Osborne told me that his men, carrying enormous bergens, were exhausted, hungry, suffering from trench foot, frostbite and severe diarrhoea, and desperately needed dry, warm shelter and clean water; could we help them? Our farm manager refused to answer his door to receive the news and, for the next three hours, Janet, Gavin and I led 3 Para to shelter in the shearing sheds, workshops, cow milking sheds and stables. Mark Cox and friends came back to spend the night in our house.

At 4am, I had to go to milk our cows and found the milking parlour full of very hungry, wet and cold Paras who asked: 'Can you get us some food, mate?' There were many men around our houses, and to get help quickly I collected all the dehydrated food they carried. Janet and I mixed it up in buckets to get hot food to them. We had a plentiful supply of meat and vegetables, and so we set to work preparing stews for the men. I realised that a major problem was the men's wet and cold feet, and so I collected as many pairs of socks from them as I could and Janet filled her washing machine, while I piled up pairs of boots on and around the Rayburn to dry them (we discovered a grenade in one boot!). Due to the condition of their feet, together with other injuries, several men were not fit to go forward but stayed with us. One member of a machine-gun team had such swollen feet that he couldn't get his size 7 boots on. He was so devastated at being unable to go forward with his colleagues that I gave him my size 11 Wellington boots (with toe protectors), which fitted his swollen feet perfectly. He wore them to fight on Mount Longdon and survived to return home to marry his fiancée, Caroline.

After 24 hours with us, 3 Para had to go forward to Estancia and their ultimate goal, Mount Longdon. I walked with the men to the edge of the settlement and shook hands with them as they left. Stewart McLaughlin was last to leave, and he asked me if he could bring his family for a holiday after the war; tragically, after displaying extreme courage, he lost his life on Mount Longdon.

Later that day, a Gazelle helicopter landed by our house and two Marines asked me: 'Are you the Hutchings family from England?' After confirming that indeed we were, I was told that Major-General Jeremy Moore was on HMS *Fearless* and wanted to establish a temporary tented headquarters on the lawn by our house, and that his bodyguard, the Mountain and Warfare Cadre, would stay with us. He could we refuse? A Chinook helicopter flew in and offloaded their stores into our outbuildings, and later men of the 45 and 42 Commando began entering the settlement. Just before dusk, Scorpion and Scimitar tanks of the Blues and Royals rolled into Teal Inlet and were parked and camouflaged in strategic positions among macracarpa pine trees and dense clumps of gorse.

By now, we realised that Teal Inlet had been occupied by more than 3,000 men of 3 Commando Brigade. Our home was bulging with Paras, Marines, Special Forces, Signallers, Army Air Corps, and for the next four weeks we entertained 28 men. Military food was in short supply at first, but fortunately we had lots of meat and fresh vegetables, and Janet set up an 'open house'. Everyone was welcome to hot drinks and welsh cakes, while at dinner she served up several sittings of delicious hot meals; her meat loaves became quite famous! As the supply ships *Sir Galahad* and *Belvedere* gradually made their way down Salvador Water to Teal Inlet, quantities of 10-man ration packs came ashore, and Janet made use of these supplies to produce meals as our own stores dwindled.

I was asked to help move stores and ammunition, and soon half a mile of essential items stretched from the beach to the settlement. Early in the occupation of Teal Inlet, troops had only hand-held 'blowpipe' missiles to defend the settlement, and when the air raid warning sounded we had to hurry into a slit trench or our own deep air raid shelter. Luckily, we had a 'Cymbaline' radar unit by our home, which gave us a three-minute warning of the approach of incoming enemy aircraft. Eventually the Royal Artillery set up several Rapier Missile batteries around the settlement and we felt a good deal safer. I was told that there was so much ammunition on Teal Inlet that if one Skyhawk got through the defensive screen and dropped its bombs, the settlement would disappear. Hooray for Rapier!

Fighting was already taking place on Mount Longdon and the Two Sisters, and a forward field dressing station was set up in the cook house to cope with the many wounded that were being helicoptered back to Teal Inlet. Eventually the hospital could not cope with the sheer numbers, and Janet and I took into our home a number of wounded Paras; later we took in four men who had escaped the horror of the *Sir Galahad* disaster. They were not physically wounded but severely shocked; these men were present on the *Sir Galahad* both times it was attacked and each time escaped

Men of 2 Para sit down to a rations meal after settling into a sheep pen on a farm at Fitzroy.

unhurt but lost all their equipment. Another of my duties was to clean through the settlement sewerage system every hour of daylight. It was designed to cope with the needs of 23 people and now it was being used by 3,000 troops, plus all the 'throwaway' items from the dressing station. During these work days, I 'bumped' into a medical officer against whom I had played cricket and rugby during my schooldays, a Royal Artillery Sergeant and a helicopter pilot who lived in streets adjoining Janet's parents in Northampton and a Harrier pilot who, in his pre-military days, had worked as our local postman.

In the midst of all this activity, I had rescued a badly oiled rockhopper penguin that had been washed ashore. I cleaned off the oil with margarine, but this process removed its natural water resistant oils, and consequently we had to keep it in our bath for three weeks.

I was asked by the medical team in the hospital if I would go in the evenings to show their patients coloured slides of the Falklands wildlife, and also if I would take the penguin to be photographed with the injured troops. I agreed, but at a price – I charged one tin of pilchards taken from the 10-man ration packs for each photograph, as this was the only way I could get to feed 'Rocky'. He survived the war and was safely returned to the sea.

At last the fighting ceased and the troops moved forward very quickly. A number of soldiers were left on the settlement to safeguard the large quantity of ammunition still remaining, while we set about clearing up the settlement, filling in innumerable slit trenches and getting things back to 'normal'. We felt very flat and missed our military friends very much, particularly WO2 David Rowntree of 3 Para who had worked hard throughout in all activities on the settlement. We were so happy for those who would be returning safely to their loved ones, and devastated for those families whose loved ones would not be returning home. We felt overwhelming gratitude to everyone of the Task Force who had risked everything to restore our freedom.

My last memory epitomised military humour. As he left for home a Royal Artillery Sergeant from a Rapier Missile Battery told me he had enjoyed the Falklands so much that he was thinking of applying for a return posting. To his colleagues' astonishment, he explained: 'Every time I go home until the end of my leave, the wife and I row continuously; weatherwise it is so dreadful down here in the Falklands, I'm sure that this is the only place in the world my missus wouldn't follow me!'

Our proudest memory was being asked to tend the war graves at Teal Inlet, and to erect the war memorial overlooking the burial site.

NORMAN TEBBIT

Cabinet Minister, 1981–87

My experience of the Falklands War was confined to the Cabinet room, where I shared the burden of responsibility, the anxieties, the grief of war and the eventual joy of the peace and liberation. I made only one unique contribution. The Prime Minister formed a Falklands inner group of herself, the Foreign and Defence Secretaries and her deputy, Willie Whitelaw, but it was at my suggestion that she included Cecil Parkinson. As Chancellor of the Duchy of Lancaster, Cecil was in effect a non-departmental Minister who could bring a detached view to bear and effectively represent all the rest of the Cabinet. It was a significant move, making him a national figure and giving him far greater personal authority almost overnight.

Among the casualties of the Falklands War was the relationship between the Government and the BBC. While the BBC correspondents with our forces in the South Atlantic upheld the highest standards of courage and journalism of their wartime predecessors, the unctuous 'impartiality' of the BBC's editorialising was a source of grief and anger. Few of us directly concerned will ever forgive the phrase 'the British authorities, if they are to be believed, say . . .' or the regular references to British and Argentine forces rather than 'our forces' and 'enemy forces'. The elaborate even-handedness jarred cruelly with those whose lives were at risk, those of us who took the ultimate responsibility for committing our forces, knowing the human costs of what we had to do, and with the general public. Nor did the excuse that the Overseas Service broadcasts would lose credibility with their foreign listeners unless the BBC remained 'impartial' hold water because it confused truth with impartiality and balance. It was not impartiality that impelled Germans to risk punishment by listening to the BBC during the Second World War. For me, the British Broadcasting Corporation might have better called itself the Stateless Persons Broadcasting Corporation, for it certainly did not reflect the mood of the British people who finance it. The wounds inflicted by the BBC have still not healed. Its decision in the early 1990s to broadcast one play hostile to the campaign and to block another presenting a favourable view ensured that the wound would fester. [5]

SIMON JENKINS

Journalist

As time passes, small wars easily disappear into the out-tray of history. Two decades on, the Falklands War already seems quaint and memories of it dated. What I shall never forget, and we should never forget, were the arguments. Was the game worth the candle? Did the cause justify the cost in life and limb, in expense and bitterness? Was open war over a tiny spit of land a justified projection of arms, or a silly overreaction to a diplomatic incident?

My memory is of sensible people disagreeing. They disagreed over the importance of the Islands and the validity of the British claim. They disagreed over the chances of military success, which were not great. Americans disagreed with the implicit colonialism of the Task Force to recapture the Islands. To many across the Atlantic, the British seemed to have gone mad.

To me, the armed seizure of foreign territory was wrong and should be resisted if possible. This particularly applied if, whatever history said, the inhabitants demanded the protection of their sovereign Government. If the Falklands could be recaptured by diplomacy, well and good; if not, then by force. It never occurred to me, at least until the Task Force was in the South Atlantic, that recapture might be very difficult and the outcome open to doubt. It was a good case history of the pursuit of diplomacy to the moment when it had clearly failed and then, and only then, the use of force.

The recapture was a military triumph, especially for the British Land Forces who were deprived of air superiority and heavy-lift helicopters. They were crucially aided by American logistical support in fuel and weapons. The alliance worked. British defeat had, eventually, to be unthinkable. But force was not excessive. I still believe the sinking of the *Belgrano* was necessary. The decision not to bomb the Argentine mainland was right. Afterwards, I remain convinced that some United Nations joint-authority lease would have been preferable to Fortress Falklands, but that is largely a nuance. That the war brought the downfall of the military dictatorship in Buenos Aires and a return to a form of democracy in Argentina was a beneficial by-product of the war, not its justification.

The same is true of the fishing and minerals licences that now offer the Islands a sort of self-sufficiency.

Yet the problem has not gone away. The Falklands remain a grumbling imperial appendix off the coast of a distant continent. Some way must still be found to bring them closer to their mainland, if only because that makes sense. But it was a war that needed to be fought. Unlike more recent overseas adventures, it was a war to guard the United Nations principles of self-determination and the integrity of frontiers. It was a just war and can be remembered with pride.

Survivors from HMS *Sir Galahad* are hauled ashore at Bluff Cove.

ANDREW COPPELL

HMS *Broadsword*

As part of the guns crew of HMS *Broadsword*, one of my jobs was rescue-boat coxswain. This is my account of the aftermath of the bombing of *Broadsword* and the sinking of the *Coventry* and the recovery of her survivors.

Coventry left it too late. She fired Seadart, more to frighten the pilots than anything else, but it didn't work. They had two direct hits amidships which crippled her. We pumped thousands of rounds at the Skyhawks but it didn't work. The *Coventry* seemed to lean over to port quite a lot, and then they began to abandon ship. I was told to go and look for survivors in the water using the Gemini. After launch, we headed towards the *Coventry* to begin the search. I noticed two 30-man life-rafts trapped alongside the port side of the ship. By this time, the ship was almost on its side and threatening to crush the trapped life-rafts, so we went to the rescue.

The first one was amidships, which was in the most danger. The men inside were panicking and some were badly burnt. As we approached the raft, some jumped out of the raft in panic so we dragged them into the Gemini. We thought that the ship was going to explode at any moment: there were flames and thick black smoke billowing from the funnel, but we carried on with the job and somehow managed to drag the raft out to safety. We used a small nylon line to tow the life-raft clear of the sinking ship, then left them with our paddles to stop them floating back into danger as we returned to the *Broadsword* with survivors.

We went back for the life-raft at the forward end of the *Coventry*, which was being crushed by a Seadart missile still on the launcher as the ship keeled over to port. On our approach to attach a line, mass panic was evident and people were scrambling from the life-raft to get to the safety of our boat. At this point, it became very dangerous and we had to fight with the survivors to establish some control. We had 16 people inside the boat and around 10 in the water hanging on to the side. We couldn't pull away from the ship. The engine was just not powerful enough. A hovering helicopter saw our plight and used his down draught to blow us away from the ship until we could make some headway. We tried to pull the life-raft away from the ship, but the towing line parted and it was not safe for us to return and pass another line. It must have taken 45 minutes to get 1,000 yards; the boat had six inches of water in it, the engine was straining and some of the men clinging to the side were freezing to death so we had to drag them into the boat and try to warm them up. The boat was heavily overloaded and was threatening to capsize, but we managed to reach the sea-boat, which was straining its engine pulling another life-raft. Our first job was to get the men out of the water who at the time were suffering from hypothermia; these were helped into the sea-boat, then winched up to a hovering helicopter, and the rest were distributed between the two boats. Most of the men had hypothermia, a lot had burns and other injuries, so we set off to the *Broadsword* with as much speed as the overloaded boat would allow.

On the way over, the engine stopped: a rope was wrapped around the prop which had to be cut off. We eventually reached the ship and the survivors had to clamber up a scrambling net; a lot made it, but the majority had to be winched up because they were too weak or their injuries were too great.

By this time, the *Coventry* had turned over; it was pointless to send back the Gemini, so we went under the Davit for recovery. The boat was completely filled with water and the engine was spluttering.

When we were hoisted up, the back broke, folding the boat in half. Tug the bowman managed somehow to climb the man rope on to the deck of the ship.

The boat was eventually recovered and a nice warm mug of tea made available.

LORD ARMSTRONG

Cabinet Secretary, 1979-87

I suppose that my chief memory of the Falklands War is the daily meetings of the 'War Cabinet' (technically the South Atlantic Sub-Committee of the Overseas and Defence Committee of the Cabinet) and what flowed from them.

Typically, the War Cabinet would meet in the morning each day, to be briefed on the course of the campaign in the South Atlantic during the previous 24 hours and related events, and on relevant international political developments, and to take the decisions that were required of Ministers as to rules of engagement and so on. The Chief of the Defence Staff, Admiral of the Fleet Sir Terence Lewin, was in attendance at these meetings, and I was there as Secretary of the Cabinet.

As soon as possible after each meeting of the War Cabinet, Terry Lewin and I would meet in my office with the Permanent Secretaries of the Foreign and Commonwealth Office and the Ministry of Defence, Sir Antony Acland and Sir Frank Cooper, with one or two other senior people brought in as might be appropriate:

- to make sure that the decisions reached by the War Cabinet were clearly articulated and understood, and that they were communicated as quickly as possible to those who would have to act on them;
- to identify the issues on which the War Cabinet was likely to be asked to take decisions the following day; and
- to put in hand the preparation of the papers and briefing required to support consideration of those issues.

This arrangement proved to be useful and effective for its purpose. It was never formalised as part of the structure of Cabinet Committees, but it became widely known in the relevant parts of Whitehall as 'the Armstrong Group'.

I have recounted elsewhere [*Memories of Maggie: A Portrait of Margaret Thatcher*, Politico's Publishing, 2000] the episode of the transatlantic telephone conversation in which President Reagan was unable to convey to the Prime Minister the message which he had been asked to call her to transmit. She wouldn't let him get a word in edgeways.

Sir Robert Armstrong was raised to the peerage in 1988 as Lord Armstrong of Ilminster

Prime Minister Margaret Thatcher and Admiral of the Fleet Lord Lewin, who masterminded Britain's victory in the Falklands, are pictured at the Falklands Memorial Service in St Paul's Cathedral.

JOHN ADAMS

Royal Marines

We had returned from a winter deployment in Norway, where we had been for three months on Arctic Warfare Training. After being in camp for about five days cleaning stores, we were sent on leave.

I remember that day very well, the day the news was released of the Argentine invasion of the Falkland Islands. I heard it early in the morning on the news broadcast. As my wife is a Falkland Islander, I had a keen interest when I heard the name mentioned. When the newscaster reported that the Argentines had invaded the Islands, I felt not shocked, but incredulous. When I was on detachment in the Falkland Islands (1974-75), there were continuous alarms of one sort or another. In fact, the day we were married, in Stanley, 20 December 1974, we were on alert as it had been announced in Argentina that a group funded (it was claimed) by the newspaper *La Cronica* had chartered three or four Boeing 707s to land at the temporary airstrip and claim the Islands as Argentine. It was a bit of a joke really because, due to the length of the runway, they may have landed and gone off the runway, but they would never have taken off again.

Anyway, I told Marj, my wife, what had happened. She was concerned, as her father still lived there. About two hours later, her cousin Landy called to say that her husband Grahame had been recalled. He was with Commando Logistics Regiment, Medical Squadron. At the time, he was Petty Officer Medical Assistant (POMA). I thought then that, as I was in a Commando Unit (42 Cdo RM), it would not be too long before I was recalled to barracks. We had intended to go shopping that morning – it was a Friday, I recall. Anyway, I went for a bath to carry on and, sure enough, the call came as I was in the bath.

I drove to Bickleigh, only to find the majority of people hanging around waiting for decisions to be made as to how stores were to be loaded, what stores were to be taken and whether we were to take Land Rovers. My job was the Commanding Officer's Signaller; it was known that I had been to the Falklands with Naval Party 8901 (NP

Royal Marine John Henderson mans a machine gun above the flight deck of HMS *Hermes* as dawn breaks over the South Atlantic.

8901) and I was therefore asked many questions about the place – terrain, climate, settlement, locations, etc.

We later embarked the *Canberra* and sailed south. I knew we would land to retake the Islands. Many doubted it and thought it was just a show of force. Having been on the Falklands, and knowing the Argentine mentality about the place, convinced me that a fight would ensue. What the outcome would be no one really knew. We kept getting updates of troop strengths and thought we really would be outnumbered. But there was never any thought that we would not win. As the PM of the time said: 'That is not an option.'

We arrived at Ascension Island and conducted training ashore and the transferring of stores between ships. We went ashore for a route/speed march from the Wideawake airfield to English Bay. It was with Fighting Order (CEFO) and my radio – about 35lbs in weight, plus SLR rifle (9lbs). Before we left the UK, I got a new pair of Cairngorm Fell boots from the stores and religiously waterproofed them with dubbin all the way down from the UK to make them supple. After the first half-mile, I had blisters on both heels. After two miles, my heels were raw and bleeding. I carried on to the finish in more than slight agony. The stops were the worst, getting up and starting again. The total distance was, I think, about 10 miles. I wore flip-flops for the next week on board to dry out the raw skin. I still continued waterproofing my boots, as I knew the ground would be wet when we landed.

When we did eventually land, I knew my waterproofing efforts had worked. We had what is known in the trade as a 'wet landing' – off the landing craft right up to my waist. My boots were waterproof all right: they kept the water in!

When we came down off Sierra Montevideo, we moved into the settlement of Port San Carlos. My 'billet' was a disused hen house (the Argentines had eaten them). I used the coops as shelves and cupboards. When in my sleeping bag, I could stretch out with my knees slightly bent, but it was warm and comfortable. On one occasion while we were at Port San Carlos, the CO and myself had to go to 3 Commando Brigade HQ, to be briefed by Julian Thompson, the Brigade Commander, for a task the unit was required to undertake (the night helicopter move to Mount Kent). We flew to San Carlos by Gazelle helicopter at very low level and in an air raid. It was also very windy. I was sure the rotors were going to hit the water as we weaved and banked all over the place at what seemed to be only feet off the ground and sea. That was one 'hairy ride'.

The night we were due to fly out to Mount Kent was a tense one for all those involved. As I was getting all my kit together to leave, there was an air of nervousness about. We were all tense and nervous of the unexpected. We were, to all intents and purposes, going into what we expected to be an opposed landing. As we were all waiting in the community centre, the main accommodation for the signals troop, someone started singing, 'I'm just mad about shrapnel, shrapnel's mad about me', to the tune of Donovan's 'Mellow Yellow'. That seemed to break the ice. All broke out in a nervous laugh. As it turned out, the flight was postponed until the following night. The Chinook had to return from the first flight due to bad weather. It could not land because there was so much snow and white-out conditions. On its return, it damaged its rear landing gear when it hit the water of a lake – it was flying that low. I was told that the relief was visible on my face when we heard that our flight had been postponed, only to go through the whole waiting game again the next night. This time, we did go. We were all loaded down with our kit, plus I had all my radio equipment. Just before we got on to the Sea King helicopter, we were each given two 81mm mortar bombs. The helicopters were well over the peacetime safe loading limit. We were all crammed in (about 25 of us), so much so that the crewman outside had to squeeze the last person in to close the side door.

As it turned out, the SAS on the ground at the landing site (LS) did come across an Argentine patrol about to fire on one of the Sea Kings as it prepared to land. The SAS did not allow that to happen, and took out the Argentines. That was on the first wave with K Company; I was on the second wave with the CO and Tactical HQ (TAC HQ).

After we had taken Mount Harriet, we found shelter as best we could, as it was snowing and windy. My place was on the north side of the feature under an over-hanging rock. Daft, I know – I thought so at the time. Anyway, at one point, I went for a call of nature. Where I went, not far from 'home', I could see Stanley Race Course. The Argentines had their guns there. I saw the puffs of smoke as the guns fired. Automatically assuming that they were firing at us, as it was our turn (they alternated between us and Two Sisters), I ran back and dived under my overhanging rock – I know, a stupid thing to do . . . those around me asked: 'What are you doing?' I said: 'You will see soon.' Then the shells landed around us, one very close, about five metres away. Surprisingly, no one was hurt. We were shelled on and off for the whole day. One story I heard shortly after we had taken Mount Harriet was of another guy going for a crap and 10–15 Argentines, who had been hiding, surrendering to him. He just said to them, 'Stay there, I won't be a minute', carried on and finished what he was doing.

The rest is now history, but as I said to the CO, Colonel Nick Vaux, as we marched into Stanley: 'I think I'll bring the wife back home and live here.'

He said: 'Don't be bloody stupid, you haven't left yet, and why on earth would you want to live here?'

Major-General N F Vaux DSO RM (Rtd) has, on a couple of occasions, revisited the Islands and now realises why I returned to live here. The events of 1982 left an indelible mark on a lot of people for many different reasons, but when people who were in the Falklands in 1982 return to the Islands, they see them from a different perspective and see their beauty. That is why they came in 1982, to guarantee this peace and freedom.

I arrived back in the Falkland Islands on 1 April 1983 (exactly one year after the invasion) with D Company RM, attached to 1st Royal Irish Rangers, for three months. When they all left in July, I stayed behind with my wife and family, who came down in June.

In September 1983, I was formally discharged from the Royal Marines after 15 years of service.

PETER BLAKER

Minister for the Armed Forces, 1981–83

I was transferred from the post of Minister of State in the Foreign and Commonwealth Office in the summer of 1981 to the newly created one of Minister for the Armed Forces, responsible for all three services in virtually all matters except defence procurement. Until then, each of the three services had had its own Parliamentary Under-Secretary. When Keith Speed, the Naval one, made a speech that was regarded as contrary to the Government's Defence Review, he was sacked and the ministerial structure reorganised on functional as opposed to separate service lines.

My first task was to study the Defence Review. When I met John Nott, the Secretary of State, to discuss my impressions, my first point was to doubt the wisdom of the proposal to scrap HMS *Endurance* on the grounds that this could be seen by Argentina as indicating a lack of British resolve to defend the Falklands. John said that this had been a difficult decision, but that he had had long and painful debates with the Admirals on the Review, and when faced with the choice between keeping *Endurance* or an extra frigate in the North Atlantic they had opted firmly for the latter.

My main role during the Falklands War was to back up John Nott while he was fully occupied as a member of the War Cabinet. I remember in particular the extraordinary speed and efficiency with which the Task Force was assembled and despatched, owing to the enthusiasm of the Armed Forces and civilians (I came across the retired Rear-Admiral Sir Morgan Morgan-Siles, ex-MP, in his shirtsleeves helping to load stores on the quay at Portsmouth); the ferocity of the Conservative Party in the House of Commons at the humiliation the United Kingdom had suffered on 2 April and the steadfast support of Parliament for our forces throughout the campaign; the superb spirit of all our forces in very difficult conditions; the difficulties presented for the Government by the new methods of communication available to the media; and the anxiety of waiting for the latest news in late morning as dawn was breaking in the South Atlantic.

One of the questions that have been put to me relates to the sinking of the *General Belgrano*, possibly because it was an answer by me to a Parliamentary Question from

Tam Dalyell MP which revealed that, at the time, she was on a course bearing 270 degrees, i.e. due west, which was of course the direction of Argentina. This was claimed by some to mean that we should not have sunk her, since she was obviously heading for home. This, of course, is nonsense. She could easily have altered course at any time and headed again eastwards, which, with other Argentine vessels on the other side of the Falklands, could have involved a pincer movement on our Task Force. Though some of the feebler souls in the media seemed to take this line of criticism for a while, the British public were too sensible to swallow it and the Argentine Navy did not again present a significant threat.

Peter Blaker was elevated to the peerage as Lord Blaker of Blackpool in 1994

Argentine prisoners of war in Stanley waiting to be repatriated.

STEVE JOHNSON

Falklands webmaster

In early 1982, things were happening in my home town of Plymouth, UK, that I could hardly believe. Returning to my car one day, I heard on the radio something about some Argentine scrap merchants putting a flag on some godforsaken island somewhere. Later the radio told me that we – the UK – would be sending a Task Force to free the islands from the invading Argentine forces. Sitting in a Plymouth restaurant, I heard the sound of Royal Marines leaping around the city, crawling over cars – they were 'high', they were hyped up, they had to be. They were going to 'do it' – the unimaginable. Britain plc was going to war.

That night in Plymouth, the air was electric as hundreds of young men were going to get the chance – if diplomacy failed – to practise the skills of war which the past few generations of UK military had been trained in but thankfully never asked to use. The ships and men then left, not amid a glare of publicity as at Portsmouth, but silently. Quietly they slid seaward past Western King point, accompanied not by a band, but by the sobbing of many a woman, and a few men. Children just gazed. Service families well accustomed to tearful separations could not help but show in action and thought that this 'Goodbye' was different to all the others. To some, it would be 'Adieu' and not 'Au revoir'.

Plymouth shops went Task Force crazy, stocking up with books on Sea Harriers and Exocets, as well as quite a few publications telling us just where the Falkland Islands were. The windows of model shops were heavy with Matchbox plastic replicas of Sea Harriers, and model magazines devoted large features to the new low-visibility paint schemes of the Harriers. We all crossed our fingers and the nation held its breath.

Then victory. Relief for some, tragic loss and grief for others. Many families in both Britain and Argentina wept over these wild islands. A victory parade in Plymouth and the ships came home. Widows and fatherless children on two continents thousands of miles apart grieved amid a sea of jubilation in the UK, and amid a tide of bewilderment in Argentina.

Travelling to Portsmouth to see the Task Force Flagship HMS *Hermes* return, I was totally overcome to see and feel the effects of 'humanity in excelcis', as the *Hermes* steamed past thousands upon thousands of well-wishers who crammed every square inch of Pompey's waterfront. Balloons, flags, flares, fireworks and screams were players among the panoply of helicopters, planes, seagulls, waves, children's cries and tears, orchestrated together by the beat of *Hermes*'s engines. Onlookers at one stage entered the water in a seeming effort to get closer to, to commune with, the *Hermes*, the rusty old ship that was the focal point for countless thousands of pairs of eyes. Almost a seaside Christening, with the wake of *Hermes* as the Holy Water.

Returning to my home in Plymouth, I went down to Western King point to see the ships come. I counted them all out, but sadly I was not able to count them all back. HMS *Ardent* and HMS *Antelope* rest on the sea bottom. Their graveyard is shared with their enemy, the Argentine ship *Belgrano* – enemies when alive, separated by wildly differing political views, but united in death in the same watery grave.

Seeing the ships come back home, amid all the flag-waving and lovers' tears of joy, I often thought to myself: 'What must it be like to be loved that much?'

Steve Johnson runs a Falklands website at http://pentamar.home.dk3.com/falklands or via www.cyberheritage.co.uk

The *Canberra* returns to Southampton escorted by hundreds of boats, yauchts, tugs and dinghies, who greeted her between the Isle of Wight and Southampton

S. S. *C A N B E R R A*

On Friday 2 April 1982, *Canberra* was happily steaming homeward through the Mediterranean Sea on the final leg of her world cruise, when she received a strange message from Head Office asking for the ship's ETA at Gibraltar. A later message instructed *Canberra* to rendezvous with a small launch as she passed through the Strait – to embark a small group of men who would brief them about an 'interesting assignment'. The day before – 7,000 miles away – as *Canberra*'s passengers enjoyed the sunshine of Naples, an Argentine invasion force had seized control of the Falkland Islands.

The British Government assembled a Task Force consisting of warships, Fleet auxiliaries and 'ships taken up from trade' (STUFT). *Canberra* was to be a STUFT. Those men who had boarded the ship at Gibraltar were Commandos and Admiralty officials who would begin making preparations for her transformation into a troop ship capable of operating with at least two helicopters. Before the *Canberra* was even back in Southampton, Vosper Thornycroft had been given detailed plans of the observation deck and crow's nest, and of the Bonito pool and surrounding area. These two locations would have to be rapidly transformed into helicopter decks.

She arrived back in Southampton at 0730 on 7 April and offloaded her passengers as quickly as possible. Then the hard work really began. Military officials from Naval Party (NP) 1710 boarded and took up headquarters in Steiners. Workers from Vosper Thornycroft swarmed over the ship. Parts of the railings along sections of the games deck were cut away to facilitate the landing of helicopters, while hundreds of tons of stores and military material were loaded. As *Canberra*'s immediate future role was an open book and it was not known when or where she would be able to bunker and resupply, she had to be able to replenish at sea, or 'RAS'.

Embarked on *Canberra* were members of 40 and 42 Commando Royal Marines and 3 Para. Captain Dennis Scott-Masson was in charge of *Canberra* and the ship's overall safety. Captain Chris Burne was the Senior Naval Officer (SNO) and had overall military control. After just three days alongside in Southampton, *Canberra* had been transformed from a luxury cruise ship into a battle-ready troop ship – well, almost. When she sailed at 2000 hours on Friday 9 April, a group of Vosper Thornycroft workers went with her to finish the forward flight deck. Crowds gathered to wish her well and her 'passengers' good luck. History was made shortly before lunch the following day, when an RAF Sea King helicopter made the first of many landings on the midships flight deck.

As the ship sailed south, evasive manoeuvres and other things military were practised. On 17 April, she arrived at Freetown in Sierra Leone for bunkering at fresh-water supplies. Other things the British Consul and the P&O representative had to arrange was the delivery of 50 irons and ironing boards and 10,000 paper bags for packed lunches. Shortly before midnight, the ship sailed again – headed this time for Ascension Island. At noon on 20 April, *Canberra* anchored half a mile from Pyramid Point at Ascension Island. From there, those on board were unable to see the airfield and the frantic activity under way there. It was still unknown whether *Canberra* would actually deliver her troops to the Falklands, but things were not shaping up well and a political settlement seemed a long way off.

For the next few days, *Canberra* lay at anchor taking on stores, performing RAS drills and anti-submarine manoeuvres. Fresh water was in very short supply among the Fleet, so *Canberra*'s purifiers were employed to produce fresh water which was then delivered to other ships by tug. It was decided that the ships at Ascension were at possible risk from underwater attack and so, from 25 April, *Canberra* would weigh anchor each evening and steam around overnight to minimise the threat.

At 1654 hours on 6 May, *Canberra* weighed anchor and headed south from Ascension Island in convoy. Three days later, she was 700 miles away and steaming straight for the Falklands, which were now under air and sea attack from British forces. Each evening, the order was given to 'darken ship', whereby all the lights – navigation, deck and cabin – were extinguished throughout the convoy.

Operation Sutton was the code name for the amphibious assault to reclaim the Falklands. At 2200hrs on 20 May, everyone on board went to General Emergency stations for the final approach to the Islands. *Canberra* anchored at Fanning Head at 0017hrs on Friday 21 May. While HMS *Antrim* and HMS *Plymouth* laid down heavy bombardment of the shoreline, HMS *Fearless* and HMS *Intrepid* along with RFA *Stromness* and MV *Norland* disembarked troops of 40 Commando, 3 Para, 45 Commando and 2 Para.

At 0520 that morning, *Canberra* weighed anchor and entered San Carlos Water to begin disembarking her troops amid repeated air attacks from Argentine aircraft. The men of 42 Commando were the reserve force for HMS *Intrepid*'s 3 Para, and they began to leave *Canberra* just after 1000 hours that morning. The air attacks on the ships in San Carlos Water continued until 1600 hours, after which time HMS *Ardent* had been sunk and HMS *Argonaut* damaged. At 1900 hours, the order was given to disembark the remaining troops from *Canberra*, and at 2242 hours she weighed anchor and headed out of San Carlos Water and North Falkland Sound. The troops were ashore and fighting to regain control of the British Islands. *Canberra* had done her job and landed around 2,000 troops without a casualty and without getting hit herself. She had not finished yet, but she was lucky to have survived this far. How the Argentine pilots could have missed the ship was one of the day's mysteries.

The *QEII* had also been requisitioned as a troop ship and was heading south as *Canberra* continued to steam in her 'box' 170 nautical miles north north east of Port Stanley. The order was given by the SNO to head for Grytviken in South Georgia to rendezvous with the Cunard flagship and cross-deck her troops. *Canberra* would be going back to San Carlos Water, while the *QEII* would be going back to Ascension or England.

During the afternoon of 27 May, *Canberra* let go her port anchor at Grytviken. The *QEII* arrived at 2000 hours after being delayed by fog and ice, and the tug Typhoon soon began transferring. Cross-decking continued for most of the following day. Then, shortly before 2100 hours, *Canberra* again weighed anchor and headed back to the Falklands with the cavalry on board.

It took *Canberra* until Wednesday 2 June to get back to San Carlos Water, over 1,500 miles through heavy seas. As the day dawned foggy, the troops began to disembark in small landing craft assisted by four of the ship's own tenders. The first signal received upon the ship's return to San Carlos was for a supply of sanitary towels for the released female inhabitants of Goose Green.

By the time darkness fell, destoring supplies had still not finished, so the SNO made the unpopular decision to remain at anchor overnight in order to finish off the next morning. By the end of Thursday, more than 100 loads had been taken by helicopter and the ship was empty of stores as well as people. She weighed anchor and sailed at 1800 hours with just 620 souls on board. She was heading for the 'Trala' – the 'Tug Repair and Logistics Area' – a large area of open ocean around 400 miles from the Falklands. She arrived in her Trala 'box' on 5 June, and continued to sail up and down her allocated zone with little deviation and little excitement until 14 June, when she received orders to return to San Carlos Water to pick up prisoners of war. The Argentines had surrendered! We had won!

Canberra entered San Carlos Water for the third time on Tuesday 15 June and let go both anchors. Just after 1400 hours, the first landing craft containing 100 Welsh Guards came alongside, followed throughout the remainder of the day by three more containing 1,121 POWs. By 0200 hours the next morning, all had been searched and processed, and just before 0800 hours she weighed anchor and sailed for Port William (*Canberra*'s draft was too deep to sail directly into Port Stanley) to embark the remaining prisoners. More troops were brought on board to act as guards, followed by the rest of the 3,046 POWs.

The ship couldn't sail until Friday 18 June, until the Argentine authorities guaranteed her and her human cargo safe passage. Eventually they did and, at just after half past nine in the morning, both anchors were secured for sea and *Canberra* set course for Puerto Madryn, Argentina, where she arrived the next day – escorted to her berth by a Type 42 Frigate named *Santissima Trinidad*. The returning men got a very cool reception and were speedily bundled off into trucks. Offloading the POWs took just under three hours, and as the last men left, *Canberra*'s hands went to stations – next destination Port Stanley.

It was originally planned that *Canberra* would repatriate another cargo of Argentine soldiers, but as she lay at anchor in Port William it was announced that she would instead be taking as many troops back home as she could carry. Unfortunately, she would be unable to take 3 Para back. There would be no room, as she would carry 40, 42 and also 45 Commando Royal Marines. Both the Paras and the crew were disappointed with the arrangement, but nothing could be done.

The men of 42 and 45 Commando boarded as the ship lay in Port William – ferried across by a local craft and three of her own tenders. As 40 Commando were mainly located around San Carlos, *Canberra* would have to go and pick them up. The ship entered San Carlos Water for the fourth and last time on the morning of 24 June. By lunchtime, numbers 7, 14, 16 and 24 boats had embarked everyone from 40 Commando. Mid-afternoon came and *Canberra* left – headed back to Port William for the embarkation of the last of her designated troops before finally heading for home at 1722 hours on Friday 25 June.

Five days later, the ship was out of Argentine Air Force range and so all the blackouts on board were enthusiastically thrown overboard. The major concern of most on board now was the dwindling supply of beer – the ice cream had already run out. *Canberra* slowed down as she passed Ascension Island, the SNO and Captain Scott-Masson refusing to stop for anybody. Helicopters brought out supplies (including beer), some MoD officials and some entertainers for the troops. Accompanying the men from the Ministry were a handful of P&O representatives sent out to inspect the state of the ship and, along with the MoD, to decide how much they were going to pay for her refurbishment.

Canberra reached the Nab Tower – Southampton's pilot station – at around 0800 hours on Sunday 11 July. Those on board were awoken by the sound of Reveille played over the ship's circuits. The morning dawned a little misty, but would turn out fine and sunny. At the Nab, small boats of every shape and size appeared to escort *Canberra* to her 106 berth home. Aircraft flew overhead, and the ship was briefly joined by the Prince of Wales and other dignitaries who arrived by helicopter to the midships flight deck. The Royal Marines band played on the forward flight deck as more and more boats, fire tugs, passenger craft and even canoes came out to greet the ship.

Those on board the tired, rust-streaked *Canberra* clambered to occupy every possible vantage point – from sitting on lifeboats to hanging out of gun-port doors. Every few minutes, *Canberra*'s steam whistle would boom and a chorus of hooters and whistles could be heard among the now huge flotilla. Home-made banners were tied to railings and held up for the TV cameras, while those on the riverbanks and quayside waved and cheered. As the ship neared her berth, a mass of people (the police said later that they lost count after 35,000 passed through the dock gates) could be seen along the quay – many of them relatives of returning soldiers – waving flags and crying. The band of the Royal Marines began to play 'Land of Hope and Glory' as the ship got closer to 106 berth, to the accompaniment of 2,500 Marines and those on shore.

After 94 days at sea, *Canberra* had steamed 25,245 miles without a mechanical fault of any note, carried thousands of troops into battle, repatriated more than 4,000 prisoners of war, treated 172 wounded soldiers and sailors . . . and won the hearts of a nation. She docked at 1100 hours and, within three hours, all her passengers had disembarked. Two days later, P&O bid a fond farewell to the 129 British volunteer seamen who had replaced the Asian crew members for the duration.

Courtesy of Steve Matthews and www.sscanberra.com

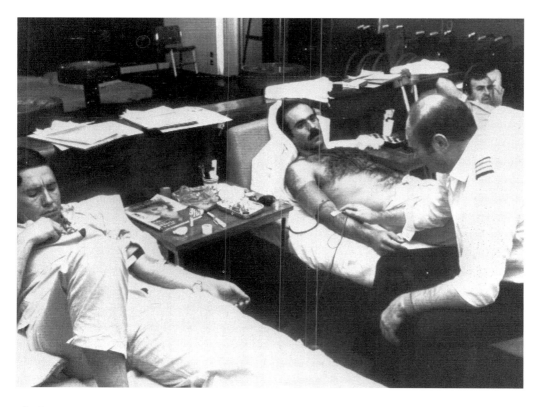

Ship's Surgeon Dr Mayner taking blood from Argentine prisoners who volunteered to give blood for other casualties, aboard HMS *Canberra*.

HAROLD BRILEY

BBC Latin America Correspondent, 1979-83

'They also serve who only sit and scribble!'

I landed from the sea at Port San Carlos in January 1981, 18 months before the British Task Force went ashore in May 1982 to liberate the Falklands. 'What kept you?' I sometimes ask my friends in the forces.

The Falklands were just one of 25 countries on my patch as BBC Latin America Correspondent from 1979 to 1983, eight million square miles from northernmost Mexico to Cape Horne. Most were cruel right-wing military dictatorships that objected to my reports of their murderous activities. I was arrested and came under fire several times covering various conflicts in Nicaragua, Guatemala, El Salvador and elsewhere.

A BBC editor told me not to file stories for the British audience because, he said, 'no one's interested in South America'! Three months before the invasion, I warned all BBC news editors that I expected trouble approaching the 150th anniversary of what the Argentines say was Britain's seizure of the Falklands in January 1833.

Concerned that Argentina might go to war over the Beagle Channel Islands with Chile or over the Falkland Islands, I made reconnaissance trips to both to check the terrain and communications . . . which is why I landed at Port San Carlos in 1981 from a Falkland Islands Government Air Service seaplane. 'If the farmer does not row out to pick you up,' they told me, 'you'll have to wade ashore, chest-deep, carrying the mail!'

I gathered much material about Islanders' feelings over Argentina's claim and made useful contacts, most of whom are still my friends 20 years on. Islanders, who felt no one cared about them, implored me: 'Tell the world who we are and where we are. Please put us on the map.' After the conflict that made San Carlos, Stanley and Goose Green famous names, I went back and said: 'There you are. You're now on the map!'

The previous December, I reported General Galtieri's military coup and was told by Argentine contacts that his talk of 'creating a Greater Argentina' and the appointment

British paratroopers clean out a mortar before the final push on Stanley.

of Dr Costa Mendez as Foreign Minister meant: 'we're going to get the Malvinas back!'
Questioning the British Ambassador, Anthony Williams, I was astonished by his
complacent reply: 'Relations between the British and Argentine Armed Forces have
never been better.'

My bids to see Galtieri and Costa Mendez were refused, but I interviewed the head
of the Malvinas and Antarctic Department, a Senor Blanco, and asked him point-blank:
'Are you going to invade the Falklands?' 'Good God no!' he replied, but I was told it
was their top foreign affairs priority.

Two months later, they did invade. I was the first correspondent to broadcast to the
world details of the crisis on South Georgia and of the invasion itself on 2 April. The
BBC recently re-broadcast my despatch from Buenos Aires, still preserved in the
archives.

Having been forced out of Buenos Aires in 1981 by death threats from the military
regime for reporting mass kidnap, torture and murder, in their own internal 'Dirty War'
of suppression, I returned there from Rio de Janeiro a few days before the invasion. I
was alerted because, uniquely, I had been authorised by the Admiralty to accompany
what was to have been the last voyage to the Falklands of the Antarctic patrol vessel
HMS *Endurance*, due to be scrapped with other vital warships as part of John Nott's
economy cuts. As I prepared to join the ship in Montevideo, an urgent call from the
Embassy Naval Attaché in Buenos Aires told me that *Endurance* would not pick me up
as 'she was stuck in South Georgia'. Sensing a crisis, I took the next flight to Argentina,
beating by a week the subsequent ban on British correspondents when diplomatic
relations were broken.

Most other Latin America Correspondents had gone north to cover the El Salvador
elections, as my perplexed BBC editors agonised over why I wanted to get bucketed
about on some old ship in the South Atlantic!

Filing dozens of despatches leading up to the invasion, I felt no one was taking much
notice. Covering a big anti-Government demonstration in the famous main square of
Buenos Aires, the Plaza de Mayo, I was tear-gassed and had guns thrust in my stomach
by the police, who wanted to know what I was doing. Four days later, I was back in
the square with several thousand ecstatic Argentines, jumping up and down, shouting:
'Argentina! Argentina! We've got the Malvinas!'

Trying to file my invasion report, I was refused a transferred charge call because, the
Argentine telephone operators told me, 'Your country has cut off relations with ours',
to which I retorted: 'I'm not surprised. You've pinched our Islands.'

The Argentines, ever helpful in overcoming my countless communications problems,
linked me instead to the New York BBC office, whose new telephone operator, in the
early hours of Saturday, refused to accept my call on the grounds that she had never
heard of me nor the fictitious name in BBC traffic we used to make collect calls! I was
saved by Canada's CBC, who asked me to file an invasion report to them, which I
agreed so long as they patched me through to the BBC.

For 12 hectic weeks, I filed hundreds of reports, not just to the BBC, but to Canada,

Australia, New Zealand, South Africa, the United States and various newspapers, which had heard me on the BBC.

A senior Argentine Navy Captain, whom foreign correspondents dubbed 'Dr No', daily briefed us on Argentina's version of events and always asked to join me privately to share my Scotch whisky (exports were cut off along with diplomatic relations!) and to listen to BBC broadcasts on my radio to find out the truth – a practice I've encountered in so many conflicts. The Argentines also uniquely delegated six plain-clothes police officers to watch or guard me 24 hours a day, as they patiently continued to do long after all the other correspondents went home. After sleepless nights, they used to ask every morning: 'Mr Briley, when are you going to leave?' I did not do so until my 'tourist' visa expired. I was never granted a working visa.

As well as news, I instituted a weekly personal 'Letter of the Air' to the Falkland Islanders, who, skilled in radio communications, were able to circumvent blanket Argentine jamming of BBC broadcasts, and showed their appreciation later.

I received many messages of thanks from, among others, the Chief of the Defence Staff, Admiral of the Fleet Lord Lewin; Task Force commanders; Captain Nick Barker of *Endurance*; BBC executives and fellow correspondents, including Brian Hanrahan on the Task Force; Sir Rex Hunt, who said there was no more reassuring voice than that of Anthony Parsons (the UK Ambassador) at the United Nations and mine from Buenos Aires; and especially from Islanders.

Free drink for life!

Their most senior Government official, Harold Rowlands, thanked the BBC and me in particular. I was made an honorary life member of the Falklands Association Stanley Committee, of the Goose Green Social Club and of the Falklands Club ('the Gluepot'). They presented me with an ashtray made from a Royal Navy shell, soldered with Falklands coins, and with an inscription reading: 'In appreciation of your excellent reporting from enemy territory.' Their letter said: 'Your courageous effort boosted the morale of the Falklanders during that very trying and dangerous period. We, Sir, will never forget you.'

They gave me a key to the door authorising me at any time, day or night, to help myself to free drink for life. It's a long way to go for a free drink!

At the request of the Foreign Office Minister, Cranley Onslow, I accompanied him on his visit in the immediate aftermath and ran into a huge banner across the road to the Governor's residence, reading: 'God Bless You Harold!'

I was amused when Lord Shackleton told me I was the only journalist whose name he could remember because we spent so long together flying to the Falklands from RAF Brize Norton via Dakar in West Africa and Ascension Island. I reminded him I had to do an extra 16,000 miles to and from Rio de Janeiro!

I've since interviewed many of the combatants on both sides, including Dr Costa Mendez; the Captain of the *Belgrano* and of the *Conqueror* submarine that sank her; and all the chief British and Argentine commanders, including the Military Governor, General Mario Menendez, who gave me tea, in courteous contrast to the death threats I previously had from many of his colleagues.

I've been back to both the Falklands and Argentina several times, most recently to Buenos Aires in January 2002, where I again joined and broadcast about protests in the Plaza de Mayo against the latest Argentine Government and its punitive actions. What a contrast! Economically, Argentina has never had it so bad, and the Falklands have never had it so good, enjoying unprecedented prosperity in a land full of vigour, opportunity and promise. Let us hope it remains that way as, astonishingly, Argentina continues to pursue its claim to sovereignty.

Argentine soldiers captured at Goose Green are guarded by a British Royal Marine.

BROOK HARDCASTLE

Falkland Islander

In hindsight, to Eileen and me the war in the Falklands was an unnecessary evil in our lives. One is automatically inclined to remember all the unnecessary death and destruction, the uncertainty and the abject fear of what might happen to us. We had suddenly lost our freedom and had no control over anything.

One remembers, too, the sacrifices made on our behalf which brought many benefits to all who live in the Islands now.

Except in sombre mood, we are more inclined to put all that to the back of our minds and bring to the fore the many amusing things which inevitably happened during that time in 1982.

One hundred and fifteen of us – the total populations of Darwin and Goose Green – were rounded up at gun point by the Argentine soldiers and locked up in the Goose Green Recreation Hall. Six trigger-happy guards made sure we stayed inside. We were told that we had been put there for our own safety. We felt more like hostages as we helplessly watched the troops move into our homes.

We had no option but to face the many problems with which we were suddenly confronted: how to keep clean, get enough to eat, sleep on bare boards, boil water to drink and how to keep the two toilets functioning. In time, we had even persuaded a platoon of Argentine troops to carry sea water from the beach to keep the loos flushed.

The farm shop was in full view from the hall windows, a few yards away across the green. Argentine soldiers broke into the shop and carried off chocolate and many other goodies. They were found out by the officers. Their punishment after returning the goods was to run around in a circle, egged on for speed by bayonet-toting officers standing in the middle. A fascinating ring-a-ring-a-roses! A guard was subsequently put on the store door. He must have been told never to leave his post. One morning, after he had been on duty all night, we were treated to a silent comic opera. Too frightened to leave his post, the guard had no option but to fill his pants. To put this right – and never letting go of his rifle – he swept back his heavy poncho and undid his trousers.

Maintaining an incredible balancing act, he managed to get one army-booted leg out of his trousers. He repeated the act, getting his leg out of his 'long johns' and back into the clean trouser leg. It was first-class entertainment. The whole performance was repeated for the other leg. He then proceeded to clean himself up, threw the 'long johns' away, did up his trousers and carried on with his war. In our minds' eye, we can still see him and his brown spindly legs.

A few days later, I was summoned and, under the inevitable guard, taken to Darwin by a Major Moore. He told me his grandfather went to Argentina from Liverpool. I told him my wife was a fifth-generation Falkland Islander. The reason for the unusual visit was so I could start the Lister generating engine, a job seemingly beyond them. The Major wanted the electricity for his equipment so he could listen to a 1,000lb unexploded bomb lying on the green among the houses. While he was working away, I took the opportunity to free three pigs that had been left enclosed in a stone corral when we were rudely rounded up. Out they came and drank water from the puddles on the dirt road. The large boar, having had his fill, wandered over to the bomb and, finding it just the right height, leant heavily against it to have a good old scratch. The honourable Major hurriedly retreated, leaving his white tape behind, and indicated that we should return to the green at once. The bomb, joined later by a second one only a few yards away, was still there when we were liberated on 29 May. They were both defused on 30 May by the British EOD and detonated on a nearby beach. The blast was deflected over the sea towards Goose Green less than a mile away by a small cliff. Much to one Islander's surprise, the blast broke his conservatory windows, which he had just finished replacing.

Even as a winner, life is never easy, but one can find an amusing side to it all. What a treat it is to be free again and masters of our own destiny.

RICHARD LINDLEY

Journalist

I'd been a *Panorama* reporter for nearly a decade when the Falklands crisis blew up. With the British Task Force on the high seas, the Conservative Government was determined to keep the country united behind military action. *Panorama* decided that it should consider the minority view that a peaceful solution was still possible.

After the programme, we had a call from the Conservative Party Chairman, Cecil Parkinson, who'd been interviewed in the studio. 'There's a bit of a stink going on down here at the Commons,' he told us. Next day, the programme was denounced by Sally Oppenheim MP in the House as 'an odious subversive travesty' that 'dishonoured the right of free speech'. Margaret Thatcher did not dissent.

Panorama's distinguished presenter Robert Kee had not liked the film he'd had to introduce from the moment he first saw it. A former bomber pilot and prisoner of war in the Second World War, he was understandably very sensitive to anything that might conceivably undermine military morale. Now he wrote to the *Times* disassociating himself from *Panorama* and the programme he had presented. The BBC couldn't have this, so the editor of *Panorama* sent for me to replace him – on what the military call a 'local, acting, unpaid' basis. The next Monday, the Falklands was again *Panorama*'s subject.

It was a difficult occasion. I had to make it plain to viewers that we would not be deterred from continuing to discuss the issues without further inflaming a situation in which the BBC was being seriously savaged by the Government and its supporters. In what I hoped was a polite but persistent way, I interviewed the Defence Secretary, John Nott.

'I felt furious,' fumed a correspondent in the *Daily Telegraph*. 'I am sure many others felt the same to see Mr Nott, the Defence Secretary, wasting an hour of his precious time listening to, and sometimes being interviewed by, Mr Richard Lindley . . . he was subjected to a disgraceful interrogation about the future of the Falkland Islands by a man who holds no responsibility whatsoever.'

Quite right of course, I had none of Mr Nott's heavy responsibility for deciding on war or peace. But I did have the journalist's job – particularly at the moment when somebody's shouting 'Charge!' – of saying: 'Hang on a minute; why are we doing this exactly?' I'm glad to say that, as we reported in the same programme, research showed that eight out of 10 viewers thought the BBC was acting responsibly in its coverage of the Falklands crisis and should continue reflecting a full range of opinions.

Richard Lindley reported for the BBC's Panorama *from 1973 to 1988. His book,* Panorama: Fifty Years of Pride and Paranoia *is published by Politico's Publishing*

Gurkha troops dug in on a hillside at San Carlos Bay.

Men of the 1st Battalion, Royal Regiment of Wales on an exercise in the Brecon Beacons in preparation for mobilisation for the Falklands War, April 1982.

SIR IAN SINCLAIR

Legal Adviser to the FCO, 1976-84

By March 1982, I had been Legal Adviser to the Foreign and Commonwealth Office for more than six years, having been called upon to advise successive Foreign Secretaries on the legal aspects of what were at the time major international issues, including the settlement of the Rhodesia problem provoked by the UDI of 1965, and the continuing argument over the future status of Namibia.

Among other potential sources of conflict was the long-standing claim by Argentina to sovereignty over the Falkland Islands and their Dependencies (including South Georgia). A considerable heightening of the temperature between London and Buenos Aires occurred in March 1982 with the arrival on South Georgia, under suspicious circumstances, of a group of Argentine scrap merchants claiming to be acting pursuant to contractual arrangements which they had entered into for the removal of scrap from the island. But they had landed without permission and were told they must either leave or obtain the necessary documentation to regularise their presence. This was of course the precursor of intensive Argentine military preparations leading up to the invasion of the Falklands on 2 April 1982.

My most vivid and compelling recollection of the ensuing conflict is indeed of its very first day. Having heard of the Argentine action by radio early on the morning of that day, I arrived betimes in the office. At the normal meeting of senior officials at 10.30am, Michael Palliser (who took the chair) began by saying that we had all no doubt heard the news and then continued: 'By the way, Ian, the Prime Minister would like legal advice within the next half-hour as to whether we should declare war on Argentina.' I simply said: 'Well, I had better go and dictate a note for her on that point.' Which I duly did. It was perhaps the most momentous piece of legal advice which I ever had to give during 34 years of service in the Legal Branch of the Diplomatic Service; but it was also one of the easiest. I pointed out that, under Article 51 of the United Nations Charter, the United Kingdom had the inherent right of individual self-defence in the case of an armed attack against United Kingdom territory; and as the

Falkland Islands were under the sovereignty of the United Kingdom, it was entitled, by virtue of that inherent right, to take whatever action was necessary to restore the situation, including the use of force, provided that any forcible action was consistent with the principle of proportionality. I also advised that action by the United Kingdom in reliance upon the right of individual self-defence (including the despatch of a Task Force to the South Atlantic) did not require a declaration of war and that, indeed, a declaration of war could have far-reaching side effects, including, among other things, the activation of the Trading with the Enemy legislation, which would have serious economic consequences.

I also recall the intense discussions that were subsequently undertaken between Ministry of Defence, FCO and Cabinet Office officials about the declaration of a 200-mile exclusion zone around the Falkland Islands during the period when the British Task Force was steaming towards the Islands. The wording of that declaration contained a saving clause designed to ensure that action by British Naval vessels to protect the advancing British Task Force could still be taken in exercise of the inherent right of self-defence of the Task Force itself, even if the action were taken beyond the limits of the exclusion zone.

I might add that, during the period of the conflict, I, together with the late Lord Havers, the then Attorney-General, was a regular attender at OD(SA) [War Cabinet] meetings and at most of the weekend meetings of Ministers and officials at Chequers; but there is not much that I can add to descriptions of these meetings given in Nico Henderson's diaries covering the period (Mandarin, 1994) and also in Peter Hennessy's book *The Prime Minister* (Penguin, 2000) (but subject to what is said above about legal advice on a declaration of war).

I had, incidentally, been a junior Assistant Legal Adviser in the Foreign Office (under Sir Gerald Fitzmaurice) during the Suez adventure in 1956 and had indeed been marginally involved in some of the very early planning work. Sir Gerald made his junior colleagues aware at the time of the extent to which both he and the then Attorney-General (Sir Reginald Manningham-Buller) had been deliberately excluded, during the final stages of the crisis, from consultation by Sir Anthony Eden because it was (correctly) suspected that they would have strongly opposed, on legal grounds, reliance upon a collusive Israeli attack in the Sinai as justifying the use of force against Egypt. I was accordingly impressed in 1982 that the proper lessons seemed to have been drawn from the Suez disaster. In particular, an effective forum, consisting of a limited group of Ministers, senior officials from the Cabinet Office, Foreign and Commonwealth Office and Ministry of Defence, together with the Chief of the Defence Staff (Sir Terence Lewin, as he then was), was constituted as OD(SA), under the chairmanship of the Prime Minister, shortly after the invasion of the Falklands in April 1982, its purpose being to supervise and co-ordinate the conduct of every aspect – diplomatic, Naval and military – of the conflict in the South Atlantic until the recapture of Port Stanley in June 1982. In this forum, it was possible, sometimes not without considerable difficulty, to reconcile potential conflicts between ongoing diplomatic efforts being made by the Americans to resolve the crisis before the British Task Force arrived in the South Atlantic, and the basic British objective of securing the total and unconditional removal of Argentine troops from the Falkland Islands. The influence of the Prime Minister in eventually securing United States support for the military action that had to be undertaken to recapture the Islands cannot be overestimated; though the securing of that support equally required a major diplomatic effort which certainly tried the Prime Minister's temper and patience at times!

An officer from the Royal Marines examines ammunition and equipment abandoned by Argentine troops at Goose Green.

SIR GEORGE GARDINER

Conservative MP, 1974–97

I have never witnessed a more dejected and fractious House of Commons as that which met in emergency session on Saturday 3 April, the day after the Argentine junta had invaded the Falkland Islands – British territory beyond dispute and recognised as such under international law. I had cancelled my constituency surgery to attend, and most other MPs had done the same. Labour was naturally critical that the warning signs had never got through to Whitehall, and on the Tory benches we felt shame that we had allowed British territory to be invaded under our Government. It was a considerable feat of Thatcher's to raise our spirits from the depths, announcing that a Task Force of Naval destroyers, aircraft carriers and troops would be despatched to the South Atlantic to free our subjects, but still there was a desire to find scapegoats. Foreign Secretary Lord Carrington and Defence Secretary John Nott were given a very rough time that evening at a special meeting of the 1922 Committee, Carrington – who as a hereditary peer had no experience of Commons politics himself – faring particularly badly. By Monday, he had resigned.

The effect on the public was much the same as when Winston Churchill called the nation to arms in 1939 and 1940, with only a left-wing/pacifist fringe objecting. In the Tory party, the old conflict between Wets and Dries appeared suspended, though before long it re-emerged in different form, with some Wets arguing that even when our forces reached the Falklands they should never invade to regain British territory so long as there was the remotest chance of agreeing a compromise (i.e. a sell-out) with the Galtieri regime. A leading Wet, Michael Mates, argued in the Smoking Room that public opinion would change 'once the body bags are flown back home', and, predictably, Edward Heath used Commons debates to argue that the exercise was futile and would gravely damage Britain's trading interests throughout South America.

In such a situation, the role of the back-bench groupings like the '92 Group' is pretty minimal. However, we did play a role at one crucial stage. Our suspicions that there might be a weak link in the War Cabinet came after a Commons statement by Francis

Pym on 20 May, in which he implied that our Task Force would not make any landings until the full potential of negotiations had been exhausted. Later that evening, Pym was ordered back to the Commons to insist that this was not what he had meant at all – but by then our suspicions were aroused. Any wobbling by Pym when it came to retaking the Falklands was very serious – especially as he was flying to Washington the following day to continue the dialogue with Alexander Haig! Patrick Wall, the Chairman of the '92 Group', strongly smelled a rat, and we agreed to summon an emergency meeting of the group to consider the situation. This revealed that many of us would feel obliged to resign the Tory whip if the merest fraction of sovereignty over the Falklands were to be ceded to the Argentine aggressor. But how best to make this threat known? We decided to bypass the usual whips' channels and go straight to the top. Party Chairman and War Cabinet member Cecil Parkinson agreed to receive a deputation from us later in the evening, when we warned him of 20 to 30 resignations. Parkinson promised to convey our warning to the Prime Minister and other members of the War Cabinet, and I have no doubt that he did.

I have no doubt that Thatcher would have stuck to her guns in any event, but it is quite possible that our warning served to strengthen the mettle of other Ministers.

Later, on 30 May, as our troops were closing in on Port Stanley, I wrote in the *Sunday Express* of the effect the war had had on us as a nation:

> *First, we have rediscovered our national unity. Second, we have rediscovered national leadership. Third, we have rediscovered national pride – the pride that comes from fighting alone for an undisputably just cause. Finally, we have rediscovered national confidence. For a quarter of a century the British people have lived under the shadow of the Suez fiasco in 1956, when we tried to act boldly in defence of our interests and failed. That single disaster cast a terrible blight on our view of ourselves and what we were capable of doing. Perhaps the greatest thing the Falklands invasion has done has been to lay the ghost of Suez. We have fought for our interests, and indeed for those of all free peoples, 8,000 miles across the world, and we are succeeding. We are masters of our own fate, once we fix on our objective, and pursue it with ruthless determination. Our years of psychological retreat are at an end.*

The final surrender came on 14 June. The Prime Minister announced it to the Commons that evening, and the Opposition leader, Michael Foot, was generous in his congratulations. All acknowledged her sheer determination and fortitude, but only those close to her knew the emotional strain she had suffered with every report of casualties. This was the only occasion in the Commons where I have had to fight back the tears.

GERALD CHEEK

Falkland Islander

I was managing the Falkland Islands Government Air Service (FIGAS) prior to the Falklands War. Around midday on Thursday 1 April 1982, the Chief Executive, Dick Baker, telephoned to say he needed to come down to Stanley Airport, where I was on duty in the Control Tower, to discuss the passenger bookings for the following day. This surprised me somewhat as he had never visited me at the airport before.

The Governor, Rex Hunt, and Mrs Hunt, together with a number of other dignitaries, were booked to fly to Roy Cove settlement the next day. Roy Cove had recently been subdivided into six smaller farms and the purpose of the VIPs' visit was to carry out a formal handover ceremony. When the Chief Executive arrived at the airport, he informed me that tension had increased quite dramatically between Argentina and Great Britain over the sovereignty of the Falklands, and that the Governor had decided he could not afford to be absent from Stanley during this crisis and therefore would not be flying to Roy Cove the following day, 2 April.

However, I was to include him on the passenger flight list, so as not to raise any queries from those persons who were expecting the Governor to travel, and on no account was I to inform anybody of this development. (Flight schedules for the next day, including the names of passengers, were broadcast on the local radio every evening and many people listened in to find out who was due to fly.)

Later during the afternoon of 1 April, the Chief Executive's secretary telephoned to inform me that all heads of departments were to attend a meeting at Government House immediately.

On arriving, I was shown into the Governor's office, where His Excellency and the Chief Executive were discussing a signal first received from the Foreign and Commonwealth Office, which stated that reliable sources were indicating that an Argentine Naval Task Force had left Argentina and was planning to invade the Falkland Islands. It appeared that it was estimating to arrive off Cape Pembroke, approximately six miles east of Stanley, at dawn the following day.

Captured Argentine explosives are examined by an officer of 9 Para, Royal Engineers.

All three of us then proceeded to the drawing room where the other heads of departments were waiting. Shortly after the meeting commenced, the Governor's private secretary appeared with another and much more detailed signal from the FCO about the Argentine Task Force.

The signal stated that the Argentines knew the likely number and disposition of the Royal Marines detachment on the Islands and, somewhat more worryingly, the Argentine Deputy Task Force Commander was already in the Islands. It transpired later that he had arrived on a recent scheduled flight from Comodoro Rivadavia posing as a member of a gas installation team that was in the process of setting up a storage facility for the importation from Argentina of domestic gas for local consumption.

The Governor continued the meeting by outlining his proposals for the tasks to be performed by the various departments in the event of the invasion becoming a reality.

The schools were not to open as normal, and the children were to stay at home and indoors. The hospital was to have all the doctors and nursing staff on duty, preparing for possible casualties. The broadcasting studio was to remain open (it normally closed down at 10pm) and relay news bulletins from the BBC together with any updates from the Governor if and when the enemy Task Force was sighted. The Royal Marines would maintain communications with Government House both from the local patrol ship MV *Forrest*, which would be patrolling the outer harbour and Cape Pembroke area, and from the Marines on shore at observation points.

The single Islander aircraft operated by FIGAS was to be repositioned from Stanley Airport to the racecourse at the west of the town immediately after the meeting. The reason for this was a) to move it from the airport, which would be a strategic target, and b) for the aircraft to carry out a reconnaissance flight at first light to see if the Argentine Task Force was approaching the Islands. Stanley Airport was to be denied for aircraft operations by parking vehicles across the runway. This was complied with, but as soon as the Argentine armoured personnel carriers came ashore at York Bay, just to the north of the airport, they bulldozed all of the vehicles clear of the runway.

The CO of the Falkland Islands Defence Force (FIDF) who was present at the meeting was instructed to deploy the FIDF troops to guard the following strategic points:

Argentine fuel depot
Transmitting station
Power station
Telephone exchange
Broadcasting station
Cable & Wireless
Islander aircraft (on the racecourse)

In addition, the football field adjacent to Government House together with the racecourse were guarded against attempted landings by enemy helicopters; such helicopters, if they came into range, were to be shot down.

Prior to closing the meeting at about 1800 hours, the Governor advised all those present not to mention the matters discussed during the meeting. He went on to say that he would be making an announcement on the radio to advise the population about the present situation, asking people to remain indoors in the event of any action taking place in Stanley. His announcement would also include a mobilisation order for all active members of the FIDF; they were to report for duty at 1930 hours at the drill hall.

I held the rank of Sergeant in the FIDF and, with some 34 other soldiers, presented myself for duty as instructed. Following a briefing from the CO, we were assigned our area of responsibility, and collected our weapons (SLR rifles) and 100 rounds of ammunition.

My assignment was to guard the Islander aircraft at the racecourse with five other ranks. We arrived at around 2130 hours. It was quite an uneventful night; we rang into the headquarters every hour to report if anything untoward was happening and, because the headquarters staff were listening to the BBC (short-wave service) every hour for the world news, we would learn what the developments were from that source.

At about 0600 hours, the CO telephoned to advise that the Governor had learnt that the Argentines had landed by amphibious vehicles on York Bay and all units of the FIDF were to lay down their weapons.

The first indication we had that enemy forces were actually on the ground was at about 0630 hours, when we heard a burst of machine-gun fire followed by one or two explosions which sounded like hand grenades at the Royal Marines Barrack at Moody Brook.

It did not sound as if there was any exchange of fire – in fact, the actual attack was all over in a few minutes and nothing further was heard. We later learnt that all of the Marines had left the barracks and were patrolling etc, as mentioned above.

An Argentine patrol arrived at the racecourse later in the morning and marched us back to the FIDF headquarters, from where we were told to return to our homes, take our uniforms off and not wear them again.

As we were being marched past Government House, an Argentine Naval Lynx helicopter landed on the football field. This only added to my depressed state of mind given the circumstances at the time, as this was the first Lynx helicopter, which of course was British-built, to have landed in the Islands.

Argentine flags were flying from every available flagpole; an enormous one had been hoisted up the flagpole at the Secretariat (the FIG's administration centre) which, during a particularly severe gale a few days later, caused the pole to break in half – to the delight of the locals.

During the afternoon, the Argentine air traffic controller, a warrant officer in the Argentine Air Force who had worked with me in the control tower over the past year during movements of the Argentine aircraft at Stanley Airport, arrived at my home. He explained that he had been sent to collect me to go to the airport. Although I expressed considerable animosity about having to accept orders from him, I was actually very interested in having the opportunity to visit the airport to see what was happening there. Indeed, I would have made my own way there but the occupying forces had issued a decree telling all the local population that they had to remain in their homes. If anybody wanted to go out, they would first have to attract the attention of an Argentine soldier by hanging a white flag out of their window.

On the way to the airport, we passed lots and lots of Argentine soldiers along both sides of the road, marching from the airport to Stanley and beyond. They were all wearing American-style helmets with large goggles on the front. Their goggles were twinkling in the sunlight like fairy lights on a Christmas tree. They could be seen from a mile or more away. Decidedly non-tactical, I remember thinking.

When we arrived at the airport my escort seemed to lose all interest in me, so I wondered upstairs to 'my' control tower, where several Argentine Air Force personnel were congregated, some operating various types of mobile radios. A Fokker F28 aircraft together with two C130 Hercules were parked on the apron, the latter unloading troops and equipment. Some helicopter traffic was also in evidence. I particularly recall Sea Kings shuttling military personnel to the airport from an Argentine ice-breaker anchored off the coast.

Indeed, it was the busiest scene I had ever witnessed at Stanley Airport; in peaceful circumstances it would have been good to see, but certainly not on 2 April 1982. In fact, some years later I came across an Argentine Air Force account of their bridge during the Falklands War, which stated that, on their busiest day at Stanley, they had 76 aircraft landings.

While in the tower, word must have got around as to who I was and a young Argentine Air Force officer, who had discovered a small amount of petty cash in the desk drawer, insisted that I take it provided I signed for it.

After being asked about the workings of some of the standby radio equipment and its power supply, which I could not remember about, and being equally unhelpful on other work-related matters, I was driven back to Stanley.

On the way back, we called in at the Cable & Wireless transmitting station where some of the airport radio equipment was located. There I met one of the local radio technicians who told me (out of earshot of the Argentines present) that the BBC World Service had reported that Maggie Thatcher had announced that a Naval Task Force was being prepared and would sail in a very few days to recover the Islands. That was obviously the greatest news I had probably ever heard in my life. Having not slept for some 36 hours and been subjected to the trauma of enemy occupation, I then felt extremely uplifted and immensely grateful to the Prime Minister and all those who supported her for taking such a momentous decision principally for the sake of fewer than 2,000 people.

The rest of the war was long and tedious – but, having said that, it was a remarkably short period of time in which to prepare a Task Force, have it sail more than 7,000 miles, and then for the troops to march over difficult terrain carrying enormous loads in often severe weather conditions and, at the end of it all, to successfully engage the enemy forces and defeat them in hard and well-fought battles.

Some three weeks after the invasion, I was arrested along with 13 other civilians for reasons of which I am still unsure – perhaps they thought we posed a threat to their war efforts – and put on a helicopter and flown to Fox Bay on West Falkland, and interned there for the remainder of the occupation.

The next uplifting moment for me, and I know for the entire Falklands population, was when the surrender was signed. I heard the news, again, via the BBC World Service and, if I remember correctly, we had a wee dram to the strains of 'Rule Britannia', which was played at maximum volume in the hope that the Argentines would hear it.

During the following morning, 15 June, a Lynx helicopter from HMS *Avenger* landed at Fox Bay with a Naval party to implement the surrender of the Argentine forces. It was truly a wonderful sight to see this helicopter landing – indeed, a completely different experience to witnessing the Argentine Lynx landing in Stanley some 10 weeks earlier. We were liberated: fantastic!

JOHN KISZLEY

Commanding Officer,
2nd Battalion Scots Guards, 1981-82

I don't remember who it was who said that war consisted of long periods of sitting around doing not much, punctuated by brief moments of frenetic activity. Whoever it was, he knew a thing or two. It was certainly true of my experience in the Falklands War, but curiously it's not how I remember it, 20 years on. Quite the opposite, in fact. My memory is almost entirely of the frenetic activity, although it can't have lasted for more than seven or eight hours.

However well you are trained – and I reckon we were very well trained – you are not fully prepared for the real thing. Your training stops short of the real thing. Perhaps my most vivid memories are of things that surprised me. First was the noise. With artillery and mortar rounds exploding close to you, your ears are ringing and you become partially, sometimes almost completely, deaf. You realise this only when you shout at someone to do something and it's quite clear that they can't hear you. The only way to get your message across is to run over to them, grab them by the arm and shout into their ear. Then there is the effect in the dark of immensely bright flashes of light as the shells and grenades explode. You are blinded, and just as your eyes get accustomed to the dark again, the same thing happens. You also become entirely focused on the enemy to your front, and miss what's happening to the sides or behind you. The result of all of this is disorientation and confusion.

When things start to happen, they do so very quickly. Your mind races to keep ahead of the enemy, to make sense of what is happening and react accordingly. If you are in command, you have so much to think about that you don't have time to be fearful, even in the lulls. It's those who are being commanded who have the really difficult job. They have time on their hands. And they need courage and discipline to conquer their fear. I remember gasping with admiration at the courage of the people in my Company, and drawing strength from them. But then, they were an exceptional bunch of people, that Company, both as individuals and as a group.

I remember a curious flashback, when things looked particularly grim. As part of what the Army called 'Adventurous Training', I had been skippering a yacht in the Fastnet Race three years before. My mind went back to the moment when, in the middle of a vicious storm that claimed 20 lives, we were dismasted close to a lee shore. Things looked grim then, but we did the right thing and got through it. Doing the right thing now would get us through it as well. As dawn broke, we got to the top of the hill, and the following Company passed through to secure the remainder of the objective. I remember very mixed emotions. First, elation that we had done it. We had actually done it! And Tumbledown was ours. But as the casualty reports came in, it became clear that the cost to the Company had been seven men dead and 18 seriously wounded. That was a sobering moment for a Company Commander in the cold, grey light of dawn.

I also remember, after the conflict, being furious when we were told we would be among the last to go home. We were sent to a farm on West Falkland where we lived in the barns and haylofts for several weeks. In the event, it wasn't too bad. We unwound, and most nights we all met for a few beers, had a sing-song, talked about those who hadn't made it, that sort of thing. By the time we eventually got back to Britain – needless to say, by sea, not air – we had got a lot of it out of the system. People who flew home straight after the war and dispersed on leave didn't have that advantage. And it just didn't seem relevant to talk about it to outsiders.

Looking back, the other thing that strikes me about the Falklands was just how brief it all was. Compared to the experience of those Second World War veterans who fought through a war that lasted years, the Falklands was just a skirmish, and Tumbledown a one-night stand.

BOB MULLEN

Leading Seaman, HMS *Sheffield*

4 May 1982

Having been in the total exclusion zone now for three days, who could tell what tragic events lay ahead for myself and the rest of HMS *Sheffield*'s Ship's Company. A day that would change the lives of so many people for ever. At the time, I was a 23-year-old Leading Seaman (Radar), my Action/Defence watch station was as SPS (Surface Picture Supervisor), and I had been on the forenoon watch in the operations room. After being relieved at 1155 hours, I went and had some lunch, had a dhobey (wash), and went down the mess (3Q stbd) to get some shut eye, as I was due back on watch a few hours later.

The day was an 'on it' day. We had 'in it days' and 'on it days' as the weather was nice up top, which meant good flying weather. We took off only our boots and lay on top of our bunks. I wrote a couple of letters and decided that now was the time to get my head down, as it was about 1345 hours. At about 1400 hours, a main broadcast pipe – 'AAWO report to the ops room at the rush' – woke up me and the rest of the lads in the mess. Being radar operators, everyone knew something was happening. It must have been about one, maybe two minutes later that we heard a dull crump (which actually sounded like someone had dropped a hatch); about 10-15 seconds later, black smoke was pouring into the mess through the air-conditioning. At this moment, we all knew we had been hit.

Amazingly, as I look back, there was no panicking: people just got on with whatever they were supposed to do in an emergency. As we left the mess, we were all picking up firefighting equipment and started towards the fire. I remember having a fire hose in my hand as I turned to go forward from 2N flat shouting for someone to turn on the water. We could not get any further forward, as the door leading to the canteen flat was stuck, so after a quick think the Leading Stoker from the after section base told us to start boundary cooling against that bulkhead. It was at about this time that we realised the water had not been turned on. We then found out that there was no water pressure and the hose was useless. All the above had happened in a couple of minutes. At this point, no one knew if we were sinking or what was going on, so everyone went up top to 1 deck to see what was happening.

As we came out on to the upper deck, everyone was leaning over starboard guardrails. As I looked over, all I could see was thick black smoke pouring out of a big gash in the ship's side, and I actually felt relieved that we had not been hit below the water line and were still afloat. The next few hours are a bit confused. I can remember lots of different jobs and tasks that I was told to do while we tried to save our ship, but it is still quite hard to put these events in any order. I remember emptying the top part of the ship locker of all the paint that we had stowed there, and throwing it all over the side, then using heaving lines with buckets tied on to get water for boundary cooling the ship's side, and screens. After that, I think we had to empty the entire two-three inch ammunition lockers and hoof them over the side. All this was being done because, with the decks as hot as they were, the command feared that ammo or paint might cook off and spread the fire.

After the two-three inch, the buffer told us to lower the Chevy (boat) into the water so we could get a firefighting team to pump water into the gash in the ship's side. This never happened because, with no hydraulics, we could not lower the boat. So we went to the after gun deck and lowered the Gemini and got a team around the starboard side that way.

I then reported to the hangar and we emptied the air weapons magazine. I was then asked to report to the tiller flat to man the emergency steering position. This is when the reality of what was happening actually sunk in. I was in the tiller flat with only two other lads and it was dark, with no information coming in, so we had time to think. I don't know how long I was down there, but I do know that it felt like years. Eventually I was relieved and reported to the quarterdeck.

On reaching the quarterdeck, we had to try and start the rover pump. I think this was about the third or fourth one that people had tried to get working; they were being flown over from HMS *Hermes* as ours were either damaged or unreachable. Eventually we got one working and I went to the flight deck. By this time, HMS *Arrow* and HMS *Yarmouth* were station-keeping off our port and starboard sides and spraying water to boundary cool the ship. *Yarmouth* was also firing her Mark 10 mortars at what they believed were submarine contacts. HMS *Arrow* eventually tied up along side us and I was in charge of the after spring, and that is where I stayed until the captain ordered abandon ship.

As I said before, some of the events may be in the wrong order, but, as you can imagine, it was a very confusing time. I am still reminded of other things that happened when I meet other ex-Shiny Sheffs at reunions. Looking at my watch after I had jumped on to the *Arrow*, I could not believe how much time had actually passed. I would like to say that the Ship's Company of HMS *Arrow* were fantastic that day, as were the crews of HMS *Yarmouth*, RFA *Fort Austin*, RFA *Resource* and the BP tanker British *Esk*, who, by being there, got all the survivors of HMS *Sheffield* back home safely. Sadly, we had to leave some of our shipmates behind, but think of them always.

HMS *Sheffield* after being hit by an exocet missile. She later sank with the loss of 20 lives.

SIR GEOFFREY PATTIE

Junior Defence Minister, 1979–83

The British are often described or like to be described as hugely innovative. One is frequently told of numerous inventions that were made here and then produced elsewhere subsequently. It is at times of national crisis that the innate genius of the Brits seems to be particularly stimulated.

When I was in the advertising business, I worked for a Chairman whose wartime work had concentrated on designing and developing exploding cowpats, which were capable, when fully effective, of causing serious disruption to the Wehrmacht rear echelon areas. My Chairman was most eloquent on the chemical formulae necessary to attract flies, for without the mandatory covering of hovering flies the cowpat was clearly a British mine and not a cowpat.

By the time, in 1982, the Falklands conflict looked as though it would become a war at any moment, I was junior Procurement Minister at the Ministry of Defence. As the lowest form of ministerial life, I was the obvious choice to receive, entertain and deal with the surge of wartime inventors who were eager to put themselves at the nation's disposal.

I have always approached such people with caution. I am not scientifically qualified and am nervous about adding my name to the list of those who have failed to recognise genius – 'that idiot Whittle with the clearly unworkable jet engine' and 'Barnes Wallis with the bomb that will never bounce, you can take my word for it'.

I imagined myself looking out into the waiting room full of men with brown paper bags on their knees.

It was decided that it would be better for morale and the 'conflict effort' if such people did not come into the Ministry of Defence. Instead, they were invited to the People's Palace of Varieties, otherwise known as the House of Commons, presumably on the grounds that the eccentrics would not stand out there.

I went to the Central Lobby of the House and approached the policeman at the desk. 'Is there a Mr Wattenchop here to see me?' I asked. The policeman indicated a tall, red-haired man wearing an overcoat and standing with his back to me. I approached him and he turned round. I half expected him to give me a Clapham Common full-frontal reveal, but his hands remained at his side and he had no paper bag. We talked.

He owned a light aircraft and had developed a device for shooting a stream of glue over objects on the ground – he had in mind Argentine gun crews.

The man with the plan for building an aircraft landing platform made entirely from ice was getting closer to the world of reality, but he and the others had to be put on hold for the duration of the conflict.

The procurement process became positively supersonic – nine-month programmes were completed in a matter of days – but there was no avoiding the fact that, in the end, it was the quality of the fighting services which gained the victory.

Seargeant David Newton is reunited with his children Jed and Caroline in Portsmouth on his return home from the Falklands

DENZIL CONNICK

3 Para

I joined the Parachute Regiment's Junior Parachute Company based in Aldershot as a 15-year-old boy soldier straight from school in September 1972.

In hindsight, I realise that I never had the slightest clue what I was getting myself into. As a boy barely in puberty, I suppose that my own idea of life in the country's top regiment was completely at odds with reality – as I quickly found out!

As Junior Paras – or 'junior sparrows', as the adult soldiers called us – we were instructed and cared for by serving adult NCOs and Officers of the regiment, who, compared to our mothers and fathers, were fearsome maniacs. After a period of 'culture adjustment', I enjoyed my adventures as a 'junior sparrow' and, after some two years, newly adorned with my maroon beret and jump wings, joined my regiment's 3rd Battalion (3 Para). Less than 10 years later, by the time of the Falklands War, I was a 25-year-old Lance Corporal who had seen service in much of the then 'free' world and had completed three separate tours of duty in Northern Ireland. I suppose I was an experienced 'old sweat', well versed in the art of soldiering and already 'blooded' with the initiation test of being at the wrong end of bombs and bullets.

At this time, I was stationed with my Battalion at Candahar Barracks, Tidworth, on Salisbury Plain. My job was now Platoon Radio Operator for the Anti-Tank Platoon. In fact, I had three jobs, as I was also a gun crew member, when needed, on the 120mm WOMBAT (Weapon of Magnesium Anti-Tank) and the platoon store man, the latter of which was a tedious, thankless task, but one that required a reliable, responsible person to do it. I did not consider myself *that* responsible then.

My Battalion was already on standby as the country's 'spearhead' unit. This meant that we were on 24 hours notice for deployment anywhere in the world for whatever emergency to do with national security or (tongue in cheek) binman strike duty.

We were all briefed, prior to being sent on Easter leave, about potential 'trouble spots' – typically the likes of Northern Ireland or the Middle East. Certainly, there was not the slightest mention of trouble brewing in the Falkland Islands.

When the 'call-up' for the Falklands eventually came, I was enjoying a weekend at the Army Gliding Club at RAF Upavon. I was a keen glider pilot and also ran the club bar. It was well into the evening when, after copious amounts of Wadworths 6X ale, the telephone rang and I spoke to my Colour Sergeant Steve (Shakespeare) Knight. It should be known that Steve's nickname of 'Shakespeare' was not given for his great command of the English language – indeed, quite the opposite.

Shakespeare said to me: 'Denzil, get your fookin spunkin fooking arse back here now, we're off to war in the fookin Falklands . . . wherever that fookin is!' He also had this nice gentle Yorkshire accent. My reaction is now legend at the Upavon Gliding Club bar, as I turned to those present and said: 'Sorry, folks, the bar is closed. I'm off to war.'

It was not long before 3 Para were assembled at the dock side in Southampton to embark the P&O *Canberra*. The *Canberra* – or 'the great white whale', as she later became affectionately known – was STUFT (ship taken up from trade) and was now a troop ship and our home for the coming weeks.

There was much cheering, tears and flag-waving as the *Canberra* slipped her mooring and nudged gently away from the quay. We lined the decks and waved back to the crowds on the quayside, and I was rather moved by all the fuss as the bands of the Royal Marines and the Parachute Regiment played us off to the music of 'Sailing' by Rod Stewart. Getting under our own steam and heading off through the Solent, it was almost dark as we watched our coastline get further away. The roads lining the coast were crowded with cars, which flashed their headlamps and honked their horns, until finally we were alone. I remember thinking to myself as I leaned on the ship's rail getting a last glimpse of England: 'Will I see my homeland again?'

Our voyage south was interrupted by a short stay at Ascension Island, a rocky volcanic spot close to the equator in the mid-Atlantic. I was impressed by the gathering ships that joined our Task Force laying at anchor. Their was much activity as helicopters buzzed about like attentive bees transferring stores from one ship to another. This stopover was also a good opportunity for us Paras to practise the alien art of going into action by landing craft – or 'floating rubbish skip', as we called them, much to the irritation of our Royal Marine comrades. On this dusty baron island, we test-fired all our weapons, including our WOMBAT and MILAN missiles. The blast of these heavy weapons created an immense cloud of volcanic dust, and a moment later, as the warheads exploded, another cloud of dust rose, accompanied by flocks of frightened seabirds. Bill Oddie would have had a fit should he have witnessed this.

As we were preparing to return to *Canberra*, this time by helicopter, we waited at the airport close to the Vulcan Bomber that had just returned from its record-breaking long-distance sortie to bomb Stanley airfield. The ground and air crews were celebrating under the shade of the bomber's huge delta wings, drinking cans of beer sent by the Bass breweries for the consumption of all of us. We were a little jealous of this first hit by 'Crab Air' (RAF), but we were also very proud of them. We learnt months later that most of the beer donated to the Task Force only got as far as Ascension Island, and was drunk by the crabs in their shorts and bloody flip-flops.

As we continued our voyage south, the temperature cooled and the seas got rougher. Our minds were also by now very focused on the task ahead, as we knew now that we would be going into action . . . there was no turning back. The Argentine cruiser *Belgrano* was sunk by HMS *Conqueror* and we had lost one of our own ships, HMS *Sheffield*. Things were very serious now and we all knew that this was no training exercise; hundreds of lives were already lost and we were not yet at our destination.

Orders for the landings were given and we learnt that we would be going ashore at Port San Carlos; D-Day was 21 May. We cross-decked on to HMS *Intrepid*, an assault ship that could flood an internal dock that contained the landing crafts. We spent about 24 hours on *Intrepid* and were shocked by the terrible loss of life when a Sea King helicopter with SAS soldiers on board crashed into the sea just as it was about to land on our ship. This was not good news, especially since we were on the verge of going into action, and it served to hype my nerves up to a terrible level. Sleep was impossible, besides being very cramped in the accommodation, and adrenalin was pumping around me so much that I thought my heart was going to burst.

Weighed down with our equipment, we finally gathered on the landing craft and set off towards the beaches. This was meant to happen under the cover of darkness but, because of delays, we were heading towards the beaches in bright sunlight, giving us even more jitters. The landings were almost completely unopposed – a great relief, as we were expecting some resistance. There was an Argentine force of about platoon strength in and about San Carlos, but they decided wisely to 'leg it' on seeing the vast gathering of warships and landing craft in San Carlos Water. Sadly, they decided to attack a small Gazelle helicopter that had strayed too close to them as they retreated; they shot it down, and then shot and killed the two-man crew as they were escaping their stricken craft close to the shore. I remember seeing the body bags containing the two men being carried into the settlement of Port San Carlos and felt very sorry for their bad luck and angry with the cowardly action of the enemy soldiers. This first action during the landings infuriated us Paras and Marines, and we were more determined than ever to avenge the aircrew.

A day or so following the landings, we broke out from the beach-head area of San Carlos and the big march east began. This was not before we watched the air attacks from the high ground surrounding San Carlos Water. We had this grandstand view of our ships at anchor as they were bombed and strafed by the Argie Hawks and Mirage fighter jets. This gave many of us the chance to vent our frustration at the attacking aircraft by firing at them with our rifles and just about anything we could lay our hands on. We even had one of our MILAN lads fire his anti-tank missile at one jet as it flew past at eye level through the valley. The missile was wasted of course and the firer was given a great bollocking for his cavalier action. It did, however, provide us with a good laugh too, as this missile ran out of steam at the end of its guiding wire and exploded on the opposite hillside containing dug-in Marines. Orders were soon given to stop shooting at the aircraft with small arms because, besides being of little use and a waste of ammunition, it was becoming a serious hazard to the troops on opposite sides of the valley.

The long forced march – or 'tab' (Tactical Advance to Battle), as the Paras called it – was one of the hardest things I had ever done in my whole service. We were required to march with our kits weighing around 100lb each to Stanley, which was 70 miles away. Our first objective was Teal Inlet, a small farming hamlet. The march took us over the most inhospitable terrain imaginable. The peaty ground was always wet and boggy, interspersed with glazier-like stone runs that were a nightmare to walk on. The weather was getting worse, with blizzards and high winds. Some casualties were being taken with trench foot and frostbite and with twisted ankles. The weather and terrain conditions were as much a challenge to us as the fighting itself, and it was just as well that we were quite accustomed to this through our training in the Brecon Beacons in Wales. Indeed, the Brecon Beacons were almost identical to the land we were now on.

The cold weather and lack of food was a distraction from the fighting to come. We became very resourceful in finding fresh food by having our snipers shoot wildfoul to supplement the bland rations we were given.

Our sister Battalion, 2 Para, were advancing to our south and were given the job of taking Goose Green settlement. It was after this epic battle that we learnt of the great bravery of our many friends and brothers in 2 Para, with the loss of their CO, Lt Col 'H' Jones and 13 other comrades, against overwhelming odds. 'H' Jones was later awarded a posthumous VC. We were by now cold, tired and hungry, and wanted desperately to get the job finished.

We arrived at Estancia Farm about ten miles from Stanley and would spend nearly a week here to prepare for our battles. The enemy had retreated in front of our advance and were now cornered like rats on the high ground that encircled the town of Stanley.

The objective given to 3 Para was Mount Longdon. Longdon was a long, saddle-like feature that was a key enemy stronghold lying in direct sight of Wireless Ridge, Moody Brook and Stanley. To the side of Longdon were the imposing features of Tumbledown and Two Sisters, the battlegrounds of the Marines, the Scots Guards, Welsh Guards and Gurkhas.

I remember vividly the reconnaissance patrol on to Longdon that I took part in. We were looking for a suitable position to site our 'Support Fire Team' with their SF GPMGs, MILAN and mortars. We needed to get close in to Longdon and were within about 200 metres of the first line of Argie troops. We were about finished with our recce when we noticed that a small group of trucks had arrived to deliver hot food. The food was being served up to a growing queue of soldiers when we thought this would be a super opportune target for our ship and shore artillery to play with.

As the radio operator, I transmitted the co-ordinates for the 'fire mission' and we watched as the shells screeched over our heads and hit the target with the first salvo. I gave orders to 'neutralise' for two minutes and then saw the target destroyed and the mission ended. We all ran off like naughty schoolboys into the night, giggling over our mischief, even though we had wreaked death and injury.

Two days later, on the night of 11 June, we retraced our steps back to Longdon ready for our battle. We knew that the objective was defended by about a company of enemy troops (this was to be nearly two companies). Our B Company was to lead the Battalion for a 'silent' assault. This meant we wanted to be into the first of the enemy trenches before they realised what was happening, relying on the advantage of surprise. Most assaults are preceded by a barrage of artillery, and therefore the enemy can expect an attack. By denying ourselves this, we were hoping to have the greater advantage of surprise. Alas, like all great plans of mice and men, this was ruined when Cpl Brian Milne set off a mine, which blew off his foot, just yards away from the first enemy trenches.

We set up our support fire base as our rifle companies lined up on the 'start line', fixed bayonets and began their advance to contact. When Brian set off the mine, all hell broke loose. The enemy, being alerted to the attack, began firing down on to the advancing Paras. The tracer fire arched up and towards us; it seemed to begin in slow motion and then, as it closed, flashed by at supersonic speed, making whip-cracking noises as it did so, then the gun itself could be heard firing with a deeper pop-pop-pop sound. The shouts of our lads in English soon blended with the Spanish shouts of our enemies.

Our fire base became unusable as our advancing troops were in danger of being cut down by our own fire, so we needed to move to a position that would provide them with better and safer supporting fire. We were ordered to move to the summit of Longdon, where fighting was still happening. The enemy bunkers here still contained Argentine soldiers and we arrived in time to witness one of these bunkers being cleared with grenades by Jerry Phillips of D Company. I was rather perturbed when, after the crump of the HE Grenade exploding inside the bunker, terrified enemy soldiers clambered out of the smoking exit without so much as a scratch, giving more credit to the old Mills Grenade, or pineapple grenade, which would have killed them all inside the bunker.

We quickly set up our GPMGs and MILAN missiles and began our job of locating targets and firing on them. There were halts in the attack, created by very accurate enemy snipers. We were getting a hold on these when there was an almighty noise and breathtaking explosion behind us, just yards away. An enemy 106mm anti-tank recoil-less (the US equivalent of our WOMBAT) had fired at us, killing the whole three-man detachment of Cpl Ginge McCarthy and wounding one of our signallers.

Moments later, the 106mm fired another of these horrendous shots, just missing us again. Once we had finally put down enough fire from our GPMGs and MILAN, we were back on our uppers.

The rifle companies of young JNCOs and private soldiers were magnificent. They took the fight to an astonished enemy who met our boys at their best. That night, during 12 hours of ferocious hand-to-hand fighting, more than 20 of 3 Para were killed and some 50 were wounded; the enemy lost more than 50 men, and about 100 were wounded. That night, among countless other brave acts, Sgt Ian McKay of B Company won a posthumous VC, making a total of two VCs for the regiment in the Falklands War.

Just before first light, the Argentines, realising that Longdon was lost, began to shell us with very accurate fire from heavy mortars and their 105mm Howitzers. This was the most scary time of my life, even more scary than the attack itself, because at least when you are fighting you have some control over your destiny. Under shellfire, you're at the mercy of God and luck, and nothing is more frightening. As we reorganised post-battle, the full reality of the fighting became apparent. Corpses of friend and foe lay around with the litter of battle. I shall always remember the strange smell of the place. It is said to be the smell of death, a sort of sweet, sickly smell, and it caught in your throat. I had the terrible job of bringing off the mountain the body of a dear friend. It was the most distressing thing imaginable to see the sightless eyes of dead friends whom, just moments before, you were comforted by, and were laughing and joking with, crying with. That is the memory I have every single day since . . . the dead. We were getting ready for the next battle, the battle for Stanley itself. This was going to be street fighting, house to house, and slow and very dangerous. Up to now, civilian casualties were extremely low, but street fighting would surely change this. Our sister Battalion, 2 Para, were our reserve for the battle of Mount Longdon; now we were the reserve for them while they finished the last remaining resistance outside of Stanley on Wireless Ridge.

I was listening to the chatter on my radio set when I heard that a cigarette resupply had arrived at the Battalion CP (command post). My bosses, Major Peter Dennison and Captain Tony Mason, needed enemy maps found on dead enemy bodies taking to Battalion Intelligence, and I volunteered with the selfish motive of ensuring my own supply of fags. Incidentally, I ran out of fags due to the raiding of my supplies by so-called 'non-smokers' who had come ashore without any fags and decided that smoking was suddenly good for you in moments of high stress.

During my errand, I was walking along the side of Longdon keeping a wary ear on the shellfire from Stanley when I met up with the Battalion Armourer Craftsman Alex Shaw and Private Craig Jones coming the opposite way on an errand of their own.

We were stood chatting when suddenly the screech of a shell coming very close made us start. For a split second we stared at one and other, resigned to the fact that there was nothing we could do to save ourselves. The shell was a direct hit and exploded between us, blowing all three of us into the air. I landed on my stomach. The wind was blown out of me and I gasped for air, spitting out earth from my mouth. My ears were ringing from the explosion. I watched my helmet as it rolled and bounced away down the hillside, and ridiculously cursed that I would have to go and fetch it back. My arms were outstretched in front of me and I noticed smoke coming out of my cuffs. I felt a burning sensation in my legs and wanted to see what was wrong. I rolled on to my back and sat up; it was now that I witnessed my appalling wounds. My left leg was blown clean off and my other leg was a mass of blood and raw flesh. I could not believe what I was looking at and laid back as the horror dawned on me: I was going to die and soon. I began to scream horribly like a frightened horse with a broken leg.

As always, the lads were brilliant. They were with us in moments and quick to begin the first aid. I heard either Craig or Alex groaning nearby. I was calmed by the lads' presence. They gave me morphine and carried me on a stretcher to the RAP (regimental aid post).

At the RAP, my good friend and medic SNCO Brian Falkner was chatting away to me, telling me I would be fine; a drip was set up and, after what seemed like a long time but was only about 10 minutes, a small Scout helicopter from the Army Air Corps landed to collect us and take us to the field hospital at Fitzroy. Unbeknown to me at the time, there was only room for two casualties on this tiny helicopter and one of us was destined to be taken overland to the field hospital. I was not considered likely to live more than a few minutes more and was put aside while Craig and Alex were prepared to be flown away, as they were considered to have a better chance of survival. Craig and Alex died before the lift, and as I was still alive, I got the lift to the hospital. The journey took about 15 minutes.

My memory of this is hazy; however, I do remember the freezing cold. On landing at Fitzroy, they carried me into the tented hospital where I fell unconscious. The next day, I was taken to the hospital ship *Uganda* and underwent four weeks of operations before I was fit enough to be flown all the way home to more hospital treatment at the military hospital in Woolwich, London. These were months of great pain and anguish. In the field hospital, I was, to all intents and purposes, clinically dead, but was brought back from the brink by the skill of the surgeons. I am very grateful to my comrades in 3 Para, the helicopter crew who bravely flew in to get me under shellfire, and the surgeons at the field hospital, the hospital ship and the hospital in the UK, including the fantastic nursing staff throughout.

Now, 20 years on, I am happily married with two sons who are young men, and of whom I am proud. I am grey and 'slightly' overweight, have a bald patch and enjoy listening to Radio 2.

I am the co-founder and Secretary of the South Atlantic Medal Association (82). I have close contact through the association with many of those who served with the Task Force of 1982 and have made many new friends, including the leaders of the day.

The association motto is 'From the Sea . . . Freedom' – most appropriate, I think, even for the Airborne Warriors among us!

NORA MONK

Falkland Islander

I was on my own, of course, at the time of the invasion. It was all so unreal. On the evening it all happened, I had walked past the school hostel, empty, peaceful and quiet in the twilight. There were children's toys in the road as I neared home. Well, why not? Everyone fully expected that the children would be playing there the next day. They never did. Not after 2 April.

At home I listened to the announcements from the Stanley Radio Station. Patrick Watts, the announcer, said that the Governor, Rex Hunt, would shortly be making an important announcement.

He did. 'The Argentines might be landing in Stanley, this – yes, *this* – evening.'

The phone rang. It was an invitation from Dick Baker, the Chief Secretary, and his wife, Connie. 'Nora, you cannot stay on your own.' With Adrian away in camp, it was very kind and tempting.

Two more guests were expected, I was told. I left our little kitten asleep by the peat fire which looked so peaceful, my quiet evening finished.

Towards midnight, the other two house guests arrived. The Governor's wife, Mrs Mavis Hunt, and Tony, their son on holiday from school in England. Government House, Dick said, would be a prime target in the event of an invasion.

I woke on 2 April, after a couple of hours' sleep, to hear Dick coming into the house – and heavens, what was that? Shooting? From the direction of Moody Brook, which was the Marine Barracks.

'Sporadic firing,' Dick said. 'Do make some tea!'

Connie came downstairs. A bullet sailed through the window and into the wall behind us. Dick had to go out again. We had a small transistor radio on all the time, and I must say that Patrick Watts kept us very well informed of what was happening – until he had a gun stuck in his back.

We decided it was time to call Mrs Hunt and Connie's two little daughters. For the next two hours, we sheltered in a little corridor that had no windows. About two hours later, the firing died away. While we were eating breakfast, we saw from our window a troop of our Civil Defence force being marched along the sea wall. Then, fresh horror, made to stand against the garden wall. To be shot? No, only counted, to our relief.

Then: 'Mummy, two Argentines are coming into the house.'

It is very difficult to look unconcerned with two 'foreign' soldiers snooping around suspiciously. And to continue washing plates as if nothing is happening.

Then Rex Hunt, the Governor, came to lunch, accompanied by Argentine officers. Rex, Mavis and Tony were given only a couple of hours to pack a few belongings before being deported to England. I must say that the Argentines looked a bit sheepish. It was really very British. We had drinks before lunch in the sitting room!

Dick had to go as far as Government House with the Hunts. 'Could I,' I asked one of the officers, 'go too and on the return collect my kitten?' 'Mad Englishwoman' was written on his face, but he said yes. Government House was swarming with Argentines. There were even soldiers sunbathing in the gardens.

My problem next day was hens. They had to be fed. We were told on the radio that we could now go about our business, providing we carried white flags.

So, via the school hostel, no longer quiet but with Argentine guns already positioned on the roof, I drove hopefully homewards by Land Rover. But soon I was pulled up by a patrol.

'Out,' they said. I 'outed'. I was searched by tough-looking Argentine soldiers. So was the Land Rover, and even the hen bucket (a bit smelly by now). I was escorted to some very startled hens. And finally I was interrogated for about two hours.

Very suspicious of someone with two homes, they were – even to the extent of searching the bungalow we were living in the following day.

They were looking for guns. I thought we had left ours at San Carlos, where we had lived until a few months previously.

'No,' I said firmly. 'No guns.' One of the 'bully boys' glanced in a cupboard. Horror – I had forgotten my husband's pistol. They really went to town then: cupboards, drawers, the lot.

More questioning, this time me sitting in a chair, with two guns pointing at me. The kitten thought this great fun and succeeded in rolling her favourite toilet roll round the room.

All right for her, I thought. I'm not finding it amusing. About time Adrian came home.

BRIGADIER DAVID CHAUNDLER

2 Para

Dawn comes slowly in the southern latitudes of a Falkland Islands winter. We had crossed the start line some 10 hours before. It was our third night without sleep and we had not seen a ration pack for 72 hours. We fought all night with blinding flurries of snow in our faces and, as dawn broke, we were counter-attacked twice, but D Company, on our final objective of Wireless Ridge, saw them off. Almost imperceptibly, as it became lighter, Port Stanley came into view. Some of our artillery had overshot their targets, and buildings were burning on the outskirts. Once Port Stanley was captured, the war was over. It was an exhilarating sight.

Suddenly, below us, we saw the Argentine Army collapse and, looking like black ants, hundreds were pouring out of Moody Brook below us and off the mountains across the valley and were walking back to Port Stanley – heads down, dejected, demoralised. I ordered the light tanks from the Blues and Royals forward, and they were firing into the valley, as were the Battalion's machine-guns and mortars. Tony Rice, the Battery Commander, was in a gunner nirvana firing a regimental fire mission. Twice, John Greenhalgh's Scout helicopters came up behind the ridge and fired SS11 missiles until I ordered them off, as they were attracting too much incoming fire.

The adrenalin was pumping, but the euphoria was short-lived when something inside me said: 'You can't do this any more; you are firing on a defeated enemy.' I ordered a ceasefire. The plan for that night was a Brigade attack to capture Port Stanley. Fighting among the houses could be costly, and besides the Argentines would have had time to reorganise. I realised that we had to get into Port Stanley as fast as possible and bring this war to an end. Frustratingly, communications back to Brigade HQ were poor and I was unable to impress the urgency of the situation. I ordered the Battalion to advance with Johnnie Crossland's B Company on the high ground on the far side of the valley, Dair Farrar-Hockey's A Company along the Port Stanley Road and Phil

Neame's D Company in reserve.

We started to move when Julian Thompson, the Brigade Commander, arrived by helicopter behind the ridge. Seeing me standing out on the forwards slope, no doubt thinking 'I've already lost one Commanding Officer from 2 Para', he rushed out and rugger-tackled me. Climbing to my feet, I said: 'It's all over, Brigadier, we must get into Port Stanley.' He took one look at the situation and agreed. And so he and I walked down the road behind A Company and, as we did so, the soldiers, realising it was all over, took off their steel helmets and out of pockets and pouches came crumpled red berets. It was a proud moment. And so we entered the outskirts of Port Stanley where we were ordered to stop – some seven hours before the official ceasefire, barely two weeks since I had parachuted into the sea to take over command of the Battalion and 11 weeks after the Argentines had invaded the Islands.

Colonel 'H' Jones died as comanding officer of 2 Para in the battle for Goose Green. He was posthumously awarded the Victoria Cross.

The reburial ceremony at Blue Beach Military Ceremony of 14 men killed in the Falklands, including Col "H" Jones.

SIR RONALD MILLAR

Margaret Thatcher's speech-writer

During the Falklands campaign, fired by the Navy's involvement, for the first and almost only time in our work together I sent in some unsolicited material which Margaret Thatcher used for her annual speech to the Conservative Women's Conference in the Queen Elizabeth Hall. Half an hour before she was due to make that speech, word came that the destroyer HMS *Sheffield* had been hit amidships by a French Exocet missile and was sinking, with 20 seamen's lives lost already. I was with her in the study when the news came through. She made no sound, just stood with her body half turned away, fists clenched, struggling for control. Then, almost but not quite silently, she was weeping.

We cut the 40-minute speech to less than 20. Wearing black and outwardly composed, she spoke calmly and well. At the end, instead of the usual triumphalist gestures, both hands held aloft like a victorious boxer, which had become her trademark in response to applause, she gave an odd little bow, left, right and left again, hands straight down by her side, to check any untoward enthusiasm from her audience, and sat down quickly. She was deeply emotional, but it was controlled emotion (just) and the jerky little bow was strangely moving.[6]

JIM LOVE

2 Para

'THIS IS THE WORLD SERVICES OF THE BBC.' I now had the Clansman 320 H.F. radio that Steve Willie had been carrying tuned in to the BBC to listen to the World Service. It was about the most reliable source of information about what was happening. Dat de dat de dah de, da da da da da. God how I was beginning to hate that tune. It really managed to get on my tits. I'll remember that tune for the rest of my life. I was squatting down in the corner of the sheep sheds writing the daily bulletin on a piece of scrap paper, quite happily listening to a man 8,000 miles away telling me what was going on in this small corner of the South Atlantic – on my own doorstep, you might say. At least he seemed to know more than what the Officers were passing on to us. It had been the result of listening to a similar broadcast that the world had learnt we were at Camilla Creek prior to the assault on Darwin and Goose Green. I hoped today would herald some good news.

We were now living in the sheep sheds at a settlement called Fitzroy. We had been here for a couple of days after having moved back from the Bluff Cove settlement about three miles away. Fitzroy was being set up as the Brigade HQ. Once it was fully established and further troops had arrived, you could bet that we would end up back on the bloody hills again. I suppose somebody had to do it, just why us all the time? A small circle of light appeared on the wooden floor next to the radio, followed in rapid succession by several more. I looked up and could see that they were coming from holes that had magically formed on the corrugated roof of the sheep sheds. From the corner of my eye, I caught movement.

Several people were charging about wildly, gesturing, lips moving frantically. I couldn't concentrate on the voice any more anyway. I stood up slowly and removed the headset. Bedlam hit my ears. Then I was knocked off my feet as an explosion rocked the building. Grabbing my helmet and weapon, I ran for the door. I hit the bright sunshine at a gallop and tried to focus. It was night vision in reverse: the interior of the sheds had been quite dark and, now I was out, the light dazzled me. Once again I was bowled over, though there was no sound of an explosion this time, just the steady whumping noise of a helicopter's spinning rotor blades. I had been knocked off my feet by the down draught of a Sea King helicopter. It was bobbing up and down by the side of the building, threatening to lift the complete roof off the flimsy structure. Now that I was outside, it was chaos: blokes were running and slipping arse over tit on the muddy grassy surface, some blown along by the chopper's down draught.

I could see a plume of black smoke rising from behind the small outcropped peninsula where the lads had been re-zeroing their weapons. It was part of the landing dock and the outcrop was linked to the main shore by the wooden jetty. It was from behind this outcrop where the smoke (now as black as the ace of spades) spewed upwards. Stark, chilling, more than just smoke, it rose like a malevolent genie against the serene blue of the sky. A bad omen for what was to come. It was also where the *Sir Galahad* and *Sir Tristram* lay at anchor. I started to run. I headed towards the line trenches we had dug over the past couple of days. As I ran down the slight slope, I could see people firing weapons from every type of position. Hip, shoulder, waist – you name it. SLRs, SMGs, GPMGs, even pistols were going off.

Then I saw it. It came in low. It popped up from nowhere, in fact. An A4 Skyhawk. I could see the pilot clearly, with a big bushy moustache and a slight grin on his face, looking back over his left shoulder. He soon lost the grin, though, when he levelled out and saw all the shit that was being sent in his direction. The pilot could only see the tracer, though; most of the 9mm was ordinary ball. He must have flown into a wall of lead. His plane must have been hit by some of it, because he kicked in his after-burners. With a flash of flames from his engine exhaust, he was soon a black dot heading for the horizon. Then, as if to confirm everybody's hopes, black plumes of oily smoke could be seen trailing behind him. He never made it past the horizon. The thin column of smoke was testament to that. More aircraft appeared from where huge explosions caused the very air to rumble. On the outcrop above the jetty was a small group of three blokes standing silhouetted against the grey rocks. It was one of the Air Defence detachments. They had the shoulder-mounted blowpipe ground-to-air missiles. They let one fly. Then I realised why the Sea King was bobbing behind our shed, and what had first knocked me off my feet.

We all watched, fascinated, as the missile they launched changed direction in mid-flight. (It had lost the Skyhawks due to their turbo-assisted exits.) Having been launched it was, however, still trying to acquire a target. It now decided to home on to the nearest heat source. It turned out to be the Sea King helicopter. He bobbed back down again. The helicopter pilot was using the corrugated sheep shed as a screen from the missile. The earlier explosion was from the first blowpipe missile that the detachment had fired and not an enemy bomb. The Air Defence detachments were unlucky. The first missile they had launched at the leading aircraft had apparently just missed the cockpit. They had fired as it was directly beside them and the missile hadn't armed until it had gone passed the Skyhawk. Being armed and having passed the Skyhawk, it was looking for an alternative or second target.

The missile now picked up the heat from the engines of the Sea King which had been unloading from the *Sir Galahad*. Dodging behind the large sheep sheds had screened the helicopter's heat signature. The missile tracking the target altered its trajectory and then, losing in effect all sight of the target, nosed-dived into the ground on the opposite side of the sheds from the helicopter, exploding on impact with the ground. This second attempt by the blowpipe crew looked like it was taking the same route as the first. This second missile, now having lost all sense of purpose, flew towards our trenches. It may have lost its target but, as the earlier one proved, it would still go with a bang. I dived into the nearest trench, landing on top of its occupants. The second blowpipe arced and exploded harmlessly in the peat near the shore. It turned out, in the end, that it was a bit of tit for tat. Apparently we had pinned down the blowpipe teams with all our small-arms fire in the first place – probably just as well for the crew of the Sea King. I was just being bodily thrown out of the trench when a third wave of Skyhawks appeared in front of us. The blowpipe detachment once again dived for cover, and I didn't blame them one little bit.

Later, when the skies finally cleared of Argentine planes and all that remained was the black oily smoke and the constant toing and froing of helicopters, I made my way to the pebbly beach. Here we met the arrival of the blackened survivors of the *Sir Galahad* and *Tristram*; the Welsh Guards had finally come ashore. They threw ropes from the cumbersome lifeboats; we waded waist-deep in the water pulling them hand over hand the final few yards to the shore.

What I Miss Most

I miss the lads.
I miss those crisp clear nights.
When the frost glistens in the moonlight.
I miss those lonely exposed hills.
Lashed by the rain.
I miss the young and innocent faces, some of whom we'll never see again.
I miss the laughter and the crack.
I miss their morbid sense of humor,
The childish pranks and their unspoken laws.
I miss that sense of belonging, that unique bond.
I miss youth at it's best.
Though I'll grow old unlike the rest.
What I miss most
I miss the lads.

Was it worth it? In the end yes.

DEREK HUDSON

Editor, *Writers' News*

HEADING ASHORE: We should have gone ashore in darkness, but delays meant we were dropped into the chilled water and clawing kelp under the full spotlight of day. Like everyone else, I was weighed down with 200 rounds of ammunition in one hand, two mortar bombs in another. Others had weapons, but there was a portable typewriter strung around my neck as we struggled down the ladders of HMS *Intrepid* and jumped into a jam-packed landing craft, carrying A Company, 3rd Battalion, the Parachute Regiment. An Argentine attack neared. Mirages, Skyhawks and Pucaras were heading our way and none of us was happy about being so exposed. The shout went up 'Air Raid Red', but as 3 Para's official account said later: 'But at this stage only the gulls, the ducks and the upland geese were noisily airborne' . . .

I'M BACK: Major Mike Norman, who had commanded the Royal Marines (79 men of Naval Party 8901, including new arrivals and those ready to return to the UK) when they fought bravely and surrendered to the invaders on 2 April, was a splendid sight when he burst into view after dashing ashore. He had been looking forward to this, and charged ahead with a determined look on his craggy features which did not bode well for anyone in his way. He had not been happy to be photographed lying in the gutter with his men. Back in April he had declared: 'We have never surrendered before. It's not part of our training.' (Once the Islands were back in British hands on 14 June, Mike and his men ran up a Falklands Island flag outside Government House, Stanley, with its motto 'Desire the Right'. He made a typically modest comment: 'It is very satisfying to be back here. We said we'd be back.') . . .

SHELTERED ACCOMMODATION: One bunch of hacks was soon carving an impressive air-raid shelter into a sloping patch of ground behind the local bunkhouse, near a peat storage shed into which I dived during Mirage and Skyhawk raids on the settlement. Although the shed's corrugated-iron roof would have given no protection

Crewmen swarm around Sea Harriers on the flight deck of HMS *Hermes* as she patrols with the Task Force off the Falkland Islands.

against cannon-fire or bombs, somehow it felt safe to be out of sight – rather like sticking one's head in the sand, perhaps. But with solid timbers and four feet of turf on top, the shelter was a much better bet, a solid refuge . . .

CORMORANTS OK: The 24-hour ration packs kept coming through with their tins of chicken curry, beef stew, spaghetti or the less convenient Arctic rations, which needed a lot of water to rehydrate their contents. So no one had to try out the survival advice given during one lecture aboard the troop ship *Canberra*: 'Five types of penguins breed in the Falklands; their bellies can be slit open and the contents eaten . . . Seals' eyes have enough vitamins to sustain a human for a week . . . Cormorants are delicious, but do not eat seagulls unless there is no alternative.' Even the dreaded tinned bacon-burger sounded tasty in comparison . . .

FRIEND OR FOE?: Up on Estancia Mountain, I learnt one lesson in staying alive. Never be mistaken for the enemy. I was trekking downhill with other pressmen, a Royal Engineers Officer and a Para Corporal. To avoid fording a creek twice – dry boots were treasured – we took a different route back to our red-roofed base, Estancia House. A Para Colour Sergeant and a Lance-Corporal appeared from behind a bluff and the senior NCO screamed at us to stay on the proper path or risk being shot. 'We thought you were f★★★ing Argies, and you could have been wasted.' It was good advice, heeded from then on . . .

COMINGS AND GOING: On Mount Kent I was taught to recognise the differing sounds of incoming 155mm fire and outgoing 105mm shells, although my instincts were not always spot on. After joining a recce to the summit early one morning, shortly after it was captured, I dived behind the nearest big rock, and a Royal Marine captain nearby remarked: 'I admire your agility, Mr Journalist, but that was outgoing fire.' Better safe than splattered, I thought, having mistaken a 'whoosh' sound for a 'who-er', or something like that . . .

COVER STORY: In their paperback *Don't Cry For Me Sergeant Major*, *Express* man Robert McGowan and ITN reporter Jeremy Hands (who died following a short illness, aged 47, in March 1999) described an attack against Brigade Headquarters on Mount Kent. Trails of smoke announced the arrival of Argentine jets and McGowan, forgetting the correct jargon, shouted out: 'What the f★★★. Run like hell!' Those of the military with blowpipe missiles or GPMGs (general purpose machine-guns) fired back. Splinters of metal and rock and peat clumps flew everywhere, but miraculously the only casualty was a case of mild concussion. The two scribes reported that everyone did run, just as the rattle of the Skyhawks' cannon began. The jets dropped parachute-delayed 1,000lb bombs across the area as newsmen and troops leaped into any bolt-hole they could find. 'After the warplanes made their first sweep and were banking for a second, a plaintive Yorkshire voice cut right through the tension and set half a dozen trenches rocking with laughter . . . "'Scuse me," said Derek Hudson, in all seriousness because he alone had apparently thought it improper to dive for cover without ceremony on top of someone else in a trench: "Mind if I come in?"' I remember McGowan, thinking about his future publishing royalties, chortling: 'One for the book, Jeremy.'

Bob, it was a joke. Nothing would have kept me out . . .

NOT ME: Begging a helicopter lift from the snow-sprinkled hillsides to organise a despatch from HMS *Intrepid*, lying off East Falkland, I had my strangest experience of the war. After more than a week sleeping rough, a blissful shower to wash away grime and lice powder preceded a steak dinner with a bottle of red something or other, and a comfy night's camp-bed sleep beckoned. But before turning in, I ventured outside on the deck for a breath of fresh air. Moored alongside was a diesel submarine, of the type used to introduce covert reconnaissance ashore, from whence one of its crew clambered on to the warship and announced from the gloom: 'Ready for you to board, sir. You can use that hatch.' Obviously some mistake here. Mumbling apologies that I was not among those going ashore, or anywhere else at that moment, I backed away from the damp, black night into the cosy glow of the wardroom, wondering whether – by some gross error – I had been mistaken for some special mission warrior. Surely not. But . . . it had been very gloomy out there, and the submariner would not have been able to see very well, otherwise he would easily have spotted the difference between a middle-aged hack and a master soldier . . .

TELL IT TO THE PARAS: After dark on 14 June, during the ceasefire and shortly before the Argentines' official surrender, pressmen and some of the military took over the bar of the Upland Goose Hotel, Stanley, as Argentine padres and other officers still billeted there loitered moodily in the background.

An angry Argentine Officer in charge of a patrol, very macho with a moustache bigger than Burt Reynolds's in his prime and grenades swinging from his combat smock, burst in to tell Des King, the landlord, that he was breaking the curfew and we could all end up as prisoners of war. As he bullied on, somebody pointed towards the window, through which some tired-looking professionals were passing by: 'Why don't you tell that to 2 Para.' He glared, swung on his heels and left . . .

V FOR . . . : Next day the Argentine Officers were removed from their cosy quarters and sent to join thousands of defeated soldiers camping in driving rain and hail on Stanley Airport – others were crowded near the Falkland Islands Company warehouses – where men of 42 Commando, Royal Marines, were to collect their weapons. How to get there ourselves? There were no taxis, so four of us stopped a passing Argentine four-wheeled vehicle and told the military driver to take us out there. Bedraggled conscripts clutching soaking blankets – the tents they might have sheltered inside had gone down along with Chinook helicopters and other valuables on the *Atlantic Conveyor* – sat around the bomb-damaged airport, utterly miserable. Suddenly, appearing from behind a hangar, there marched a company of smart and highly wound-up Argentine Marines, still in full battle order. Spotting our camouflaged British windproofs, they chanted defiantly 'Viva, Viva Republica Argentina' and 'Viva La Patria', and the Major in charge offered the press party a vigorous two-fingered sign . . .

SOUVENIR: The hijacked vehicle was taken back to town by the ITN crew, but there were no transport problems. Across the tarmac was a 'jeep' which had taken down its blue and white Argentine pennant, and two of us made a hitching signal with our thumbs, climbed in and said simply: 'Hotel, por favor.'

Held up by a straggling column of dripping prisoners of war which stretched for more than a mile, we were flagged down by the Royal Marines of 42. A familiar face appeared at the front passenger window – Major Mike Norman, whose glare turned into a wide grin. 'It's you buggers! I wondered why these two Argies were still driving about when my men had to walk. Want anything?' He pointed towards a growing hillock of pistols, military webbing, holsters, rifles, helmets and bayonets, which was growing bigger as the disconsolate line shuffled forward. We joined other souvenir hunters and I picked up an Argentine helmet, complete with goggles, which raised £100 for the South Atlantic Fund when it was auctioned a few weeks later at an Institute of Journalists garden party at Harrogate showground . . . And the most important memory of all . . .

REMEMBRANCE: 'We all feel great sadness for the many who have been killed or injured. Their sacrifice has been for a good and just cause and our thoughts are with them and their families. We will remember them.' (Signal received aboard *Canberra* from the Ministry of Defence)

ANDREW PETER

HMS *Arrow*

Was it almost 20 years ago now?

The millennium has come and gone, and some of us still remember things as if they were yesterday!

I was just a lowly LWEM(R) on HMS *Arrow* when our call to action came.

We had been doing Naval gunfire support in the Mediterranean for some junior officers during the build-up period. As usual, we were more concerned with getting ashore and having a good time, as matelot's are prone to do, than working on expensive war charriots. So one fateful day, the Captain woke us personally and said: 'For all you budding astrologers out there, you will notice the sun is on the other side of us, we are going south.' The usual rumour mill had failed us!

And so began the biggest adventure of my life. We started by RASing (Replenishment at Sea) all we could from the lucky ships headed north (and home). The group of us now heading south got larger as we neared the Ascension Islands. We were told that it was too dangerous to go swimming as it was shark migrating season. What, and going to war isn't? Serious training was the order of the day from that point on.

The next thing that stands out in my mind is the day I was to take the whaler ashore to burn garbage. We were in Bomb Alley (San Carlos inlet) and, as I and another lad were deemed 'spare', we were to do this necessary task. So off we went, beached the whaler ashore, joined another party already there and added our stuff to the pile. As we were last there, we stayed to watch that the bonfire didn't get out of hand. Next thing, the radio comes to life: 'AIR RAID. Get back here PRONTO!'

OK, back to the whaler we ran . . . Uh, oh . . . 'Um, Chief . . . we, uh, can't leave the beach' . . . 'Why not?' . . . 'The tide's left us high and dry!' . . . 'We'll send the Gemini if we have time.' Suffice to say that a towrope and lots of muscle power got us back to the relative safety of the ship. There were other things that happened, like the newspapers from home always getting the stories wrong. But it was nice to get them all the same, even if they were more than two weeks old by the time we got them.

I also remember us trying to help the *Sheffield* put out the major fire she had. We helped them abandon ship by pulling a lot of them over the railing to board us. In this sorrowful task, credit also goes to HMS *Yarmouth* and various helicopters in the area.

I was transferred to HMS *Endurance* for two years right after a short course in England, so I was sent south yet again.

HMS *Glamorgan* steaming into Portsmouth harbour, a tarpaulin covering the spot where she had been hit by an exocet missile.

JOHN WILKINSON

Parliamentary Private Secretary
to Rt Hon John Nott MP, 1979-82

During the Falklands War, I was Parliamentary Private Secretary to the Secretary of State for Defence, John Nott. He was a delightful boss for whom to work – intelligent, very capable of thinking on his feet at the despatch box of the Commons, self-deprecating and funny. His early years in the Gurkhas helped him psychologically, although he did not comprehend fully the importance of sea and air power. I greatly admired him and liked him personally also.

I had co-authored a book with Commander Michael Chichester entitled *The Uncertain Ally: British Defence 1960 to 1990*, which came out just before the Argentine invasion of the Falkland Islands. I asked John Nott if the book – which advocated a strategy of 'blue element' force projection clearly at variance with his Defence Review, which favoured the Army – was compatible with my position as his PPS. In typically generous fashion, he told me not to worry.

Before the war, I had underplayed the importance of an Early Day Motion signed by Edward du Cann and many other MPs urging the Government to keep HMS *Endurance* in commission. I should have warned John that the ship's withdrawal from the South Atlantic would lead Argentina to believe that we were not interested in the Falkland Islands and Dependencies.

I remember, when the invasion came, a worried Ministerial conclave in the corridor behind the Speaker's chair. A brief statement was made by Humphrey Atkins on Friday 2 April about the growing crisis. On 3 April, after the invasion, we had the historic Saturday sitting of the House. I felt John Nott's speech was too party political, but on reflection nothing he could have said would have satisfied the House.

Throughout the war, as it unfolded, the Government made regular statements to the Commons. When vessels went down or crises occurred, it was decided to make an almost immediate statement, which I believe was right. Otherwise rumour would grow and the Argentines could then derive more propaganda value.

Royal Marines training with anti-tank weapons aboard HMS *Hermes* on the way to the Falkland Islands.

From the start, I was deeply impressed by Henry Leach, the First Sea Lord. He was a pugnacious old sea dog whom I much admired. Likewise, it was invaluable to have John Fieldhouse as Commander-in-Chief Fleet at the time. The relationship of mutual trust which he had with the Prime Minister was crucial to our success. Without Margaret Thatcher's courage and determination, the outcome would have been different. We were lucky, too, that Rear-Admiral Sandy Woodward, who commanded the Task Force, and Major-General Jeremy Moore, Royal Marines, who commanded the troops ashore, were the right men for the job.

Every weekday morning at 8am, the three PPSs concerned – the late Ian Gow for the Prime Minister, the late Spencer le Marchant for the Foreign Secretary, and myself – would meet at 10 Downing Street to concert strategy, pass on political intelligence and try to ensure that the back benches remained supportive.

My fear as an ex-aviator was always for the damage that would be wreaked by Argentine land-based air power on a British Fleet without airborne early warning aircraft. I wrote a paper to John Nott suggesting that we operate Andover aircraft modified for airborne early warning from Goose Green airfield.

It was clearly vital to get the troops ashore fast and to establish a big beachhead. This was rapidly achieved thanks to the elan of the Parachute Regiment and to the effectiveness of the Royal Marines, who owed much to their Arctic warfare training in Norway.

The capture of Goose Green and the death of Colonel 'H' Jones leading 2 Para's assault made a big impression on me. He had been an exact contemporary of mine at Eton, but I felt ashamed I could not remember him.

Likewise, the achievements of the handful of Fleet Air and Sea Harrier pilots on *Hermes* and *Invincible* helped to secure victory; in part, thanks to their American sidewinder AIM9L missiles. We owed much to Lieutenant Commander Sharkey Ward and other aircrew who flew over icy waters with no diversions, often in atrocious weather. I remember, too, Wing Commander Peter Squire, the Commanding Officer of No. 1 Harrier Squadron, Royal Air Force, bringing his aircraft out to the theatre – a crucial reinforcement.

Finally came the bloody battle for Mount Longdon, and it was soon all over. It was an intense spring and early summer for us – a cruelly demanding early winter in the Falklands for the combatants.

I had few criticisms of the conduct of the war either politically or militarily. Indeed, I felt Margaret Thatcher's small War Cabinet was the ideal instrument for the rapid high policy formulation that the conflict required.

When it was all over, I never lost my interest in the conflict. I remember a visit with the Defence Select Committee to East Falkland in 1989 – climbing Mount Longdon and seeing the detritus of war and paying homage to the dead at the evocative war cemetery in San Carlos Water.

I now study South American and South Atlantic policies deeply. I love the Islands and Patagonia on the mainland. I hope we never forget our duty to our compatriots and that the right to self-determination is supreme.

RICHARD VILLAR

SAS Doctor

It is difficult to tell this story. Difficult because I have never been so scared. I think about it even now, nearly 20 years later. When I read what others have to say about the Falklands War, it is a conflict I do not recognise. Either I was somewhere different or they are unable to feel fear.

While Britain hovered on the brink of war, I was hard at work as a trainee orthopedic surgeon. My role had been established as one of caring for casualties once they returned to the United Kingdom. The South Atlantic Medal was not one for me.

It was at half past midnight in mid-May that my life changed for ever. I had been out on a stag night and was feeling terrible. I had had far too much to drink. The telephone rang in my central London flat. It was the Ministry of Defence – Major N, who had been trying to find me for three hours. The bleep system had let him down at every turn. I was summoned to an urgent meeting at the hospital and was given 30 minutes to attend. Major N did not explain the reasons over the telephone.

I met him in a small room in the building's administration wing. There was no one else present. Considering a war was in progress, his briefing was remarkably limited. The operation was highly sensitive. That night, he had been asked to find two surgical teams for an SAS operation. My name had been given as a starting point. There was no time to lose. He could not say what the operation involved, but it would mean working in the back of an aircraft. There would be no facility for fancy surgery. Our task would be to keep operatives alive as long as possible, until they could reach established medical care.

At 2am, forming two three-man medical teams by dawn is a difficult task. I had a free hand. By 4.30am, the MoD had its teams. I was astonished how readily everyone agreed to help, particularly when I could tell them so little about the operation. One assistant was due to move house that very morning.

We were told to be ready to move to a tiny airfield in central England by 1.30 that afternoon. I still had no idea what to expect. Even the destination after the airfield was kept from us.

Major N had also asked me to collect the equipment needed for the job. As I had no idea what the task was, this was an impossible order.

'Where are we going?' I asked.

'Dunno,' came the reply.

'How many casualties can we expect?'

'Dunno.'

'OK then. How long will we have to keep them alive?'

'Dunno.'

I got the message quickly. We were on our own.

The final hours before one goes to war can be immensely confusing. There is certainly no time to worry. From all corners came strange items of equipment that, during peacetime, the quartermaster hotly denied existed. Suddenly they miraculously appeared from a hidden shelf, somewhere in a back room. Everything for this operation was spanking new.

That morning, before leaving London, I made one vital telephone call. To my mother. I could not tell her where I was going, even if I had known. With a husband in intelligence and a son in the SAS, she had become highly skilled in the art of veiled conversation. I suppose this was one more episode to add to the already lengthy list of worries I had given her since leaving home.

'I've got to go away for a while, Mum,' I said. 'I'm not sure for how long.' I tried to sound as jolly as I could. Mum picked it up immediately. I could sense her distress, even though she would never admit it. Dad, the voice of reason, came on after her. Having been sunk three times in the Second World War, I was sure he knew what faced me. Neither asked any detailed questions, just calmly wished me well. Mum whispered, 'Be careful', and hung up. While I was away, she listened to almost every news bulletin, at least 12 a day. She also faithfully stuck pins into a model of Galtieri daily.

At 3am the following morning, we left for a tiny location in the middle of nowhere. The six of us were squeezed, like sardines in a tin, into the tiny recesses that a Hercules's huge freightload would allow. It took 20 hours of juddering to reach our destination.

As I stumbled from the tailgate of the C130, I was greeted by numerous smiling, familiar faces – men I had known well when I was RMO at Hereford. 22 SAS was here in force and had been stood by to act for three weeks already. Major D ushered me in the direction of his Land Rover, as he wanted to brief me, which meant there was probably little time to spare. His first words, spoken as soon as I had slammed shut the Land Rover door, set the scene. 'Doc, it's great to see you,' he said. 'I wondered whether it would be you who volunteered for this.'

Who the hell had said anything about volunteering? At no stage had anyone in the UK said anything about an opt-out.

The operation was enormously risky, depending almost exclusively on surprise. Scheduled to strike many miles from the front line, the SAS would be stranded, or even annihilated, if events went wrong. The Argentine forces were not a placid enemy. They were well trained and very well equipped. This was not the Third World, whatever the news bulletins had suggested. Furthermore, intelligence sources had warned the enemy we might attack and they were upgrading their defences as a precaution. It was as if they were waiting for the SAS to arrive.

It is difficult not to mope when you are told you are going to die, especially if it is unexpected. What impressed me was the self-control of the operatives. They knew the exact nature of the operation and the risks involved. Most had families and loved ones at home. For three weeks they had been stood by to kill themselves for Queen and Country. At first appearance they seemed remarkably relaxed and accepting. 'That's why we're here, Doc,' one old hand remarked. But behind the facade, many were deeply and significantly affected. As the days passed, I was to become introduced to their worries on frequent occasions.

By the end of May, it was becoming apparent, to my mind anyway, that Downing Street could not decide about us. At times we were stood by to move at 30 minutes' notice; at other times the operation was altered to two hours' standby. Once we even climbed on to the buses that would take us to the aircraft before being told of a further postponement. Each time, you prepare yourself physically, and psychologically, for what you are certain is imminent death. Each time, your emotions having been raised to fever pitch, the rug is yet again pulled from under you. This happened 30 times or more. It must be similar sitting on death row in the US, waiting for that last-minute reprieve.

At the midday orders, we were informed that the operation had been postponed. Instead, I was told to be ready for immediate departure by passenger aircraft, destination to be advised. The plane was scheduled to leave two hours later, so there was no time to spare. The remaining members of the medical team would return home to the UK. No sooner had I prepared myself than the plans were changed again. Something had happened to the main fighting forces, though the exact reasons were never made clear, and the original operation had been reinstated.

With such toing and froing, it was difficult to keep everyone suitably occupied. The medical teams had by now gleaned snippets of information from a variety of sources and were clearly concerned.

By now it was becoming clear that life was not going well for the Fleet. Despite the main troops landing in East Falkland, the Naval casualty list was becoming longer by the day. There appeared a great disparity between what the media now reported and what was truly happening on the ground. Downing Street had to be sweating.

At this point, I felt we were as close as we would ever be to the operation being launched. Again, we were in short standby to move. As if to emphasise the situation further, I was asked to update myself on a variety of weapons. 'Just in case, Doc,' I was told. With the upgraded training, and horrifying reports from the Task Force, all of us were convinced that Downing Street was a hair's breadth from letting us on our way. The operation must surely be launched?

It never was and the reasons not explained. I imagine you feel as let down as us when you learn this. Probably, the sensitivities and the risks were too great. For those of us poised to strike, we had lived and relived the operation for weeks. My mind had pondered all manner of grizzly ends. Our masters, for most likely very good reason, had developed cold feet.

By early June, we had returned to the UK, happy in some respects, disgruntled in others. My first port of call was to Major N. I told him my mind, even though tact, rank and diplomacy might have suggested otherwise. How could the Army, I asked, send its people on a projected suicide operation without warning them beforehand? Why were we not properly briefed? Why was I not stopped from taking married men with me? Of course, now the operation had been cancelled, I had no argument. It was as if it had never happened, that the idea had never occurred. Major N was shaken and there was not much he could say. My objections were passed up the lines, though I do not know who received them.

As for myself, I always swore I would not tell this story. In many respects, I still feel ashamed that I reacted as I did, that I felt such immense, sometimes uncontrollable fear. For years I avoided the subject of the Falklands completely. For those who knew I had been involved, I preferred to talk as if I had been part of the more traditional activities. My true role is an aspect of life I wish to forget. Much has been said in closed Regimental circles about the operation that never was. Emotions do run very high. I have seen brief, partially accurate mention in the press of what we were supposed to be doing. I have seen outlines presented in several books. None effectively describes the terror and hopelessness felt by many involved. You do not need to be shot at to be scared. [7]

SIR KEITH SPEED

Minister for the Navy, 1979–81

Friday 2 April 1982 was a bad day. I was at home in my constituency having a major correspondence session with my secretary, who also happened to be my wife. We both listened with incredulity to a series of ever-more depressing broadcasts from the BBC. Confusion seemed to reign in both the Ministry of Defence and the Foreign Office. Such information that was given to Parliament and the media was both late and inaccurate. That evening, I was addressing the annual general meetings of the St Michael and High Halden Conservative branches. Needless to say, there was only one subject for the speech, and the subsequent questioning showed that my supporters shared my sense of outrage and dismay.

Just prior to the first meeting, BBC2 and *Newsnight* had been in touch asking me to take part in that evening's programme. Unsurprisingly, they could not get a Government Minister, but John Silkin, Shadow Defence Minister, and David Owen – then Parliamentary Leader of the Social Democrats and a former Foreign Secretary and Navy Minister – would be taking part.

I knew the timing would be tight. From my constituency to the BBC studios in White City was a good hour and a half. Fortunately, Mike Thomas, my brother-in-law and a teacher, was spending Easter with us and volunteered to whisk me there on time.

The journey to London allowed me to concentrate my mind on the crisis. Ever since I first trudged up the hill to the Royal Naval College as a young cadet back in September 1947, I had been educated in the effectiveness of sea power when properly deployed and had had practical experience as a midshipman in the Korean War.

I concluded that this was a classic situation for a Naval blockade, where ships could establish a cordon around the Islands both on and under the sea, later adding an air blockade by carrier borne aircraft and an electronic blockade by electronic warfare methods. This would limit severely the Argentines' capability to supply their occupying forces with fuel, ammunition, stores and food, would interrupt their communications and, if need be, pave the way for an amphibious assault to recapture the Islands if, in

A Wessex helicopter hovers overhead as HMS *Antelope*, still burning fiercely, slips beneath the water of Ajax Bay.

the meantime, diplomatic efforts to resolve the problem had failed. Very much in my mind was President John F Kennedy's blockade of Cuba by the US Navy 20 years before.

I think that the live interview with the three politicians, which concluded the programme, was constructive and gave some hope to the large and influential audience who were watching in their homes.

I was the junior MP and came on last in the discussion. John and David were both gloomy and tending to put more faith in the United Nations than I was. My strong advocacy of a Naval blockade and Task Force were well received and we all agreed it was an initiative to be advanced while diplomatic talks took place simultaneously.

As far as I'm aware, this was the first public suggestion for such maritime action and would transform our national stance from being reactive to proactive.

The *Evening Standard* on Monday 5 April, in a favourable review of the programme, used phases like 'the road to Damascus'. I would counter that these ideas and the successful operations that followed proved Henry Ford wrong in his famous dictum 'History is bunk'. The lessons of history for us as a maritime nation were, when properly applied, both invaluable and successful.

ALISON AND MICHAEL BLEANEY

Falkland Islanders

Alison Bleaney

The Falkland Islands in 1982 – a long time ago, yet snippets as from a film often surface in my mind for no apparent reason. Sometimes this results in an emotional release triggered as though the events had just occurred.

My memory of the war is that it went on for ages, though I know that it was really only a matter of weeks. There was very little sleep and I think the blackout and curfew made it difficult to keep track of the passage of time. With the constant interruptions to sleep, this had the effect of blending night and day.

By the time the conflict had reached the outskirts of Stanley, I was distressed that I had put my two little children in so much danger by opting not to leave when this had been possible soon after the Argentine invasion. This gave the impetus to my efforts to assist in organising the Argentine surrender.

However, I found that I could negotiate with angry Argie soldiers much more effectively when breastfeeding Emma! I always took her with me in a sling on my front when I wished to speak with senior officials, as the sentries' guns would be lowered when they spotted her.

In retrospect, I am grateful that I was young and foolhardy and had not the experience to recognise the danger I was in.

I am also grateful that I had the experience of finding that there are good people in the world who show their true colours when the chips are down. I was helped and taken care of by many individuals: Islanders, British military and Argentines alike.

Other random memories: my husband, Michael, looking like a monk in a hooded dressing gown, reading aloud to us in the middle of the night to settle us down. Also, when the floor of our small room in the hospital was covered in sleeping bodies, him telling me anxiously in the gloom at 3am that he had counted three more heads than when we had retired!

On the first day of the liberation, I ended up as a runner in hospital theatre for the field hospital team. Dark, no electricity or water, and the team in field-stained uniform, boots and all. I don't know who was more bemused – Matron with this flouting of theatre dress code or the team at the sight of their 'runner' nursing a baby in a fluffy pink outfit while sorting their equipment.

One thing I have learnt from it all: *carpe diem*.

Michael Bleaney

When things started to hot up and we decided to move out of our house into the hospital, I stealthily buried all our most precious possessions – photographs, prints, silver, jewellery, etc – in a trunk in the garden.

One of the first things we did after the liberation was to move back home and eventually dig up our buried treasure. The hole had flooded and our treasure was mostly damaged. Our reaction was to look at each other and laugh. What did we care for these 'things'? We were ALIVE!

Casualties from HMS *Sheffield* are taken from a helicopter aboard HMS *Hermes*.

A crewman mans a machine gun mounted on the hatchway of a helicopter on
patrol over San Carlos Water.

DAVID OWEN

Deputy Leader of the SDP, 1982-83

The House assembled at 11am on Saturday 3 April for the most dramatic debate I have ever participated in. At Prayers, the House was packed and the mood sombre. Immediately afterwards, the Lord Privy Seal rose to apologise for misleading me and other Members in the House the day before. We then had a rather irritating vote on whether the debate should take place for longer than three hours, a fairly typical House of Commons diversion.

I believed, as I said in my own speech, that Margaret Thatcher had misjudged the atmosphere of the House quite seriously when she said: 'It would have been absurd to despatch the Fleet every time there was bellicose talk in Buenos Aires. There was no good reason on 3 March to think that an invasion was being planned.' This was, I felt, no time for self-justification and I said directly to her in my speech that she now had to 'examine ways of restoring the Government's authority and ask herself why Britain has been placed in such a humiliating position during the past few days'. Fortunately, Mrs Thatcher agreed that these issues should be examined when the war was over. An inquiry was established and all political parties agreed that Lord Franks would be a suitable Chairman.

The Naval deployment in the Southern Atlantic in the autumn of 1977 had been revealed to the House by Jim Callaghan on 30 March 1982, just before the invasion on 2 April. He was, I felt at the time, giving the Government the chance to claim that Naval vessels were in the area – even if they were not. The question once the invasion had taken place was: could it have been prevented?

The Cabinet Overseas and Defence Committee met three times in November 1977. As Foreign Secretary, I felt it was important that we should not be obliged to negotiate over the Falkland Islands from a position of total vulnerability, and equally important that, if the Argentines were ever to attack our shipping or invade the Islands, we should not be seen by public opinion to be unprepared. I had recommended that the Secretary of State for Defence be asked to prepare urgently contingency plans for the defence of

British shipping in the area of the Falkland Islands and for the eventuality of an Argentine invasion of the Islands and their Dependencies; also, for the preliminary deployment of an SSN to be considered if there was any expectation of an Argentine use of force.

Clear and specific rules of engagement were then drawn up for Ministers to endorse, and ships and a submarine despatched to the Southern Atlantic, and these were drawn to the attention of the Franks Committee of Inquiry.

Rules of engagement

It is highly desirable that the following broad guidelines as to the degree of force which may be used in differing circumstances should be approved by Ministers before the ships sail.

(a)   Once Argentine forces have committed a hostile act, minimum force may subsequently be used against military units displaying hostile intent.

(b)   In the event of intelligence indicating that invasion is imminent, an exclusion zone should be established within 25 miles of the Falkland Islands. If Argentine warships or military aircraft violate this exclusion zone, they are to be ordered to withdraw. If they fail to do so, ascending degrees of force from warning to the discharge of conventional weapons may be used to compel them to do so. (HMS *Dreadnought*)

Definitions for the purpose of the rules of engagement

Hostile act is defined as any act of Argentine aggression against or armed presence on the Falkland Islands (excluding their Dependencies), their air space or territorial waters, and British shipping on the high seas, ie outside the territorial limits of the Falkland Islands and Dependencies and outside the respected territorial limits of other countries (12 miles in the case of Argentina).

Evidence of hostile intent is considered to be when:

(a)   a ship, submarine or aircraft unmistakably prepares to fire, launch or otherwise release weapons, including mines, against British forces, shipping or territory, or land military forces in the Falkland Islands (excluding their Dependencies), or

(b)   one or more surface ships, submarines or aircraft clearly manoeuvres into a position to attack British forces, shipping or territory.

The Governor of the Falkland Islands was also advised at the time in 1977 that if the talks go well the Task Force will quietly withdraw. But if things go wrong we will be in a position to counter any Argentine threat to the Falklands or to our shipping in the area . . . What we are doing is taking a number of precautions since we believe it will be prudent not to leave ourselves unprotected or unprepared . . .

Winding up the first of the debates in 1982, John Nott, the Secretary of State for Defence, made a disastrous and defensive speech. He dismissed the key question about why he had not put a hunter-killer submarine on station a few weeks earlier, as if he were still debating in the Cambridge Union. This provoked me to intervene, saying: 'If the Rt Hon Gentleman, the Secretary of State for Defence, has not understood the value to a Foreign Secretary of being able to negotiate in a position of some military influence and strength, he should not be Secretary of State for Defence.' It was a sentiment which most people in the House that day shared. When John Nott sat down at the end of the debate, there were few people in the House who believed that both he and Lord Carrington could stay on. At least one of them, perhaps both, would have to resign.

The House of Commons spoke for the nation that day, reflecting the humiliation that millions felt and a resolve to put this humiliation behind us, to restore our reputation and to retake the Islands.

The Government's conduct of the actual war was exemplary; even the sinking of the *Belgrano* was a necessary military operation that effectively trapped the Argentine Navy in their ports for the rest of the war. The British people, during the Falklands War, began to see the formidable benefits of our voluntary but highly professional armed services. For me, as Devonport's MP, the actual war was an emotional experience. Thousands of my constituents were in the Southern Atlantic. I visited the wives and families of a number of servicemen who were killed or injured, and it was a harrowing experience. For the people of Plymouth – who felt that a significant part of our city, with Royal Marines as well as the Royal Navy, were participating – this was no remote war. The mood was not, however, jingoistic. People sensed the danger and the risks involved. The *Sun*, with its headlines 'Gotcha!' and 'Up Yours Galtieri' may have upset the liberal intelligentsia in London, but in the provinces it was taken in good heart; more as an amusing morale-booster than a sign that jingoism was running rife in the UK.

The inescapable conclusion of any fair-minded reading of the Franks Report is that the Falklands War was an avoidable war, and that the events of 1977 should have given us the knowledge and experience to have prevented the 1982 invasion. It was a bizarre omission that the Franks committee decided not to recount in the report the evidence they were given about the invasion scare that the Callaghan Government had dealt with four and a half years before.

David Owen was raised to the peerage in 1992 as Lord Owen of Plymouth

SIR EDWARD DU CANN

Chairman of the 1922 Committee, 1972-84

At the time of the Falklands crisis, I was Chairman of the 1922 Committee. Not the least responsibility of that elected office is to keep Government informed about opinion among Conservative Members of Parliament – either through the subject committees or, if the importance of the subject warranted it, to report their views directly to Ministers or to the Prime Minister.

Before the invasion of the Falklands, there was a growing unease among Tory MPs about Britain's intentions and policy in that part of the world. Rightly or wrongly, there was a suspicion that there was a covert agenda on the part of the Foreign Office and its Ministers in some way to cede Britain's sovereignty over the Falkland Islands to Argentina (no doubt similar anxieties were being expressed in party committees on both sides of the House of Commons at the end of 2000 about Gibraltar).

There had been the visit of a Foreign Office Minister to Argentina which raised suspicions. The decision to reduce Britain's physical activity in the South Atlantic by withdrawing a ship, apparently on the pitiful grounds of economy, heightened the worries.

Then came the bombshell – the invasion. Now opinion in the Conservative Party in the House of Commons (as in the country at large) was fully aroused.

An emergency debate was called in the Commons on the first available day, a Saturday. I cancelled all my constituency engagements. My own mind was absolutely clear. I was fortunate to be the first speaker to be called by Speaker Thomas from the back benches in the debate. I stated as clearly as I could that our country had a duty, notwithstanding the obvious physical difficulties, to liberate the Islanders, our British compatriots.

Plainly it was necessary for this grave situation to be discussed privately by those Conservative Members of Parliament that were present in the House that day, a large number. I took the view that it would be best of this were done by the Defence Committee, rather than its parent, the 1922 Committee. This was arranged for the mid-afternoon at the end of the debate in the Chamber. Ministers attended. It was a difficult meeting for them. The opinions of those who spoke at this meeting were universally critical of the impression of weakness that had been given to the Argentines, and clear that the invasion was intolerable.

After the meeting, I was asked by many lobby correspondents if Ministerial resignations were imminent. I have to confess that this was the only occasion in the 12 years that I was Chairman of the 1922 Committee that I gave misleading replies to my questioners. I said I thought it unlikely. It seemed to me that mass resignations of Ministers at that moment would hardly help the Prime Minister and the Government. It would be wrong to send the wrong signal to the invaders. In the weeks ahead, the Prime Minister would need to depend upon experienced counsel, not least in soliciting support from the United Nations and the United States. Ministers should stand resolute at her side. Nonetheless, Ministers took the honourable course and resigned.

Looking back on those days, I have one regret – namely that the warnings that were given to Government were ignored. Hindsight comes easy, but I never was in any doubt that we were right at the time strongly to press for the invaders to be ejected, and I am glad we were proved right.

NICHOLAS HENDERSON

British Ambassador to the United States, 1979–82

On a hot, humid May afternoon in Washington, something was said to me during a party in the garden of the British Embassy that lifted me instantaneously out of the steamy atmosphere and contradicted my long-held scepticism about the conceivable value of such social functions.

It was the height of the 1982 Falklands War and the US Government was providing our forces with crucial material of war and invaluable intelligence and communications support. After prolonged negotiations by the Secretary of State, General Alexander Haig, Washington had decided at the end of April to back the British, who, they realised, were defending the right of self-determination of the people of the Falklands in the face of blatant aggression. Nevertheless, it was far from clear to many high-ranking people in Washington how we were going to oust the Argentines from the islands they had occupied which lay 8,000 miles away from their home base. Besides, there were prominent people in high places in the Government who were doubtful of the wisdom of the US commitment, fearing that it would jeopardise the country's relations with much of Latin America.

Suddenly Caspar Weinberger, the US Secretary of Defence – thanks to whom, personally, American help had been so immediately and generously forthcoming – took me aside and said that he would be prepared to make a US carrier available in the South Atlantic if the military situation required it.

I don't recall my response, but I must have said something about passing the offer immediately on to London. I hope I indicated my appreciation of its generosity and courage. It struck me immediately as something unique in the annals of the Washington–London relationship. I know how it transformed my hitherto somewhat maudlin feelings about the sweltering hot garden party. No longer did I swoon in the languid air. The leaves and flowers of the magnolia trees became in my eyes shinier and more exotic than ever. It made me love my fellow men – most of all, of course, Caspar.

CHRIS OWEN

Journalist, *Portsmouth News*

I closed the front door, idly switched on the TV, walked into the kitchen and filled the kettle. For the first time, the horror of war was about to affect me directly. Before the kettle had boiled, a grey man in a grey suit appeared on the screen and started relating even greyer news. If ever there was a harbinger of doom, civil servant Ian McDonald embodied it. At an excruciatingly slow pace – a tempo that has lived with me to this day – the man from the MoD sombrely revealed that HMS *Sheffield* had been hit by an Exocet missile. As a reporter with the *News*, the previous four weeks had been a period of intense excitement. In Portsmouth, I'd watched the mood of the city switch from despondency as dockyard workers were served with redundancy notices to elation as the Task Force was cheered from the city, helped by the same men whose jobs were about to end.

Everyone thought it would be a walkover – the 'might' of the Royal Navy and the other services against a ragbag bunch of Argentine conscripts. No one really thought it would come to much. And then the nuclear submarine HMS *Conqueror* sunk the Argentine cruiser *General Belgrano*.

Two days later, HMS *Sheffield's* life was ended. As I toured the city that night, a palpable air of despair hung in the atmosphere.

On the Naval estates, groups of wives huddled in rooms with the lights switched off, not knowing whether their men were dead or alive. Many were too afraid to answer the door.

Some spoke to the *News*. They were desperate for any information from the South Atlantic.

Their stories were heart-rending. There was the wife from Southsea whose husband was just finishing his last tour in *Sheffield*. He had written from Gibraltar full of excitement at the good times ahead. But when she opened the letter, some uncanny sixth sense told her it would be the last time she heard from him. Again the city was left mourning its war dead.

Prince Andrew and the crowd gathered in Portsmouth to welcome
HMS *Invincible* home from the Falklands.

As the war progressed, the newsroom at the *News* became a focus of attention for the world's media.

Through our Naval contacts, we were able to establish much that was happening 8,000 miles away before it was officially released.

It was like that on 25 May, when HMS *Coventry*, another Portsmouth-based Type 42 destroyer, was sunk after an air attack.

For the second time in three weeks, the city had the stuffing knocked out of it. We knew about it first and published the news before it was confirmed officially.

For all the relief and joy across Portsmouth when the Task Force returned, there was always the memory of the men at the bottom of the South Atlantic who would never return, and the wives and sweethearts who would never again stand on a quayside to welcome home their men from the sea.

Seven months later, I was privileged to fly to the Falklands with the relatives of those who died.

The stories they told were as moving as the immaculate lawns surrounding the pristine graves at San Carlos war cemetery, hewn out of the rock by the Commonwealth War Graves Commission.

As a journalist I was lucky to be intimately involved in covering a war, even if it was not at the sharp end.

But I was also able to see at first hand the dreadful futility of it all: the wasted lives and indelible physical and mental scars it leaves on people for ever. [8]

RODNEY LEE

Falkland Islander

The Governor came on the radio one evening and said he had an important announcement. He said it was inevitable that, by dawn the next morning, the Argentines would be planning an invasion.

We were just a small island and led such a sheltered life that we didn't really know what to think. We didn't have a clue what chain of events was about to be triggered.

We had very mixed feelings, but I didn't feel fear because I didn't know what to be afraid of.

Because we lived in West Falkland, the start of the conflict was a bit of an anticlimax, as we didn't actually see any Argentines until 26 April. We are rather remote here and cut off from the capital, Port Stanley.

One morning we were having breakfast and helicopters started flying in. We ended up with about 1,000 Argentines surrounding our settlement area.

They came to our houses and told us to stay indoors. One of the most striking things was that conscripts who had come straight off a boat from Argentina were stunned that we could not speak Spanish and were not welcoming them with open arms.

They firmly believed they had come to liberate us and couldn't understand why we were not glad to see them.

There was a curfew, so we were not allowed out after dark. Nor could we leave the settlement area without a guide, so we couldn't do much in the way of work.

The Argentines didn't have food, so we had to kill some of our sheep. That is virtually all they ate.

Ships used to shell this area at night and Harriers dropped cluster bombs. They hit a few of the houses and the Argentines evacuated some of the women and children to a house about seven miles outside the settlement. It was becoming a little bit dangerous.

A Sea Harrier was shot down over here, and the pilot, Geoff Glover, ejected just before it hit the ground. He was the only prisoner of war to be taken to the Argentine mainland. They kept him in our social club for a couple of nights.

It was before the Task Force landed and was a most depressing time for us.

Captain John Hamilton of the SAS was also killed here in Port Howard and we have a memorial service each year. It is a time to remember and we shan't forget the lives that were lost. But apart from that, it all seems a very long time ago.

We were actually liberated on 15 June. It was a big relief, but the first few days of the war were far worse than any others because, by the end, we had learnt to accept what was happening. When you are in the middle of something like that, it never seems quite so serious.

I think it must have been much harder for relatives of servicemen back in the UK. They didn't know what was going on. That must have been horrendous.

If we had another conflict tomorrow, we would be a lot more scared. It was because of our ignorance that people were in good spirits.

Things got back to normal fairly soon. The Royal Marines and the Scots Guards were the last to leave Port Howard. They tidied up all the mess left by the Argentines and were tremendous. Things like our air service and mail service took a long time to get back to normal, but within a year you wouldn't have known there had been a conflict.

The British people were exceptionally good to us and sent us all sorts of things. They were showered on us to an almost embarrassing extent, but were all gratefully received.

Any gift, however small, seemed big to us because our population was only 2,000. In our settlement, we ended up with pool tables and carpets for our social club.

If Argentina had won the war, I wouldn't be here now. I would have left for Britain or anywhere else that would have us. I am proud to be British and I still refer to Britain as home. Even though I have never lived there, I have relatives in Britain and visit once every three years.

But I really enjoy living in the Falklands. It is a peaceful way of life without such things as crime rates.[9]

T. M. LE MARCHAND

Captain, HMS *Valiant*

Valiant was on a deep and fast passage across the Atlantic when Argentina invaded the Falklands. News does not travel easily to submarines when deep, and it was by means of the BBC World Service that we discovered the reasons for the Prepare for War signals that had emanated from the Flag Officer Submarines.

Perhaps we could go straight down there. No, after two months at sea there was not enough food – as ever, the human machine is the limiting factor in a nuclear submarine. So the plan evolved: get home fast, top up with stores and torpedoes, and deploy for a long trip, which in the end was to last exactly 98 days under water.

Earnest preparations at base ensued. Our weapon system was upgraded to the most recent Tigerfish development, stores and provisions for 95 days were stuck down below, and one member of the Ship's Company married his fiancée. From the outset, we were utterly convinced that this was going to be a shooting war, and that our task was going to be to take the Argentine Navy out of the equation.

The submarine entered the war zone on 1 May after a high-speed transit south. Drills every watch on attacking and torpedo evasion had made us confident that we could do our part; recognition was honed – strangely difficult when our enemy had until recently been friends: it has always seemed 'not cricket' to gather intelligence on those whom one expects to be on one's own side.

More importantly, we practised and became very skilled at operating the Tigerfish MoD 1 weapon system – in effect an underwater guided missile – which was to be our prime weapon against all targets, surface or submarine. Not for us the Second World War Mark 8 – which was in fact the weapon that the *Conqueror* employed with such devastating effect against the *Belgrano*.

On one occasion, while at periscope depth, we suffered a near miss from a stick of six bombs, the fourth one of which was close enough to spill cups of tea. Having to assume that we may have been detected, though there was no other indication that we had, it was prudent to get some distance between us and where it happened. We later assessed that it was returning aircraft jettisoning their unused bombs before landing back at base that had so nearly scored a fluke hit. The moral was to get off track from their return route. We were lucky, but a few feet closer and it might have been something of a bad luck story.

A word about the Ship's Company. We numbered 105, and kept to a six hours on, six off watchbill for the whole deployment. Keeping the highly sophisticated but 21-year-old nuclear submarine at peak performance for night after day was a fantastic achievement. Heroes daily dealt with steam leaks, hydraulic bursts and even the odd fire; one person, the smallest man on board, had to slide 12ft down between the pressure hull and the port main condenser (a space of nine by 18 inches cross-section) to replace a flange from which steam was leaking. Unrepaired, we would not have been able to use full power – a crucial get-away requirement.

Discipline and morale were outstanding – the more so because no one was conscious that such characteristics were under trial. Throughout the deployment, all were acutely interested in how the 'real battle' was going and determined to do all possible to contribute. There were no defaulters; no one was even ill.

Valiant returned to base in Scotland in early August. There was one single frozen chicken in the ship's fridges.[10]

W. R. CANNING

Captain, HMS *Broadsword*

It was for me the greatest privilege to have been in command of 250 young men who accepted the quite exceptional challenges of this modest little war (eg, months continuously under way, an 8,000-mile line of communication, weather, etc) with the greatest fortitude and good humour.

Furthermore, *Broadsword* was in at the start and was one of the last of the original players to withdraw. Also, in view of my seniority at the time, *Broadsword* occupied a busy 'scrum half' position during the hectic period of the landings and the days that followed.

I remember the peaceful scene in Falkland Sound at first light on 21 May, followed by the mayhem of air attacks shortly thereafter and throughout the hours of daylight; first air parties being called to attend casualties; the call 'handbrake' being received, indicating an imminent threat of Exocet missiles in the area (even today, this buzzword raises the hairs on the back of my neck!).

There was the calm, professional way that my people got on with the job while under fire and short of sleep; my petty officer cook managing to bake a loaf of wholemeal bread during an overnight lull; the irksome business of refuelling, seemingly every other night while darkened and in most weathers of the South Atlantic winter.

Broadsword's lowest ebb was reached on 25 May when, in company with HMS *Coventry* during anti-air operations north of Pebble Island, we were attacked late in the evening.

It was not our day. Seawolf failed at a critical moment as the attack developed and, despite our combined efforts with Seadart, gun and an assortment of small arms, both ships were bombed at low level. The upshot is well documented: *Broadsword* survived while *Coventry* was lost.

These were moments of great anguish, but my recollections remain clear. We strove to sort ourselves out and to prepare for re-attack against the haunting knowledge that the *Coventry* survivors had abandoned ship.

My mind was criss-crossed by self-analysing thoughts: how could this possibly have happened? Had I given *Coventry* enough help and direction? Indeed, in the heat of the moment, I gained the impression, quite falsely, that my ship was trimming by the stern following the bomb strike aft.

Chiefly among the many reports flooding into the ops room during this quite short-lived incident, I shall never forget a very controlled statement from my officer of the watch saying that *Coventry* 'has blown up'.

Surprisingly, no future air attacks developed and our situation was relieved by the arrival of a pair of Harriers to provide top cover, thus enabling us to concentrate on recovering the *Coventry* survivors, in which we were ably assisted by a fleet of helicopters sent out from San Carlos.

What do you say to *Coventry*'s Captain when he is ushered to your bridge sopping wet, frozen stiff and injured? 'Would you like a warm bath?' seemed desperately inadequate. I made a brief visit to the wardroom to see my own casualties and to offer a sympathetic welcome to some of the survivors from *Coventry*.

And so back to San Carlos in the small hours to disembark survivors. Another deeply embedded memory was the *Coventry* men raising three cheers in the total darkness as their craft bore them away to shore. While very moving, this generous act seemed only to accentuate the sense of failure harboured in my subconscious. After this, things slowly returned to normal during the following six weeks until our departure on 11 July.

Then there was our return to Devonport and to a memorable welcome from hundreds of well-wishers and families. So absorbing was all this that I all but rammed the jetty and had to call for 'full astern' to avoid doing so. Lack of recent practice, I suppose!

And so, the less favourable memories from the previous three months faded from the mind while one was left with such impressions as a splendid performance by a young Ship's Company; the support from home; the huge part played by the RFA and the Fleet train in keeping the Task Force supplied; the good luck that *Broadsword* enjoyed in so many ways despite being in the thick of things; the vagaries of the South Atlantic winter weather – sometimes hostile, sometimes strangely benign, but always cool. [11]

The Duke of Edinburgh awards the Atlantic Medal to Simon Weston
at Buckingham Palace.

SIMON WESTON OBE

Welsh Guards

When thinking about writing this piece regarding any memories I might have about my short time in the Falklands, I was acutely aware of the fact that so much has already been written or recorded. However, one memory that sprung to mind that I have never spoken of before happened during my stay on the SS *Uganda*, just after the bombing of the *Sir Galahad*.

Nobody can imagine the feeling of frustration and helplessness that I experienced, when lying immobile and in pain during the first 11 days following my injuries. It was so bad that it threatened to suffocate me at times. My eyelids had been burned and had shrunk, and seeing, even in the daytime, was impossible. I kept having to have my eyes cleaned all the time to clear away the debris and muck that just persisted on gathering there, and dressings covered my eyes to prevent them from drying out and being permanently damaged.

I remember feeling so desperate that I was so far away from home, from my family. It was during this time that I recall watching, or rather listening to and catching glimpses of, the film *Car Wash*. This short period of time watching that film allowed me the chance to become distracted from what had happened to me. As I look back on this moment, I realise the value of those two hours of entertainment. Aircraft were still flying overhead, the horror of the attack on the ship still vivid in my mind, the pain and fear of what had been done to me were momentarily lost in a blissful moment of escapism. That was invaluable in the reality of my situation.

Soon after this I was sent home, against normal medical procedure, as the powers that be realised that the frustration and isolation of the ship would kill me, and I might as well die trying to get home as die out there.

COMMANDER C.J.S. CRAIG

Captain, HMS *Alacrity*

On 10 May, we receive special orders – to detach from the task group under cover of dense fog before proceeding far to the west, probing harbours and inlets along the southern coasts of East and West Falkland. And if that is not risky enough, we are also to enter the slim strip of water that divides the two islands, Falkland Sound, and complete the 50-mile transit in darkness to emerge at the northern end. My Ship's Company are less than enthusiastic. We enter the Sound at precisely 2300 hours, more than 130 miles from meaningful British support. We are in the 'Ultra Quiet State', the minimum of machinery running, our speed but five knots through the narrows, thereby stirring only minimal cavitation around our propellers. At half past midnight, we are no more than one-third of our way through, and still in confined waters.

Radar contact, bearing 079, range five miles. Moving north-east inside the channel. Speed eight knots. The sudden whisper comes from the surface-picture radar plotter.

Minutes passed. Range closing. Course 020. Speed nine knots. Large contact.

An eternity passes before the radar plotter speaks again.

Contact merging from the channel, moving out into clear water. Range 4.8 miles. I have him on the A scope. He's a big feller. A pause.

The blast of the gun is shattering: the whoosh of nearly 3,000 feet per second muzzle velocity as the shell leaves the barrel is very audible. For men not in the ops room and thus unaware that it is ourselves taking the initiative, it must be terrifying.

'Nothing seen,' comes the report. He had to be the enemy.

'Engage!' The noise is deafening, cordite reeks. The rounds continued.

Lookouts are reporting flashes on the bearing of our gunfire. More reports of flashes through the rain. There seem to be some secondary explosions. Then a report that is chilling in its finality. 'Huge orange flash on the bearing, sir. Right up into the cloud. Radar contact fading on all displays. Cease firing.'

Some minutes later, our helicopter reports flickering lights close inshore but nothing else. We have to leave any rescue work to the Argentines and be gone.[12]

VELMA MALCOLM

Falkland Islander

On 27 April, at about 3pm, I came downstairs from trying to peer at Stanley Airport to see if I could see any activity happening down there. A number of Argentine soldiers were banging on the wall of the house. The leader was a very big Sergeant who said: 'You are going to camp, you and your husband.' They came in and said they were going to search my house, to which I replied: 'Help yourself, I have nothing to hide.' He accompanied me upstairs to pack. When I turned from the drawer with some clothes, I was amazed to find that he was holding a pistol in my back.

He taunted me for not liking Argentines, and so on, to which I replied: 'That is why – we don't live with guns.'

We were taken out and put in a Mercedes jeep and whisked away. Had I been told they could abduct us in Stanley, I wouldn't have believed it, but it happened.

When we entered the jeep, the result of their search was evident in the form of a small box of miniature flags that we normally distributed to schoolchildren when visiting dignitaries called in on us.

We were taken to the airport and placed in the south-east corner under guard. Later, Brian Summers and the Wallace family arrived, but we were kept apart. Eventually we were taken inside the building, but were not allowed to talk. A Hercules had been revved up on the tarmac during this period, and we all breathed a sigh of relief that it left without us.

After a couple of hours, we were all herded out and put into yet another jeep, where we found two more comrades, making our party 14 – nine adults and five children. We were put in a Puma helicopter and away we went. Knowing the land, we were able to locate the area we were in until we left East Falkland and crossed the Falkland Sound, whereupon I no longer had accurate bearings.

Eventually we landed at Fox Bay East. One or two Argentines jumped out but came back to ask us where we were going. We had no idea, but they took us across the bay to Fox Bay West and landed us.

Next day, Richard Cockwell came around with the Argentine Major from Fox Bay East and offered us accommodation at Fox Bay East to ease the congestion. We had a long discussion because the Knight family had been very good to us. We also decided the 14 of us should stay together. Eventually it was agreed that we would cross the Bay, and our Puma came back to collect us.

At Fox Bay East, the Major addressed us and told us we could move around the settlement but not to go over the fences dotted around us – they were mined areas.

Five of us billeted in another house and it was necessary to go outside the perimeter of the house fence to get peat and water. The reservoir supplying the settlement had been contaminated by the occupying forces.

On 1 May, I think it was, the Harriers had attacked Stanley Airport, and when one of our number went outside the house boundary to get water, he came scurrying back and said: 'I don't think they want me out there, they fired at me!'

Troops appeared shortly after and put us under house arrest, a situation that remained in force until 14 June 1982.

Later in the day, we were allowed to go to the Manager's house and join our colleagues, so all 19 of us were in one house.

The *Bahia Buen Suceso* appeared at the jetty from time to time. Eventually she came to retire.

The Cockwells had a yacht and Richard asked permission to go to the yacht to collect bedding, taking three members of the house party with him. All went well until they started back, when shots were fired over them. The guards had changed while the men were on the boat, and the guard going off duty had forgotten to tell his relief that permission had been given for the journey.

We thought we had been forgotten when, one Sunday, the Harriers appeared and strafed the *Bahia Buen Suceso*. The sound of Harrier cannon fire will remain with me for ever.

We had three Harrier raids and I forget how many Naval bombardments, but it may have been five.

Probably the most frightening day was when Goose Green was recovered. We were ordered out of the house with fully armed guards on each side of the path and taken towards the jetty. Wondering how I was going to get up a rope ladder on to the ship, it was a relief when we were herded into the shearing shed and put at one end of the shearing floor with the severe warning that the guard had instructions to shoot us if we tried to leave the area.

While this was going on, Officers were thoroughly searching the house. About four hours later, we were allowed to go back to the house.

WILLIAM SKINNER

9 Parachute Squadron, Royal Engineers

This is my story of 8 June 1982, surrounding the Royal Fleet Auxiliary Landing Ship Logistic *Sir Galahad*.

I had joined 9 Parachute Squadron Royal Engineers from an Engineer support Squadron in Germany during April of 1981. Following 'P' company selection and parachute training at Brize Norton, I was allocated to 1 troop.

When Argentine forces invaded the Falkland Islands, we were baffled in many ways. Our first thoughts were: what does a South American country want with a bunch of islands off the Scottish coast? After we got our geography sorted out and packed the G10s (each troop has a store of basic engineering equipment called G1098), we signed out weapons and got stuck in to the training that would hopefully prepare us for what lay ahead. We later realised that Wales and Dartmoor were perfect training grounds because of the similarity to the ground we would encounter 8,000 miles south.

The Squadron boarded the *QEII* and, after a technical hitch which involved hiding around the back of the Isle of Wight, we cruised south to join the rest of the force. After the landings, I was involved in many of the operations leading up to 5 Brigade's push to Stanley. On the morning of 8 June, I was called over by the Squadron Commander (Major Chris Davies). 'Corporal Skinner, I hope you can remember your watermanship skills,' he said. I was given a requisitioned 18ft boat with a very noisy diesel engine and, along with Sapper Dave 'Gopper' Leer, prepared the small boat with our kit. After bunging up the various leaks and pumping out the bilge, we fuelled the boat with as much diesel as we could find and then reported back to the Squadron CP (command post) for our orders. Dave and I were to motor out to the *Sir Galahad* and pick up stores and personnel and deliver them to Bluff Cove. Whenever soldiers are sent on tasks, they will always take all their kit with them, as the chances are that, by the time you have finished, the Squadron will have moved and taken your scratcher (sleeping bag) with them. A night out in a Falklands winter without your doss bag and some sort of overhead cover was potentially lethal.

During the day, we had overheard others talking about the 'two big grey sitting ducks' in the bay so, as Dave and I chugged out to the LSL, we briefly considered the fact that we would also be part of the possible target. We first went to the starboard side of the ship as it was nearest; not finding any means of scaling the steep sides, we sailed around the stern and found a ladder on the starboard side leading to the lower open deck. Once aboard, Dave said he had 'a turd on a bungee rearing its ugly head' so, not wishing to miss out on the opportunity of warm porcelain, we agreed to meet up in the galley later. I set off to find the people and equipment that I was tasked to pick up. I went down to the tank deck and found the whole area crowded with troops, equipment and vehicles. A sergeant who seemed to know what I was after told me I was wasting my time until the ship's engineers had got the rear ramp sorted out. I looked to the back of the ship and could see that it was partially open by about a foot or so, but that was it. The Sergeant told me it was jammed and that they had been told to expect at least a 20 minute wait. I suggested we man-handle the kit up the gangways and over the side to my boat; the Sergeant didn't say anything but showed me the equipment boxes. It was obvious that a struggle up and along the one-man-wide gangways would be a major military task with even the smallest of the boxes.

I remembered I had to meet Dave, so rather than hang around in the cold tank deck I went off to the galley hoping to scrounge a brew. On the way, I passed a lot of other troops, mostly with Welsh accents, who were dressed casually in just shirts and denims. They were all wearing either trainers or issue PT 'daps': this was probably a ship's regulation of some sort to protect the decks. A crowd of Welsh senior NCOs were engaged in a shouting match outside the washing-machine room, arguing about whose kit was next in turn. After following the smell of food, I found the galley, but Dave was absent: I guessed he was forcing out enough to make room for a week's worth and the possibility of another porcelain later in the war.

It was at this point that I realised I was dressed for the Antarctic and stood in a small room full of blokes with the heating set at furnace level 6. My face and hands felt like they had severe sunburn; after more than a week living in the freezing and driving snow, sleet and rain conditions on land, my complexion probably resembled that of a Russian farmer's wife. I got a brew from one of the many Chinese hands working on the ship and stepped out into the middle of the room to wait for Dave. I soon got shouted at from a crowded table to 'get out of the way'. Wondering what they meant, I turned and looked round. A small TV was fixed high up the galley wall in the corner of the room, and my fat head was in the way of the latest showing of a porn video. Some soldiers can proudly boast that their lives were saved during battle by various lucky events; a porn film saved mine. (It's been 20 years now since this event and I still dare not tell my wife.)

Glancing back at the angry-looking boyos at the table, I thought it best to move. I smiled to myself as I thought that later, while they had locked themselves in the heads for a bit of self-love, my bright red face would abruptly appear in their minds during the replay and spoil the event. Walking over near to the door where I had entered, I wondered how long I was going to be stuck on this floating bull's-eye when two fast jets flashed overhead with such shocking din and speed that I flinched and instinctively bent forward. Someone immediately shouted over the ship's Tannoy: 'AIR RAID RED.' This warning is usually given more than once; on this occasion the second warning was interrupted by the shock wave and deafening explosion that erupted from the decks below. The whole ship seemed to cry out with one voice. I couldn't see and realised I was lying face down on the deck and was covered with the panelling and fixtures that once made the galley a comfortable place to eat a meal. As I stood up, the debris fell off, but I still couldn't see and I was now finding it difficult to breathe. I rubbed my face which, despite feeling gritty and very sore, seemed to be intact. I looked around for any light that would give me my bearings. Finding very dim sunlight shining in from the fore'd portholes, I could see why it was difficult to breathe. Thick black smoke filled the air; some of it even looked like it was in lumps. I looked around the room to where I had been standing when the boyos had got upset: I felt momentarily confused that I could see through to the deck beneath us. The steel decking plates were peeled back and flames lit up the area below through dense smoke. I'm sure that if the video had been *Basket Weaving For Beginners* Taffy and his mates wouldn't have moved me on and I would now be wearing wings of a different colour.

It's been said many times before that traumatic events seem to play out in slow motion, and it's true. Although the whole thing probably lasted only seconds, it seemed like long, slow minutes to me. I could see the hazy silhouettes of people moving through thick smoke near the portholes and started to head for where I thought the entry door had been. I had moved only a couple of steps when someone shouted: 'Stand still.' In such confusion, any order is as good as the next, and so everyone stood still. This was quickly followed by another voice which shouted: 'Fuck that, the smoke is killing us, let's get out.' Strangely, both commands served their purpose. The first order stopped people bouncing around the room as if in a pinball machine and gave them a few seconds to think; the second order got people's feet moving again but this time in a more controlled direction.

On getting to the door, I broke out into the bright sunlight and air that was breathable. I was coughing and could hardly see because of the tears and soot in my eyes; the surge of bodies from behind pressed me on towards a gangway descending to the lower deck. A soldier lying face down on the stairs blocked the way down; his efforts to move were hindered by the mass of troops trying to get over him. As I got level with him, I grabbed the straps of his webbing with one hand and took hold of the stair handrail to steady myself with the other. I pulled him to the bottom of the stairs; he didn't make much noise or struggle. It was then that I saw the reason: a piece of timber about 40mm square was jutting from his back. I carefully rolled him on to his side and saw that he was still conscious. I asked him if he was OK and whether he was in pain. He said that he could feel nothing, except he found it difficult to breathe. The lump of wood was well away from his spine, but I suspected that it was pressing against or had pierced a lung. I felt a hand on my shoulder and looked round to see the smiling face of a

Medical Corps Sergeant. He told me he would take over. I felt relieved that this man's life was in more experienced hands than mine. I thankfully stepped away and moved to the side of the ship and looked over the handrail searching for my small boat.

Someone was already aboard, and it was obvious that they were trying to work out how to start the engine. I climbed down the rope ladder and, without saying anything, reached into the engine compartment. The engine started first time and we set off for the other lifeboats drifting towards Pleasant Island. The stranger did introduce himself, but I can't remember his name – only that he was a Royal Marine. It was obvious what we had to do: most of the other lifeboats did not have engines and the strong Falkland winds were blowing the boats away from the mainland. We headed for the nearest boat, which was one of the big lifeboats that had been lowered from the side of the mother ship. The more able passengers were desperately trying to row for the opposite shore, but the wind was clearly getting the better of them and they were tiring quickly. When we got close enough, I shouted for them to throw a rope, which I tied to the transom of our craft. As we towed them towards the next big lifeboat, the crew sat back, thankful for the rest and the chance to help treat some of the casualties on board. We tied the next boat to the one we were towing and then went on to the smaller, inflatable rafts. By the time we had six or so boats, we agreed to turn for shore. My little boat was hardly moving against the drag of the wind and the weight of the boats and men. Looking back, I could see many of the boats had casualties and the crews shouted to us to go faster. The little engine was already at full thrash with nothing to spare, so we plodded on at a painfully slow speed.

As we rounded the back of the *Sir Galahad*, I could see that the whole ship was now seriously on fire. We sailed through the dense smoke that drifted across the water and I could see the helicopters starting to arrive and lift troops who had escaped to the bow of the ship. Burning ammunition that was stored on the tank deck was now starting to explode, small arms ammunition and rocket motors were getting past the rear ramp and dropping into the water. We emerged from the smoke and I realised that if we didn't move further away we were in danger of being hit by some of our own ordnance. My little boat plodded on and very slowly we moved away from the immediate danger area. Now that some of the lifeboat crews had rested and done what they could for the casualties aboard their respective boats, they took up the oars and started to row again. I couldn't tell if we were going any faster, but it must have taken some of the strain off the little diesel engine.

After what seemed like an eternity, we reached the shallow waters of the shore. In all, it must have taken 15–20 minutes to cross the relatively short distance. Soldiers crowded the beach and some even braved the freezing waters to wade out and pull the boats in. I let go the line on the transom and turned the boat out to deeper waters just as I felt the keel start to bounce on the bottom.

The televised pictures only show the lifeboats with the able crews still rowing, but the chug chug of my little boat can be heard in the background as I headed back to the *Galahad*. More lifeboats were still out near Pleasant Island, although it was obvious that some were empty. Many of the inflatable rafts were grounded on the island and some had been turned over by the wind: I steered for these first. Thankfully, I found no other casualties and so I headed for the burning ship to see if anyone else had jumped in the water. Helicopters were still flying back and forth with survivors as I searched around the ship, but I found none.

For me the immediate crisis was over, but for the surgeons such as Rick Jolly, the medical staff and, worst of all, the casualties, the nightmare had only just begun.

I set my boat back to the small jetty where I had first collected it and walked back to the Squadron position. The OC (Major Chris Davies) and the 2iC (Captain Freddie Kemp) were obviously pleased to see I was still in one piece. They asked me if I had seen the other members of the Squadron, which worried me as most of the ship had now been evacuated. It suggested that they may still be trapped on board or injured in one of the medical reception stations.

The Squadron was still on air raid warning red and positioned in the trenches with weapons at the ready. As I walked back, someone emphasised the point and again shouted across to the position: 'Air raid warning red.' I ran over to the nearest trench, where Gus Hales was. As I jumped in, I could hear the rattle of weapon fire far out to the right; as they were in dead ground I couldn't see at first what they were shooting at. A Skyhawk suddenly shot into view with tracer fire following its flight path. It was very low, and because of our position on the hill we looked down on the aircraft. This aircraft must have returned either for another attack run or, more likely, for a damage recce flight. Unfortunately for the pilot, 9 Parachute Squadron, the Parachute Regiment, A Battery of Royal Artillery and many others occupied Bluff Cove at that time.

The hail of small-arms fire that went up to meet this lone aircraft was astonishing. The tracer lit up as it arced out and funnelled into the aircraft from positions scattered all over the hillside. Gus got off a few rounds with the Browning 30 cal before the old cloth belt caused a jam and I emptied most of the magazine of Gus's rifle before the Skyhawk disappeared around the next hill to the left. It is surprisingly difficult to hit a moving target and even more so if it's a pop-up target moving at fast jet speed. On this occasion, however, there was just so much ammunition in the air that some of it was clearly hitting the aircraft. Just before the jet disappeared, I saw a small part fly off and fall into the water and more smoke than I thought normal was also streaming from the engine jet pipe. We learnt later that the aircraft had crashed some way down the coast, killing the pilot.

A few hours later, the missing members of the Squadron were accounted for. Some were still helping with casualties after getting off the ship; others were involved with shooting down the Skyhawk from other positions. Sadly, two members of the Squadron who formed part of 4 Troop and were attached from other Sapper units were killed.

Later that evening, I was involved with salvaging stores and medical equipment from the still-smoking *Sir Tristram*. In retrospect, this was a fortunate mental diversion and gave me little time to brood on the day's events.

This and many of the other adventures of the Falklands conflict are with me for ever. The horror and terrible things that we, as humans, are capable of haunt me daily, but I can and will live with it because I also learnt the enormous compassionate humanity that we are capable of in the most trying of times.

For my actions on the 8 June 1982, I was awarded a mention in Despatches.

RFA *Sir Galahad* burning at Bluff Cove, 23 May 1982. The ship was later towed out into the Atlantic and sunk as a war grave.

JOE D'SOUZA

Leading Aircrewman, HMS *Yarmouth*

Our ship had been involved with supporting the San Carlos landings and we experienced many close calls with air attacks from that day. Each ship has a contingent of Royal Marines and our Colour Sergeant had recommended we man the upper deck with lots of light machine-guns loaded with 1 in 1 tracer as a visual deterrent to incoming aircraft. This proved very effective during our later days in San Carlos Water. Despite being under attack on numerous occasions, the sight of streams of tracer emanating from our decks visibly dissuaded low-level air raids, and many other ships that had not taken the same deterrent action were bombed or sunk. To support the guys at the gun posts, it was decided to fill sandbags from the shore at the same point as the field hospital and main arms dump, to use as protection around the bridge emplacements. A small boat party was sent ashore and included a member of the ship's flight to act as loadmaster. The first load was underslung and taken back to the ship without incident. After a further 20-30 minutes, we returned for a further load. It was while we were in the hover with the load attached that 'Air Raid Warning Red' came over the radio. This was immediately followed by a series of explosions on the far side of the Bay. Instead of jettisoning the load of sandbags, we gently lowered it to the ground and dropped the load strop. Several more explosions occurred around us and we saw aircraft departing at low level above where we were hovering. It was at this point that I looked toward the hospital and saw an A4 Skyhawk on an incoming bombing run. Immediately I thought of my shipmates who had dispersed on the ground to find cover and that this aircraft had an unopposed attack on the hospital and ammo dump. I could see the pilot looking at me and he was firing his cannon to knock us out of the sky. I can't say why – but I decided the guys on the ground had to have support and ordered my pilot to climb in height. Our rate of climb was clearly interfering with the A4's escape route and, what is more, his angle of attack. In order to drop his bomb load, he needed to maintain a shallow approach; we were forcing him to climb. In what seemed like an age but could have been no more than three or four seconds, he was almost on top of us. I shouted for my pilot to reduce height and the Skyhawk passed overhead at around 10ft while his bomb and retard parachute passed below at 6ft or 7ft.

We found a ravine and landed. I checked whether we had been hit, fortunately not but we were choked up from the massive adrenalin rush we'd just experienced, the knowledge that we had deliberately tried to cause an impact with a 300mph jet aircraft and that our colleagues might be injured or worse among the explosions on the ground.

When the 'All Clear' came over the radio, we returned to the cargo net full of sandbags and I jumped out to hook the load on. As I reconnected my intercom, the pilot said that he'd noticed one of the retard parachutes about 100 yards away and that it would make a good souvenir. I ran over to where the parachute lay, only to discover that a 500lb bomb was still attached and buried in the mud! I left it there.

We returned the sandbag load to the ship, then went to locate the shore party who were all thankfully OK. All six piled into the Wasp which is designed to carry three passengers! On landing back at the ship, an intercom broadcast from the captain asked if everyone was OK and then enquired as to the whereabouts of the ship's boat. Trying to persuade the shore party to go back was a struggle. Ammunition from the arms dump was still exploding and, upon departing the jetty, half an outbuilding landed very close to where the boat had been tied.

Later in the messroom, the boat party recounted what had happened to them during the air raid. They had jumped into the first trench that they came across and waited until they had seen the Wasp return for them. A soldier had also jumped into the trench but, after a minute or two, exclaimed: 'I'd rather be shot than stay in this shit hole . . .' Because that is exactly where the guys had sought shelter!

That incident is the one that I recall as being a positive input on my behalf. The decision to sacrifice myself to protect others, the feeling of inevitability and complete calm during those few seconds. Looking into the eyes of the Argentine pilot who, upon realising our game plan, had stopped firing his cannon and wasted his bombing opportunity. If I helped save lives, then it was worth it.

PHIL HANCOCK

SS *Canberra*

I remember following the lead up to the war through newspapers and news bulletins. I was on leave and one evening the news announced that the *Canberra* had been requisitioned. I was at the local pub drinking a pint when the barmaid called my name to take an urgent phone call. I had to call P&O head office urgently. I was due to return to the *Canberra* as my leave was at an end. Would I volunteer to join the Task Force? We wouldn't go anywhere near the war zone as we were a hospital ship!! This proved to be incorrect as the Argentines argued that as long as we carried troops we were a legitimate target and not protected under the Geneva Convention.

Of course I said yes. When I told my parents, my mother asked why I had to go and if I couldn't have told them I had a cold. These were the first steps down a path that would change my outlook on life forever.

I served aboard the TEV (Turbo Electric Vessel) *Canberra* as an Engineering Officer. *Canberra* was driven by two huge electric motors, one attached to each propeller shaft, with steam turbines spinning the generators. A passenger ship in peacetime, she served as a troop ship and a hospital ship for the period of the war.

At sea for 93 days, with watertight doors shut, each engineroom compartment was a potential tomb. There was no way to persuade the troops on board come down to the engine room voluntarily. Some were forced by irate NCOs to carry out small tasks down below but on the whole the troops preferred the open air.

I have never met a tougher, more dedicated group of men. All of the cheese wires were taken from the galley. If the soldiers could not break them around their wrists they were sent to the engine room and made into garrotes.

I'm glad they were on our side!

On our way to the Falklands we anchored at Ascension Island. An alert watchkeeper aboard *Canberra* spotted an Argentine tanker about two miles from the Fleet. The 12-4 engineers were on watch at the time. The engines were shut down, the boilers had only half a bar in them to keep them warm. It normally takes about three hours to warm through steam plant prior to the engines being ready to use. Well the navy decided that the tanker may have dropped midget submarines with the intention of sticking limpet mines to the ships hulls and issued an emergency sail order. You can imagine being 30 feet below the water line with the possibility of someone sticking mines to the other side of the ships hull from where you are standing. Galvanised into action the engineers, six of us, broke all the rules and the steam turbines were rotating within 15 minutes of getting the order. This meant that the *Canberra* was the second ship to sail in the Fleet. A source of astonishment to many but of immense pride to the engineers on watch. It's amazing what you can achieve when you need to.

The weather on the way down to the Falklands was at times best described as foul. Thick freezing fog and rough seas were often our only companions. Visibility was often to low to even make out our escorts. We spent many days steaming around in a square waiting for our next orders. Eager for news we waited each day for messages or briefings. A friend of mine from the Royal Navy was aboard and had the role of taking communications from the radio room to the bridge. As an officer I was allowed alcohol and spirits. The troops were rationed to two cans per day. With a small amount of haggling an arrangement was reached through which he kept us up to date with events, provided they were not classified, in exchange for a few beers or a bottle of whisky. Friendly rivalry existed between the NCOs and the engineers. We sneaked into their mess and placed a tin of beer on their bar and then proceed to join hundreds of straws together linking their mess with the officers wardroom. When the NCOs traced the straws they found us unsuccessfully sucking with all our might to get the beer from the can. We drank all of the stockpiled beer that night.

One evening we were told that the Argentines may have located *Canberra* and we were to swap TRALA (God knows what that stood for) zones with the *Atlantic Conveyor*. Image how we felt when next day we learned that the *Atlantic Conveyor* had been hit with an exocet missile. Luck was still with us but we felt sadness and a twinge of guilt. Fellow seafarers died again that night.

We slept in the restaurants on the lower decks during our time in San Carlos Bay. We worried that this area presented the largest radar cross section for an exocet missile. The sinking of HMS *Sheffield* had shaken us all. We slept under the tables, our cabins below the bridge were too exposed. The Naval Commander kept us informed of the current state of readiness using the ships PA system. Yellow Alert meant enemy aircraft were in the vicinity. Red Alert meant we were under attack.

Frequently the PA sounded 'RED ALERT – TAKE COVER' and we dived to the floor and covered our heads as we had been told. One missile was to close for comfort. The next call was issued . . . 'RED ALERT – TAKE CO . . .' then silence. We were sure the bridge had been hit, but the CO had hit the deck as well. The missile was within 300 metres of the ship before a surface-to-air missile from HMS *Fearless* destroyed it.

Lying under the tables while the ship shook from near misses, Norman Pound, the 1st Engineering Officer, asked Jack nervously: 'What kind of bombs do you think they are throwing at us now?' Jack replied: 'I don't know. First – bloody big ones.'

After being told the night before that it was unlikely the ship would survive the day intact, many of the engineers had the fatalistic attitude of 'If it happens I'll worry about it then'. We knew we wouldn't survive long if we went in the water. The temperature was just above freezing. Engineers coming off watch tried to photograph some of the air battles ignoring the danger. The Naval personnel obviously better trained took cover where ever they could.

The night before the attack was a sobering time. The Senior Naval Commander on board saw the off duty engineers drinking a cold beer after our watch and told us that the Government had written the ship off as a war loss. *Canberra* was not expected to survive the next day. We were also asked to make a will. It was not something I had considered as a young twenty year old who was going to live forever. I didn't have much in the way of an estate, so the task was not too difficult.

The Argentine pilots were offered a reward to sink the *Canberra*, a fact disputed by some. A white ship with yellow funnels made a very inviting target. Bombs exploded around us, each one a dull thud that reverberated through the ships hull. When not on duty we stayed in the restaurants near to the engine room or sneaked onto the deck to try and photograph the Argentine jets.

God smiled on us that day.

As we sailed into port back in England the atmosphere was electric. As dawn broke, the air was cool and crisp and a few small boats ventured out to be the first to welcome the ship. The few soon turned into a small flotilla. The coastline of England had changed into a sea of Union Jacks that stretched for as far as the eye could see. We had really made it home. The lump in our throats were the size of tennis balls.

The Great White Whale had returned home!

Boy scouts gave everyone disembarking a rose. At one point two buxom ladies decided to bare their breasts causing the ship to list slightly as hundreds of soldiers moved to the starboard side for a look. The engineers made a banner as well. We were all worried in case we got into trouble. The officers on the ship were supposed to set an example. It actually tore and blew away before we tied up alongside.

My parents had come to Southampton as we were allowed only two tickets to get into the dock. It was an emotional day and I'm sure that it is etched forever on the minds of all those who were there.

After the excitement of Southampton, I returned home to find the house decorated with bunting and banners. My friends and family had spent the evening before putting it all up. My friend Robert Shuttlewood had a lovely time orchestrating it. I remember seeing the house for the first time and the immediate sense of embarrassment. I was touched, but being naturally quiet (well, I was then!) preferred anonymity. I took the decorations down as quickly as was polite.

Phil Hancock runs a Falklands website called the Great White Whale at
www.comcen.com.au/~raiment/

SIR JOHN NOTT

Secretary of State for Defence, 1981–83

I hate war; the thought of sending young men and women away to fight is repugnant to me. Yet on the night of Thursday 1 April 1982, I agreed, with my immediate colleagues, that we had no option but to do so; and we sent them to the other side of the world, at huge risk, across 8,000 miles of ocean. It ended in triumph and tragedy – 255 British lost their lives and many more were wounded. Nor should we forget the Argentine dead, brought about needlessly by the fascist leaders of their country.

Those who had experienced war – Terry Lewin, William Whitelaw and Francis Pym, my colleagues in the War Cabinet – must have felt as I did. Margaret Thatcher, as a woman and a mother, must have been just as deeply affected as us men. But all of us managed, in the crisis which engulfed us, to conceal these feelings from each other. Sometimes Francis, in his determined quest for a negotiated settlement, perhaps allowed his emotions to show a little; but it was his job as Foreign Secretary to seek a diplomatic exit – an exit to a situation that had vexed successive Governments ever since the Second World War.

Throughout the Falklands conflict, Margaret Thatcher was at her best, showing great courage and determination. I had some disagreements with her when I urged restraint, and occasionally I aligned myself with Francis Pym, not entirely to Margaret's liking. But generally there was a remarkable sense of unity among us – and that was surprising, given the rather diverse personalities involved.

In time of war there is no room for the post of Defence Secretary; that role must necessarily be performed by the Prime Minister of the day. I found it difficult, because I knew that I would be the first scapegoat for any military failure. Truly, I had responsibility without power. I participated in, and I hope influenced, all the key decisions in the War Cabinet – but it was a very different set of circumstances to when I had been very much in charge on my own patch in the Ministry of Defence. I tried, and I believe succeeded, in redefining my own role within the MoD, questioning but not overly influencing the decisions of the military.

If you go to war you have to trust the system – the relevant parts of the bureaucracy must be kept informed. This was one of the principal failures of Suez. It means widening the circle of information and consultation far beyond what is wise; but in an emergency the key people must be made to feel part of a team, for exclusion breeds resentment. In the early days several of my Parliamentary colleagues were a real threat to national morale and good order, not least because of their incestuous relationship with the Parliamentary press, but with difficulty we managed to neutralise the worst speculation and gossip in the newspapers.

Our intelligence services intercepted a series of signals which left little doubt that an invasion was planned for the morning of Friday 2 April. We knew four things: that an Argentine submarine had been deployed to the area around Port Stanley (we were subsequently to learn that its task was to reconnoiter the beaches); that the Argentine Fleet, which had been on exercises, had broken up into smaller units and seemed to be reassembling for an invasion; that an Army commander had been embarked separately on a merchant ship and seemed likely to be the commander of an amphibious force; and finally, that the Fleet had been ordered to destroy all their documents.

I said to my Private Secretary, David Omand, that we must see the Prime Minister immediately. He telephoned No. 10. I saw Ian Gow, Margaret Thatcher's Parliamentary Private Secretary, and slowly we assembled in her room. I believe that this informal meeting consisted of Clive Whitmore and John Rose, the Private Secretaries from No. 10, Humphrey Atkins and Richard Luce, the two Foreign Office Ministers, and Ian Gow. Margaret Thatcher herself suggested that Sir Antony Acland, the new Permanent Secretary at the Foreign Office, should join us, and I asked for Sir Frank Cooper to come over from Defence. Our initial conversation was somewhat unstructured, but mainly concerned itself with how we could react diplomatically. A message was prepared for Margaret Thatcher to send to President Reagan asking whether he was aware of the Signals intelligence that we had just received. David Omand was sent to ensure that our Intelligence material had equally been received by our US counterparts. At this early stage it had not. A message was prepared to send to our Ambassador in the United States, Sir Nicholas Henderson, and to the Governor of the Falkland Islands.

At this juncture, a secretary took me aside and said that Henry Leach was outside the Prime Minister's room and had asked to see me. After I had suggested to Margaret Thatcher that he should join us, Henry did so in full Naval uniform. The sight of a man in uniform always pleases the ladies and Margaret, very much an impressionable lady, was always impressed by men in uniform.

She asked for Henry's views. With great assurance, he said that it was possible to prepare a large Task Force. This would include *Hermes* and *Invincible*, together with the greater part of our destroyer and frigate forces, which were exercising off Gibraltar. He declared that the Task Force could be ready to sail early the following week, so long as he had authority to prepare it, with instructions to sail to follow later. This assertion greatly boosted the confidence of Margaret Thatcher; it was met by some scepticism among the rest of us.

Eventually the meeting broke up late at night and I was left alone with Margaret. I thought that Henry had performed very well – and I have great praise for his supreme self-confidence and assertiveness. He had appeared, quite by chance, at a critical moment. I had already had a long series of disagreements with him on the Defence Review, but that Henry was a sailor in the best Nelsonian tradition. 'Sail at the enemy!' and do not hesitate about the consequences.

I expressed my qualms to Margaret Thatcher about the viability of such an operation. Reasonably enough, she has often reminded me of them. In particular, I recall the following exchange between us. She said: 'I suppose you realise, John, that this is going to be the worst week of our lives.' I responded: 'Well, that may be so, but I imagine that each successive week will be worse than the last.' It was not a helpful exchange at that particular juncture. Nevertheless, we gave Henry Leach authority to make preparations for a Task Force.

In his memoirs, John Major asserts that 'if the Cabinet had not sent the Task Force, Margaret Thatcher would not have survived as Prime Minister'. He adds that 'she took a great risk, requiring huge nerve, but the alternative was certain catastrophe'. Actually, I do not agree with that judgement. I would not have survived, but I think that Margaret Thatcher would have done so. But that is another 'What if?' of history. Who can know?

Margaret Thatcher had, I believe, made up her mind from the outset that the only way we could regain our national honour and prestige was by inflicting a military defeat on Argentina. She was sufficiently pragmatic to understand that if the negotiations could bring about a total withdrawal of the Argentines and the restoration of some kind of British administration, then her Cabinet would accept it. A myth grew up about Margaret Thatcher that in some way her word was law. It was never the case in my day; she was very well aware that she had to keep her Cabinet, her Parliamentary supporters and the party in the country with her. The painful and endless negotiations for a diplomatic settlement produced the only significant personal clashes of the war. The only positive thing that can be said of them in retrospect is that they filled a horrible vacuum, whilst the Task Force made its long, long voyage towards Antarctica – as far laterally as Hawaii.

Three weeks later our forces recaptured South Georgia without loss of life, after encountering some dreadful weather conditions. Quite late on the Sunday evening, the 25th, I went across to No. 10 with a draft statement, as I felt that this first victory should be announced by Margaret, but she was insistent that the task should fall to me. We went out into Downing Street and I read out the agreed statement. I remember the occasion for two reasons.

I had returned from my constituency in Cornwall on my RAF plane wearing an appalling spiv's suit, which had been made for me by the only tailor in my constituency. It never occurred to me that it would see the light of day; but as soon as I had completed my statement, the large number of assorted hacks and newshounds, accompanied by a huge congregation of cameramen, started shouting questions at me. 'What happens next, Mr Nott? Are we going to declare war on Argentina, Mrs Thatcher?' To which Margaret replied in a high-pitched voice: 'Just rejoice at that news and congratulate our forces and the Marines . . . Rejoice.' Somehow it was highly embarrassing, although she was only trying to get the wretched media to acknowledge our success. We retreated hastily into No. 10.

Second only to my interview – or non-interview – with Robin Day, this incident known as 'Rejoice, Rejoice' was to dog me on the television for the next 20 years. Every time I see it, I cringe at that awful suit and the millions of people around the world who have now been able to judge the quality of Cornish tailoring.

During the following week, we became aware of preparations by the Argentine forces to make a strike with their carrier-based aircraft against the Task Force. On 2 May, we were aware that a pincer movement was also being organised for the *General Belgrano* and her escorting destroyers to exploit the air strike on the Fleet. We had already given Admiral Woodward rules of engagement, enabling him to attack the Argentine carrier *Veinticinco de Mayo* wherever he found her, inside or outside any exclusion zones; the extension of this right to attack the *Belgrano*, given the clear warnings given, was really not more than a formality. The two nuclear submarines given the task of shadowing the *Veinticinco de Mayo* seemed to have lost her temporarily, but *Conqueror*, the third submarine, was following the Belgrano. Terry Lewin asked me whether there would be any political problems in extending the rules of engagement to cover an attack on the Belgrano, knowing the grave danger she posed with her Exocet and other armaments to our ships. I agreed that we should attempt to neutralise her.

As it happened, we were due to meet at Chequers on Sunday 2 May to discuss a range of matters, and Terry Lewin, Margaret Thatcher and I agreed there that we had no option but to agree to an attack on the *Belgrano*. It was one of the easiest decisions of the whole war and was subsequently endorsed by the War Cabinet at its meeting later in the morning.

Next day I received a terse, one-line signal from the Fleet just before I was due to make a statement to the House of Commons. I hardly had time to compose my statement, so I knocked the final version together in the car. My final statement was not seen – and vetted – by officials, as there was no time for this to happen. I remain astonished to this day, although knowing the House of Commons I should not have been, that anyone should consider the momentarial compass bearing of the Belgrano's passage to be of any consequence whatever. Any ship can turn about in an instant. She was sunk in international waters in strict conformity with the warnings that we had given – and for us to have taken any other decision, given her threat to the Fleet, would have been a serious dereliction of duty on our part.

I was shocked when I heard of the terrible loss of life that followed, and I regret it deeply, but I fear this was the consequence of a war that we did not initiate. I do not know why the Argentine destroyers did not stay in the area to pick up the survivors – I believe that our ships would have done so. I have no doubt that, although this incident turned international opinion against us, particularly in neutralist-minded Germany and in Argentina's cousin countries Spain and Italy, it did in fact save many British lives. If

John Nott with a sea king helicopter aboard HMS *Hermes.*.

we had been forced to contend with an aggressive Argentine Navy, as well as the courageous Argentine pilots, things might have been different. As it happened, Admiral
Anaya, the most aggressive member of the Argentine junta and more than anyone
responsible for the conflict in the first place, decided to keep the Argentine surface Fleet
in port following the sinking of the *Belgrano*. By neutralising the whole of the
Argentine Navy, our decision proved to be correct and fully justified.

My feelings at this moment of victory were surprising. I just felt an intense sense of
relief that it was over. Although I recognised the tremendous achievement of our forces
and their leaders – and the courage and determination shown by Margaret Thatcher –
personally I felt no sense of triumph. I wanted to sneak away and hide. I knew what
the Duke of Wellington had meant when he said that 'nothing except a battle lost can
be half so melancholy as a battle won'. Just over a thousand had died on both sides and
it all seemed so unnecessary.

And then there were the victory parades and dinners, the self-congratulatory
speeches about our will to resist aggression, and the strengthening of the deterrent
posture of the Alliance. All true. Great Britain emerged from the Falklands a more self-
confident nation. It had taken a quarter of a century to recover our pride after the
shambles of Suez. But I did not enjoy the celebrations.

I least of all enjoyed the stupidity of the Bishops of the Church of England when
arranging the Thanksgiving Service at St Paul's at the end of July. No one was more in
favour of reconciliation with Argentina than I; we could all say prayers privately, if we
wished, for the dead and maimed of both sides; but this was a Service for the veterans of
the war and, in particular, for the families of the British dead. It almost seemed as if our
disagreements on the form of worship were more about the Church of England's own war
against Margaret Thatcher and her policies than about comforting the families of our dead.
Archbishop Runcie had been a brave soldier, but he got drawn into a purposeless argument
about the appropriateness of the hymns and prayers. Enough said – the modern Anglican
Church is beyond my comprehension. It should be laid to rest alongside the BBC.

Margaret Thatcher had more courage and more obstinacy than a man. She really did
believe that men were 'wet', and particularly the species called 'gentlemen'. Of all the
men that I knew in my time in politics, I cannot think of any who would not have
sought an honourable settlement. I am sure that Margaret never meant to do so, but she
went along with the diplomatic game – because to 'win' she had to do so. In my letter
I said that her approach was instinctive, 'so very unmasculine'. She was confronted with
a crisis for her Government and she shut her mind to the risks of conducting such an
adventure 8,000 miles away. Of course, it is always easier to be in charge; to be leader
if you have it in you, rather than to be the staff officers who make it happen. But, in
the last resort, it was a woman's war – and the woman in her won.

A much longer version of John Nott's Falklands experiences can be found in his memoirs,
Here Today, Gone Tomorrow: Recollections of an Errant Politician, *published by
Politico's Publishing*

MICHAEL HALL

3 Para

I served with Airborne Forces from 1981 until 1987 and was attached to 3rd Battalion of the Parachute regiment during the Falklands conflict of 1982. I was a REME armourer and my rank was Craftsman. I spent most of the conflict with 3 Para's quartermasters department and was usually to the rear of the rifle companies, humping rations around etc.

Towards the end of the conflict myself and my friend, fellow armourer, Alec Shaw were flown by helicopter from Teal Inlet to Estancia House. As we arrived there the main body of 3 Para were moving out, I cannot remember if it was that night or the next, 3 Para attacked mount Longdon which I guess was ten or twenty miles away. It was a night attack with no artillery support. From Estancia House we could see the sky lit up all that distance away as the battle raged. A continuous stream of helicopters arrived and we loaded them up with ammunition and primed grenades, which they ferried back to the battle. In the HQ, which inside a big shed where we slept, you could hear the clerk, who was in radio contact with our troops on Longdon, repeating the names of soldiers who were being killed or wounded as the battle went on.

By morning it was over. I had missed my chance of fulfilling my childish desire to be in a battle and perhaps be a hero. Around lunchtime the Qm Tech (I think) confirmed that I was the armourer and asked me if I had mortar spares. I told him that I had and he informed me that a mortar bipod had broken on Longdon and that a helicopter would be picking me up in thirty minutes to take me there and fix it. I was elated! Me going up to 'the front'! I told Alec who wanted to come with me. Alec had received his first ever fathers day card that morning from his son. We jumped on the helicopter with some signals people and took off. Our flight to Longdon was low to the ground and fast. We stopped about a mile or so short of Longdon at 3 Para's Rebro station, which was located in a small rocky outcrop a mile or so from Longdon. I think a couple of Argentine spotting rounds landed close to the helicopter and the loadmaster who was getting very nervous wanted to get away as quickly as possible. Me Alec and a Colour Sergeant, who I think may have been Colour Sgt Russel from Support Company, dragged our stores off the helicopter, which included radio batteries, cigarettes for the boys, and weapon spares, and then took cover in the rocks, I was loving it! Alec was scared, he was older then me and in hindsight I think that he had a clearer understanding of the danger that we were in.

A couple of BVs picked us up and took us up to Mount Longdon. One of the first people that I saw was Corporal Ross Noble. Coming down to the Falklands, he had been very gung-ho and had been really looking forward to some action, we all had. He now looked totally different, tired maybe dazed. He began reeling of the names of those from the MT platoon who had been killed or wounded the previous night. 'Fester' Greenwood had been shot in the head and killed and I can't remember the other names. Suddenly there was hassle, apparently Argentine Chinooks had been seen taking off from Stanley, a counter attack on Longdon was suspected. We were hurriedly given sixty-six millimetre anti tank weapons and lined up facing the flat ground in front of Mount Longdon. We were briefed to wait until the Chinooks were about 50ft off the ground and then let rip. They never came and we were stood down about half an hour later.

Ross invited Alec and I up the mount a bit to a crevice in the rocks where the REME lads were making a brew. I went into the crevice with Ross. Corporal Bishenden, Lance Corporal Geoff Hamilton and Lance Corporal Simon Melton were there as well. Alec went into another crevice beside ours about twenty feet away to have a cup of tea with Cfn Steve Lint. I was standing up while Geoff made the tea, he looked up at me and advised me to get down as there were a lot of shells coming in, I loved it!! Then about three shells came in at once (I watched one land about 50ft away, but wasn't hit); I shat myself. I forced myself into this tiny crack in the rocks and froze. Then people started screaming. I recall someone in the rocks above me who was absolutely terrified, shouting out time and time again: 'I've been hit, I've been hit.' My illusions about war were instantly dashed; it was no adventure, and I was very, very scared. Geof Hamilton verbally dragged us out of our cracks saying something like: 'Come on, lads, somebody's been hit.'

We went into the next crevice and there was Alec just sitting there unconscious. He had blood spattered on his face and Steve Lint was applying a shell dressing to his leg. I saw the wound which was in his thigh, and it did not look that bad. We called for a stretcher and then ran down the hill with Alec on the stretcher. I was totally shitting myself with fear. I was just waiting for the next salvo to come in. Since then I have thought about this often and wondered how I could possibly explain my feelings at this time to somebody that had not been in a similar position. Well I would ask them to imagine themselves standing by the side of a moderately busy motorway, blindfolded and with their hearing blocked up and then being told to walk across all three lanes knowing that at any second, with no warning whatsoever, you might get smashed up. Well that's pretty much how it feels.

We carried Alec down very fast and I left him with the medics. I was told that I was now with the stretcher-bearers. That night, unbeknown to me, 2 Para attacked Wireless Ridge, which was very close by. It was very, very loud. Nobody was injured that night from 3 Para even though it sounded like a lot of shells were coming in, but on reflection, they were probably getting lobbed at 2 Para. I spent the night extremely frightened and praying to God (who I never pray to) asking him to not let me die. When I wanted a piss I pissed lying down in my water bottle. I was very scared of shrapnel.

Morning came and I was starting to get used to the shells and no longer ducking at the whine of each incoming missile; the longer the whine the further away they were going to land. I was having a shit in some rocks when I met a cook who said that it was a shame about Alec. I thought his wound hadn't looked that serious so assumed that he had been choppered out to the hospital ship Uganda. Therefore, I said that at least Alec was lucky because he would be on a hospital ship out of this crap. Then he told me that Alec had died the previous night.

We packed our kit and started walking towards Stanley. A cease-fire was declared on the way and everybody put their maroon berets on. Like everybody else walking down off Mount Longdon that morning I had left friends behind and had experienced things that would change my life forever.

JULIAN THOMPSON

Commander, 3 Commando Brigade, 1981-83

White Flags over Port Stanley?

As the winter evening light began to fade on 14 June 1982 a British helicopter clattered over where I was standing among the men of the 2nd Battalion the Parachute Regiment, stopped on Stanley racecourse by orders from above. Thinking the helicopter was bearing my boss General Moore to negotiate with the Argentine Commander, Major General Menendez, I decided to report to him how my Brigade was disposed and what troops were available should the enemy be inclined to continue fighting. So I, with a couple of my Tactical Headquarters staff and my gunman, Corporal Deane, headed for the Secretariat building in Stanley, which I guessed might be General Moore's destination. Large numbers of Argentine stragglers eyed us curiously as we walked up the muddy, concrete surfaced road, but made no attempt to challenge us. That was left to an Argentine officer in smart combat dress standing on the steps of the Secretariat.

Taking him for a military policeman, I was somewhat surprised that he appeared to know who I was, and did not question my being in a small party well forward of my own troops. I merely assumed he recognised the Brigadier's badge on my beret, for I was wearing no other rank insignia. The conversation that ensued should have told me that he was more than a gatekeeper, but only on meeting him nearly twenty years later did I learn he was Major Carlos Doglioli whose considerable knowledge of the British Armed Forces had led to him being especially asked for by Menendez to advise on British tactics. He politely asked me my business in fluent English. I asked if my General was there, indicating the Secretariat Building.

'No, but mine is, and there are two British officers with him'.

I guessed correctly, as it transpired, that the two British officers were Lieutenant Colonel Mike Rose CO of 22 SAS, and Captain Rod Bell the Spanish interpreter, conducting preliminary negotiations with General Menendez. Not wishing to interrupt what I hoped would be the rapport those two talented officers were establishing with Menendez, I thanked the Argentine officer, turned on my heels and left.

The next step was to find a base for the night. Our rapid advance and speedy collapse of the enemy, found us miles ahead of my Tactical Headquarters with its radios, rations, and sleeping bags. By now our party had been joined by John Chester, my Brigade Major, a couple more radio operators, a few more members of my headquarters, and Mike Holroyd Smith my gunner regiment CO. Sharp as ever, John Chester negotiated with Johnny Crosland commanding B Company of 2 Para for a room in a house he had commandeered. Who owned the house was a mystery It had clearly been taken over by the enemy, judging from the signs of hurried departure. Of the original owners there was no trace.

Soon after dark, I summoned my Commanding Officers to brief them on what I knew of the situation, which was that the Argentines had asked for negotiations, and for the present we were not to advance further. The Brigade was now deployed in a tight defensive posture, guns were laid on likely targets, and should the enemy decide to start fighting again, we were ready in all respects to 'rock and roll'. None of us had spotted any of the white flags that we had been told by our superior headquarters were flying over Port Stanley. We assumed this was rumour, ever present in war, often emanating from the 'blunt end', and in this case probably from the UK.

Some time later, one of my radio operators tuned his high frequency set to catch the BBC World Service, and we learned from the BBC 8,000 miles away that the Argentines had signed the surrender document in the Secretariat building about 800 yards from us. Minutes later Rod Bell came in and confirmed the truth of what we had just heard.

The three or four bedroom suburban detached house occupied by the hundred or so soldiers of Johnny's company was lit only by candles or torches. In every room heaps of soldiers slept, clutching rifle or machine gun, only the sentries outside were alert. Some soldiers had lit the peat-fired Rayburn in the kitchen. The recent occupants had abandoned tins of Argentine bully beef and plastic bottles of red wine. A large iron pot was pressed into service, and soon a stew was simmering. Our turn came, and we dipped our spoons into the delicious brew. We were lucky, some of us had breakfasted that morning, for the parachute soldiers it was their first proper meal for over 72 hours.

It was a moment to savour.

MAX HASTINGS

Journalist

Nothing has changed. Nick Vaux and I clambered among the Argentine field telephones wires still trailing between the rock screes, looking out over the battlefield between snow flurries.

'It was bloody cold, wasn't it?' I said. 'And I had a sleeping bag. How on earth did you manage, all those nights without a blanket?'

Nick grinned at his old signaller, John Adams, who was walking beside us. 'It was one of those times when the colonel and his signaller huddled pretty close together, wasn't it Corporal Adams?'

Memories, memories. There is no bond as close as that between men who have been beside each other in battle. Twenty years ago, I met Lt. Col. Nick Vaux for the first time aboard the great liner *Canberra*, as we steamed 8,000 miles south across the Atlantic towards the Falklands War.

Nick, a slight, puckish figure who shared all my obsessions for rural England was commanding 42 Commando, Royal Marines. I warned to him from the start, and I ended by following him up Mount Harriet, his Commando's brilliantly successful attack on 11 June.

Me? I was a mere passenger, a spectator, a war correspondent. I was one of a handful of men who went to the Falklands to tell the story of Mrs Thatcher's Task Force.

We spent six weeks on *Canberra*, wondering if there was ever going to be a war, and then four more ashore, watching thousands of men such as Nick Vaux doing extraordinary things in the most ordinary British fashion. We shared experiences which remain the most vivid of my life.

Last autumn, in weather as harsh and merciless as that which we knew so well 20 years ago, a few of us went back. We flew south for 17 hours in an RAF Tristar to recapture some vivid moments of the war for one of a season of Channel 4 television films to mark this anniversary.

There was Julian Thompson, who led 3 Commando Brigade, spearhead of the Land

Force; Nick Vaux and his old signaller; Goose Green veteran Private Spud Ely; and a handful more.

Again, we walked the shoreline at San Carlos. Once more, we stood on the deck of a Royal Navy destroyer as fast jets – British, this time – swung low overhead, recalling how it was when the aircraft were Argentine Skyhawks.

Julian Thompson and Nick shouted mockingly at the RAF's Tornados: 'The Argies flew lower than that!' We talked of what a very, very close-run thing it all was; of the battles and hardships; of some glorious moments, and some less glorious.

Channel 4 had tracked down in Buenos Aires and flown back to the Falklands for our film, a certain Major Carlos Dogliolo. In 1982, Carlos was a staff officer to the Argentine commander, General Menendez. When the Argentines were on the brink of surrender and 2 Para was ordered to halt its advance on the outskirts of Port Stanley pending negotiations, I walked to the Argentine lines. Carlos was the first enemy office I met, on the steps of Menendez's headquarters building.

What on earth did he think, when he saw me approaching their positions 20 years ago, I asked? 'Well, you did not look very much like a soldier,' said Carlos in his excellent English, 'and as far as I knew there was no loony-bin on the Islands. So I assumed you must be a journalist.'

I told him how grateful I was that they didn't shoot me.

Julian Thompson spent hours quizzing Carlos about Argentine tactics. Why didn't they harass our long yomp across the islands? Why didn't they patrol? Why didn't they put barbed wire in front of their defences?

The Argentine officer patiently explained how badly armed and equipped they were, compared with the British. In his Latin pride, neither he nor his country can bring themselves to acknowledge the simple truth: the British were incomparably better soldiers than their enemies; the Argentine troops – luckily for us – never really behaved as if they were serious.

A few years ago, a very silly feminist historian wrote a book – for which she was given a literary prize – suggesting that men like wars because they enjoy the opportunity to kill each other. It is true that every army has its handful of psychopaths. Yet, for the vast majority of soldiers, it is the experience of shared sacrifice, the profound nature of comradeship, which provides a consolation for war, rather than a justification for it.

I saw very little jingoism – the *Sun*'s horrid 'Gotcha' spirit – in the South Atlantic in 1982. Modern British soldiers are pretty streetwise. They knew that they were being asked to fight because Mrs Thatcher's Government had cocked up politically. They did not resent that, because they were professionals, proud to show what they could do.

But even as Britain's forces achieved wonderful things against the odds – and they were wonderful things – almost everyone felt a sense of absurdity, that we were fighting a war against Argentina, of all places, in the last years of the 20th century, for a left-over of empire in the midst of the South Atlantic.

Looking out across the stark hills and crags, those miles of peat and moss and swamp and rock, it is possible to see beauty, but hard to feel much love for the place.

The Falklands looks like an intruder, an alien presence, clinging uneasily to the seabed amid the gale-swept ocean which stretches away to Antarctica.

The wind never dies, perpetually ruffling the Union flag over the neat little cemetery at San Carlos where Colonel H. Jones, VC, and some 20 other British casualties of the war lie buried.

The deep inlet of San Carlos Water shimmers marvellously in the winter sunshine, lighting up the silhouette of the Royal Navy's guardship, the frigate *Edinburgh*, as she patrols the seas where so many men died. It is a droll thought, for those of us who watched the battles, who saw poor HMS *Antelope* explode in that terrible, dazzling Guy Fawkes display that some of *Edinburgh's* young sailors were not even born when it happened.

Walking that lonely shore again, I found myself asking the question almost all men ask, as they look back on the experience of war: why did I survive, while others did not?

Why was I chosen to be lucky, to see an Argentine 1,000 bomb explode into the peat 30 yards away without inflicting a scratch, while others suffered so much, and paid so dearly.

I lamented the absence of Michael Rose from our little pilgrimage. During the war, his companionship and support were priceless to me.

But because he commanded the SAS, today General Rose is forbidden to speak about his experiences, amid the desperate official struggle to prevent special forces veterans from telling their stories, even 20 years on.

When the British staged their dramatic night helicopter landing on Mount Kent, 40 miles ahead of the British main force, it was Michael who took me with them.

God, some of us were frightened. I shouted to Rose as we swept over the hills in the darkness, 30ft above the deck:'What happens if the Argies start shelling the landing zone?' We would be within easy range of the enemy's artillery around Port Stanley.

Michael grinned and leaned towards me, cupping his hand over my ear: 'Oh, well,' he shouted back, 'who dares wins.' And, of course, his men did.

I admired Michael as I admired so many of the men I followed across the Falklands, because they possessed virtues that I, like most journalists, lack: unselfishness; a willingness to work for sacrifice; the ability to work with others for a common cause; professionalism of the highest kind.

It is these things, not the killer streak which that foolish feminist historian professed to see, which make veterans of all wars look back with such emotion.

What mattered most in the end, of course, was that our side won. Mrs Thatcher took a huge gamble to save her Government – it was, indeed, a gamble, because many senior officers thought we could not win such a campaign 8,000 miles from home – and it triumphantly succeeded.

The Task Force came home to the wild applause of the British people, to cheering crowds on the dockside at Southampton.

Now, this is where the odd part came in. An historian might say today what many sceptics said at the time: win or lose, what had the Falklands War got to do with the real problems of Britain in 1982?

The Union flag flying again at Government House in Port Stanley after the surrender of
the Argentine forces, 14 June 1982.

What was the use of more than 300 British lives lost, billions of pounds spent, to regain this fragment of South Atlantic wilderness?

Yet, somehow, it all added up to more than that. Somehow, the Falklands War made a decisive contribution to the revival of Britain under Margaret Thatcher.

The triumph of the Royal Marines, the Paras, the Royal Navy at the other end of the world, in what was surely our last colonial war, lifted the spirits of the British people in such a fashion as few of us had ever experienced before. The ghost of the Suez fiasco on 1956, which had haunted a generation's memories for a quarter of a century was laid to rest at last.

After so many years of national decline, industrial and economic failure, we had astonished the world by displaying a resolve it seemed we had lost for ever.

We British hate to think of ourselves as a militaristic nation, but we are certainly a martial one. We like our servicemen. We know we are good at soldiering.

'The British are the last people left in the world who like to fight,' growled Dr Henry Kissinger three years ago, comparing Britain's willingness to send troops to Kosovo with the reluctance to America and the rest of Europe.

I repeated Kissinger's remark to Julian Thompson a few weeks ago, as we looked down on port Stanley from the summit of Wireless Ridge.

As his first unit marched into Stanley on 15 June 1982, Julian must have felt that the war had been the greatest experience of his life.

'Yes', he said, 'but I wasn't under the impression this was some sort of cavalcade laid on for my benefit. A lot of good people had died, to win back those islands.'

Julian, Nick Vaux, Michael Rose and the thousands of others who played their parts in winning the Falklands War command my love and admiration today, as they did back in 1982, because their deeds were in the great tradition of British understatement, matched to astonishing achievement.

I loved making our film together all these years afterwards, though I am unhappy at Channel Four's choice of title: *Reluctant Heroes*.

Heroes? Yes, though the media daily debase that word by using it promiscuously, those men of the South Atlantic were, indeed, heroes. But 'reluctant'? No, they were professionals entirely willing to show the world what they could do. They were cynical about the cause, rather than reluctant to fight.

They knew that for the thousandth time in history, as soldiers they were being asked to risk their lives to retrieve a disaster created by politicians. For anyone who, like me, had not been back to the Falklands since 1982, the most obvious change one sees on landing is the huge military complex built by order of Margaret Thatcher, at a cost of £2 billion.

She created a British strategic commitment in the South Atlantic, which her Government had never recognised before the war to justify afterwards the cost of fighting it.

Today most of the military buildings are empty. The garrison has been run down to a few hundred men, a flight of Tornados, and the personnel who service the big airfield.

But our defence of the Falklands still costs more than £25,000 a head for every man, woman and child on the island.

I am one of those who passionately supported fighting the 1982 war, to show that Britain still possessed the will to resist armed aggression.

But it seems ridiculous to sustain Fortress Falklands indefinitely, at vast cost, as a war memorial to Lady Thatcher. The island's population is that of a big English village. It cannot forever remain trapped in a time-warp of empire.

Argentina today looks an especially unappealing parent, however, with its economy in ruins. But sooner or later, for their own sakes as well as for ours, the islanders need to reach an accommodation with the mainland. South America is so close, we are so far. Like remote farming communities everywhere, the future of the Falklands on their own looks precarious.

But that is the voice of cold politics, harsh economics. In my heart, as I stood once again on the mountains of West Falkland beside those men whose companionship had meant so much to me, I found myself looking back with gratitude on the most dramatic experience of my life.

I was proud to have been there to see the British do something supremely well.

I teased Nick Vaux that he seemed to be finding the going over the rocks pretty tough. 'I keep remind you, Max,' he responded testily, 'that I'm 65 years old.'

I'm 20 years older myself than I was in 1982. But I found that surge of national pride was still there, as we took our yomp down memory lane.

Notes

1   We are grateful to Lady Thatcher for allowing us to reprint this extract from her memoirs, *The Downing Street Years*, published by HarperCollins in 1993.

2   Courtesy of Orion Publishing. *Diaries* by Alan Clark, 1993.

3   Adapted from *Endure No Makeshifts: Some Naval Recollections* by Sir Henry Leach, Leo Cooper Books, 1993.

4   Courtesy of Carol Thatcher, from her book, *Below the Parapet: A Biography of Denis Thatcher*, HarperCollins, 1996.

5   Extracted from *Upwardly Mobile* by Norman Tebbit, Weidenfeld & Nicolson, 1988.

6   Extracted from *A View from the Wings* by Sir Ronald Millar, Weidenfeld & Nicolson, 1993.

7   Adapted from *Knife Edge*, by Richard Villar, Michael Joseph, 1997.

8   Reproduced by kind permission of the *Portsmouth News* (www.portsmouth.co.uk)

9   ibid

10   ibid

11   ibid

12.   ibid

An enthusiastic girl waves her shirt to troops who sailed home to Southampton
aboard the *Canberra*

APPENDIX I

Roll of Honour

Pte Richard Absolon
PO Michael Adcock
AEM Adrian Anslow
MEM Frank Armes
AB Derek Armstrong
Rfm Raymond Armstrong
Sgt John Arthy
WO2 Malcolm Atkinson
Staff Sgt John Baker
Lt Cdr David Balfour
Lt Cdr Richard Banfield
AB Andrew Barr
Lt James Barry
Lt Cdr Gordon Batt
Cpl William Begley
L Cpl Gary Bingley
AB Ian Boldy
PO David Briggs
PO Peter Brouard
Pte Gerald Bull
L Cpl Barry Bullers
Cpl Paul Bunker
L Cpl Anthony Burke
Cpl Robert Burns
Pte Jason Burt
CPO John Caddy

Marine Paul Callan
MEA Paul Callus
L/Sgt James Carlyle
PO Kevin Casey
Bosun Chee Yu Sik
L Cpl Simon Cockton
Pte Albert Connett
Catering Assistant Darryl Cope
L Cpl Anthony Cork
Pte Jonathan Crow
Sgt Philip Currass
Lt William Curtis
Guardsman Ian Dale
Sgt Sid Davidson
Marine Colin Davison
A/PO Stephen Dawson
Guardsman Derek Denholm
Capt Christopher Dent
Elect Fitter Dis Leung Chau
Pte Stephen Dixon
A/WEM John Dobson
Pte Mark Dodsworth
Cook Richard Dunkerley
Guardsman Michael Dunphy
Butcher Dis Sung Yuk Fai
Cook Brian Easton

Sgt Clifford Elley

Sub Lt Richard Emly

Sgt Roger Enefer

Sgt Andrew Evans

Cpl Kenneth Evans

Guardsman Peter Edwards

CPO Anthony Eggington

Lt Cdr John Eyton-Jones

PO Robert Fagan

L Cpl Ian Farrell

C/Sgt Gordon Findlay

Cpl Peter Fitton

CPO Edmund Flanagan

Pte Mark Fletcher

A/Ldg Cook Michael Foote

MEM Stephen Ford

Major Michael Forge

PO Michael Fowler

Lt Kenneth Francis

WO2 Laurence Gallagher

Sapper Pradeep Gandhi

Guardsman Mark Gibby

Guardsman Glenn Grace

Guardsman Paul Green

Pte Anthony Greenwood

L Cpl Brett Giffen

Cook Nigel Goodall

S/Sgt Christopher Griffen

Marine Robert Griffin

Guardsman Gareth Griffiths

Pte Neil Grose

3rd Eng Off. Christopher Hailwood

WEM Ian Hall

Capt Gavin Hamilton

A/Steward Shaun Hanson

Cpl David Hardman

Cpl William Hatton

Flt Lt Garth Hawkins

AB Sean Hayward

Lt Rodney Heath

AEM Mark Henderson

2nd Eng Officer Paul Henry

AB Stephen Heyes

L Cpl Peter Higgs

AEM Brian Hinge

Chief Radio Officer Ronald Hoole

Cpl Stephen Hope

Guardsman Denis Hughes

Guardsman Gareth Hughes

Sgt William Hughes

A/Sgt Ian Hunt

Pte Peter Hedicker

Pte Stephen Illingsworth

MEA Alexander James

Guardsman Brian Jasper

Pte Timothy Jenkins

C/Sgt Brian Johnston

Sapper Christopher Jones

Pte Craig Jones

Pte Michael Jones

Lieut Colonel Herbert Jones

Cpl Philip Jones

Sailor Kam Yung Shui

Guardsman Anthony Keeble

L/Sgt Kevin Keoghane

Laundryman Lai Chi Keung

Laundryman Kyo Ben Kwo

LMEM Allan Knowles

Pte Stewart Laing

WEM Simon Lawson

CPO David Lee

Sgt Robert Leeming

MEM Alistair Leighton

L Cpl Paul Lightfoot

Cpl Michael Love

L Cpl Christopher Lovett

Cpl Douglas MacCormack

Marine Gordon Macpherson

Cook Brian Malcolm

Guardsman David Malcolmson

Guardsman Michael Marks

Naval Airman Brian Marsden

Ldg Cook Tony Marshall

Marine Stephen McAndrews

Cpl Keith McCarthy
AEA Kelvin McCullum
Cpl Michael McHugh
Sgt Ian McKay
L Cpl Peter McKay
Cpl Stewart McLaughlin
Cpl Andrew McIlvenny
AEA Allan McAuley
Pte Thomas Mechan
Cpl Michael Melia
Pte Richard Middlewick
A/LMEM David Miller
L/Sgt Clark Mitchell
Guardsman Christopher Mordecai
3rd Eng Off Andrew Morris
A/Ldg Seaman Michael Mullen
L Cpl James Murdoch
Lt Brian Murphy
Ldg PT Inst Gary Nelson
L Cpl Stephen Newbury
Cpl John Newton
Guardsman Gareth Nicholson
PO Anthony Norman
Marine Michael Nowak
Lieut Richard Nunn
Major Roger Nutbeam
Staff Sgt Patrick O'Connor
Cook David Osborne
A/WEM David Ozbirn
A/PO Andrew Palmer
Pte David Parr
Guardsman Colin Parsons
L Cpl John Pashley
MEM Terence Perkins
Guardsman Eirwyn Phillips
Marine Keith Phillips
Seaman Po Ng
Guardsman Gareth Poole
Staff Sgt James Prescott
Pte Kenneth Preston
Cpl Stephen Prior
L/AEM Donald Pryce

Guardsman James Reynolds
Cook John Roberts
Lt Cdr Glen Robinson-Moltke
Craftsman Mark Rollins
Sgt Ronald Rotherham
Guardsman Nigel Rowberry
Marine Anthony Rundle
L/Cook Mark Sambles
L Cpl David Scott
Pte Ian Scrivens
Lt Cdr John Sephton
Craftsman Alexander Shaw
Seaman Shing Chan Chai
L/Cook Anthony Sillence
Sgt John Simeon
Pte Francis Slough
Cpl Jeremy Smith
Pte Mark Holman-Smith
L Cpl Nigel Smith
Cpl Ian Spencer
L/Radio Op Bernard Still
Guardsman Archibald Stirling
AB Matthew Stuart
Steward Mark Stephens
MEA Geoffrey Stockwell
L Cpl Anthony Streatfield
Steward John Stroud
CPO Kevin Sullivan
Cook Andrew Swallow
L Cpl Philip Sweet
A/WEA David Strickland
AB Adrian Sunderland
Cpl Paul Sullivan
Cpl Stephen Sykes
Sapper Wayne Tabard
Guardsman Ronald Tanbini
L Cpl Christopher Thomas
Guardsman Glyn Thomas
L Cpl Nicholas Thomas
Guardsman Raymond Thomas
CPO Michael Till
Lt David Tinker

MEM Stephen Tonkin
A/Cook Ian Turnbull
Cpl Andrew Uren
PO Colin Vickers
Cpl Laurence Watts
Guardsman James Weaver
Guardsman Andrew Walker
PO Barry Wallis
Cpl Edward Walpole
L Cpl Christopher Ward
Master at Arms Brian Welsh
WO2 Daniel Wight
A/Ldg Mar. Eng Mech Garry Whitford
Ldg Cook Adrian Wellstead
Pte Philip West
Sgt Malcolm Wigley
A/WEA Philip White
A/LMEM Stephen White

Guardsman David Williams
MEM Gilbert Williams
Apprentice Ian Williams
Cook Kevin Williams
Marine David Wilson
Cpl Scott Wilson
Capt David Wood
Lt Cdr John Woodhead

MERCHANT NAVY

Capt Ian North
John Dobson
Frank Foulkes
James Hughes
David Hawkins
Ernest Vickers

APPENDIX II

Useful Websites

Battles of the Falklands	www.naval-history.net/NAVAL1982FALKLANDS.htm
Britain's Small Wars	www.britains-smallwars.com
British Forces Falkland Islands	www.army.mod.uk/bffi/home.htm
British Forces Foundation	www.bff.org.uk
Falklands Conservation	www.falklandsconservation.com
Falkland Islands Government	www.falklands.gov.fk
Falkland Islands News Network	www.sartma.com
Falkland Islands Tourist Board	www.tourism.org.fk
Falklands–Malvinas Forum	www.falklands-malvinas.com
Falklands Memorial Chapel	www.falklands-chapel.org.uk
Great White Whale (*Canberra* in the Falklands)	www.comcen.com.au/~raiment/
HMS *Broadsword*	www.btinternet.com/~broadsword82
HMS *Glamorgan*	www.hmsglamorgan.cwc.net
SS *Canberra*	www.sscanberra.com
South Atlantic Medal Association 82 (SAMA 82)	www.sama82.org.uk

APPENDIX III

Falklands Timeline

1522, 1592

Argentine versions state that various Spanish and Portuguese seamen, and particularly Esteban Gómez of the Magellan expedition (in 1522) were the first to see the islands without giving concrete verifiable sources except their own, which are most likely revisionistic. According the Encyclopedia Britannica (an American source probably leaning toward the English), the English navigator John Davis on the Desire (1592) may (note emphasis) have been the first person to sight the Falklands. Given that both sides' claims are much debated and undocumented by the original sources, they should be taken with a grain of salt.

Circa 1600

The Dutchman Sebald de Weerdt makes the first undisputed sighting of the islands.

1690

The English captain John Strong heading a British expedition made the first recorded landing in the Falklands, in 1690. The British claim the islands for the crown and named the Sound between the two main islands after Viscount Falkland, a British Naval official. The name was later applied to the whole island group.

1764

French navigator Louis-Antoine de Bougainville founds the islands' first permanent settlement, on East Falkland. During subsequent years, a French fishery is manned by people from St. Malo (hence 'Iles Malouines' from which the Argentine name 'Islas Malvinas' is derived).

1765

The British are the first to settle in the West Falkland island.

1767

The Spanish buy out the French settlement (Port Louis) in the East Falkland island. For Spain, this implies a French recognition of the Spanish rights to the land.

1770

A Spanish flotilla arrives at the islands asking the British to leave. When first asked to leave, the British officer in charge of the garrison, a Captain Hunt, replied: "I have received your letters by the officer, acquainting me that these islands and coasts thereof belong to the King of Spain, your Master. In return I am to acquaint you that the said islands belong to his Brittanic Majesty, My Master, by right of discovery as well as settlement and that the subjects of no other power whatever can have any right to be settled in the said islands without leave from His Brittanic Majesty or taking oaths of allegiance and submitting themselves to His Majesty's Government as subjects of the Crown of Great Britain." This is the first documented sign we could find of the conflict between Britain and Spain regarding the Islands. Shortly thereafter, the Spanish revisited with a much superior force 'convincing' the British garrison to leave on 14 July 1770. [Source: 'An account of of the last expedition to Port Egmont in the Falkland Islands' , by Bernard Penrose published in the Universal Magazine, April 1775.]

1771

The British outpost on West Falkland is restored after threat of war.

1774

The British withdraw from the island (for economic reasons according to British sources). Spain maintains the settlement on East Falkland (which it called Soledad Island) until 1811, when Spain is about to lose control of its colonies in America.

1816

Independent Argentina first appears on the historical scene.

1820

The Buenos Aires Government, which had declared its independence from Spain in 1816, first proclaims its sovereignty over the Falklands.

1828

Argentine warlord (Caudillo), and later governor of Buenos Aires Juan Manuel de Rosas sent a governor, Mr. Vernet, together with a garrison and settlers for menial work to the islands. The first recorded Argentine settlement in the islands.

1831

The American warship USS *Lexington* destroys the Argentine settlement on East Falkland in reprisal for the arrest of three U.S. ships that had been hunting seals in the area.

1833

Afraid that the Americans seized the islands, the British remember the expedition of the 17th century, re-invade the islands, forcefully depose Vernet and send the Argentines back to the mainland albeit without having to fire a shot.

1885

A British community of some 1,800 people on the islands is self-supporting.

1892

Colonial status is granted to the Falklands.

1933 onwards

According to David Rock: "After the Roca-Runciman treaty [A bilateral trade agreement signed in 1933 between Britain and Argentina, benefiting Britain and exploiting Argentina's natural resources -- Ed.], a profusion of new nationalist writers and factions began to appear. For a time the nationalist movement was largely dominated by historians who sought to fuel the campaign against the British. These historical "revisionists" began to reexamine the 19th century and to catalogue Britain's imperialist encroachments: the British invasions of 1806-1807, Britain's role in the foundation of Uruguay in the late 1820s, its seizure of the Falkland Islands in 1833, the blockades under Rosas . . . A cult now enveloped the figure of Juan Manuel de Rosas, who was depicted as a symbol of national resistance to foreign dominations [In fact, he was a strong handed dictator who killed countless opponents, benefited greatly from trade with Britain, sized 800,000 acres of estate land for himself only etc. -- Ed]. . . Propaganda of this kind made a deepening imprint on public opinion and helped sustain nationalist sentiments in the Army. . ."

1964

The islands' position was debated by the UN committee on de-colonization. Argentina based its claim to the Falklands on papal bulls of 1493 modified by the Treaty of Tordesillas (1494), by which Spain and Portugal had divided the New World between themselves; on succession from Spain; on the islands' proximity to South America; and on the need to end a colonial situation. Britain based its claim on its 'open, continuous, effective possession, occupation, and administration' of the islands since 1833 and its determination to grant the Falklanders self-determination as recognized in the United Nations Charter. Britain asserted that, far from ending a colonial situation, Argentine rule and control of the lives of the Falklanders against their will would, in fact, create one.

1965

The UN General Assembly approved a resolution inviting Britain and Argentina to hold discussions to find a peaceful solution to the dispute. These protracted discussions were still proceeding in February 1982 shortly before the Falkland war started.

March 19 1982

A group of Argentine scrap metal merchants working in the South Georgia island is escorted by some military personnel. Britain calls Argentina to remove the military personnel without response.

March 26 1982

The Argentine military junta decides to invade the islands. Background: Argentina is in deep economic trouble; Throughout 1981, inflation sky-rockets to over 600%, GDP is down 11.4%, manufacturing output is down 22.9%, and real wages by 19.2% [Rock: p 375-378]. In addition, Mass disappearances of people in the hands of the military juntas causes significant unrest. The third dictatorship president since the 1976 coup, General Leopoldo Galtieri launches a military invasion of the islands, code named Operación Rosario. The invasion is planned by the commander of the Navy Admiral Jorge Anaya to be launched on one of the most important national celebrations (The revolution anniversary on 25 May or Independence day on 9 July). Its main purpose is to divert public attention from the distressing internal problems and restore the long lost popularity and prestige of the dictatorship. Due to the mounting pressures on the Government, and mass union demonstrations in late March, the date of the invasion is moved earlier to 2 April in an act of desperation.

2 April 1982

The Argentine Navy with thousands of troops lands on the Falklands. A small detachment of Royal Marines on the islands put up a brave but futile resistance before Governor Rex Hunt ordered them to lay down their arms. The marine forces are flown to Montevideo along with the British governor.

3 April 1982

Argentine troops seize the associated islands of South Georgia and the South Sandwich group (1,000 miles [1,600 km] east of the Falklands) following a short battle in which an Argentine helicopter is forced down and 4 Argentine troops are killed. General Mario Menendez is proclaimed military governor of the islands. As Galtieri has predicted, the move proves to be extremely popular: In Buenos Aires, where the unions had a week earlier demonstrated against the Government, there are massive outbursts of solidarity in the streets. The United Nations Security Council passes Resolution 502 calling for the withdrawal of Argentine troops from the islands and the immediate cessation of hostilities. First Royal Air Force transport aircraft deploy to Ascension Island.

Late March to early April 1982

Thousands of Argentine conscripts lacking basic training are drafted in a hurry and sent to the islands. Argentina rapidly accumulates more than 10,000 troops on the Falklands.

8 April 1982

The US Secretary of State, Alexander Haig, arrives in London to begin shuttle mediation.

10 April 1982

EEC approves trade sanctions against Argentina. Haig flies to Buenos Aires for talks with the Junta.

17 April 1982

Haig meets again with the Argentine junta. After a breakdown in the mediation talks, he returns to Washington on 19 April.

23 April 1982

British Foreign Office advises British nationals in Argentina to leave.

25 April 1982

A small British commando force retakes the Georgia Island. Argentine submarine *Santa Fe* attacked and disabled. The commander of the Argentine forces on the island, Alfredo Astiz, signs an unconditional surrender document on board the British HMS *Plymouth* without firing a single shot violating the military code's article 751: 'A soldier will be condemned to prison for three to five years if, in combat with a foreign enemy, he surrenders without having exhausted his supply of ammunition or without having lost two thirds of the men under his command.' Meanwhile, the main British Task Force is on its 8,000 miles (13,000 km) way to the war zone via the British–held Ascension Island.

30 April 1982

Alexander Haig's mission is officially terminated. President Ronald Reagan declares US support for Britain and economic sanctions against Argentina. The British war exclusion zone comes into effect.

1 May 1982

Harrier and Vulcan British planes attack the Port Stanley (named 'Puerto Argentino' by Argentina) airfield. Three Argentine aircraft are shot down.

2 May 1982

Belaunde Terry, President of Peru, presents a peace proposal to Argentine President Leopoldo Galtieri, who gives a preliminary acceptance with some proposed modifications. Before the Argentine junta ratifies the acceptance, British submarine HMS *Conqueror* sinks the Argentine cruiser *General Belgrano* outside the war zone and while sailing away from the islands. Almost 400 crewmen die. At this point the junta rejects the proposal.

4 May 1982

Argentine air attacks from Super Etendard fighter planes using Exocet air to surface missiles sink the British destroyer HMS *Sheffield* with twenty men on board. One British Harrier plane is shot down.

7 May 1982

UN enters peace negotiations.

9 May 1982

The islands are bombarded from sea and air. Two Sea Harriers sink the Argentine trawler *Narwal*.

11 May 1982

Argentine supply ship *Isla de los Estados* is sunk by the British HMS *Alacrity*.

14 May 1982

Three Argentine Skyhawks are shot down. Prime Minister Thatcher warns that peaceful settlement may not be possible. Special British forces night raid on Pebble Island; 11 Argentine aircraft destroyed on the ground.

18 May 1982

A peace proposal presented by the United Nations Secretary General, Perez de Cuellar, is rejected by Britain.

21 May 1982

The British manage to make an amphibious landing near Port San Carlos, on the northern coast of East Falkland. From this beachhead the British infantry advances southward to capture the settlements of Darwin and Goose Green before turning towards Stanley. The British HMS *Ardent* is sunk by an Argentine air attack. Nine Argentine aircraft shot down.

23 May 1982

The British HMS *Antelope* is attacked and sinks after unexploded bomb detonates. Ten Argentine aircraft destroyed.

24 May 1982

Seven Argentine Aircraft destroyed.

25 May 1982

HMS *Coventry* is hit by three air bombs dropped from Skyhawks; 19 British dead. The MV *Atlantic Conveyor* is hit by an Exocet missile and sinks 3 days later, 12 British dead.

28 May 1982

More air raids on Port Stanley. British 2nd Battalion, Parachute Regiment (2 Para), take Darwin and Goose Green in what was arguably the longest and toughest battle of the War.

29 May 1982

Warships and Harriers bombard Argentine positions.

30 May 1982

Shelling continues as British troops advance. The British 45 Commando secures Douglas settlement; 3-Para recaptures Teal Inlet.

31 May 1982

Mount Kent is taken by British troops. The Falklands' capital of Port Stanley is surrounded.

1 June 1982

Britain repeats its cease-fire terms.

4 June 1982

Britain vetoes Panamanian–Spanish cease-fire resolution in the UN Security Council.

6 June 1982

Versailles summit supports British position on Falklands.

8 June 1982

An Argentine air attack on British landing craft *Sir Galahad* and *Sir Tristram* at Port Pleasant south of Bluff Cove. 50 British die.

12 June 1982

The British 3-Para mounts an assault on Mount Longdon. The battle on this heavily defended position, which was supposed to last until dawn, proves much tougher and longer than expected. Mount Longdon and its surroundings are finally taken after hand to hand and bayonet fighting with the Argentine troops position by position. The British casualties mount to 23 men, one of which, Sergeant Ian John McKay of 3-Para is later awarded a posthumous Victoria Cross, 47 more British are wounded. The Argentine suffered over 50 dead and many more injured. 6 more British die shortly afterwards. British 45 Commando takes Two Sisters and 42 Commando takes Mount Harriet with support by the guns of 29th Commando regiment and Naval gunfire from a number of Royal Navy frigates.

The 2nd Scots Guards seize Mount Tumbledown in another bloody battle. nine British and about 40 Argentine die. Another 34 Argentine soldiers surrender and taken prisoners. 32 British are wounded. [Source: Tactics of Modern Warfare by Mark Lloyd].

The cruiser HMS *Glamorgan* is hit by an Exocet missile as it was bombarding on shore Argentine positions. Thirteen British die.

14 June 1982

The large Argentine garrison in Port Stanley is defeated, effectively ending the conflict. The Argentine commander Mario Menendez, agrees to 'an unnegotiated cease fire . . . with no other condition than the deletion of the word unconditional' from the surrender document which he signs. 9800 Argentine troops put down their weapons.

20 June 1982

The British reoccupy the South Sandwich Islands. Britain formally declares an end to hostilities, and the two-hundred mile exclusion zone established around the islands during the war is replaced by a Falkland Islands Protection Zone (FIPZ) of 150 miles.

Timeline is reprinted courtesy of The Vanished Gallery www.yendor.com/vanished

Royal Marine Commandos hoisting the Union Flag on the Falklands, 20 June 1982.

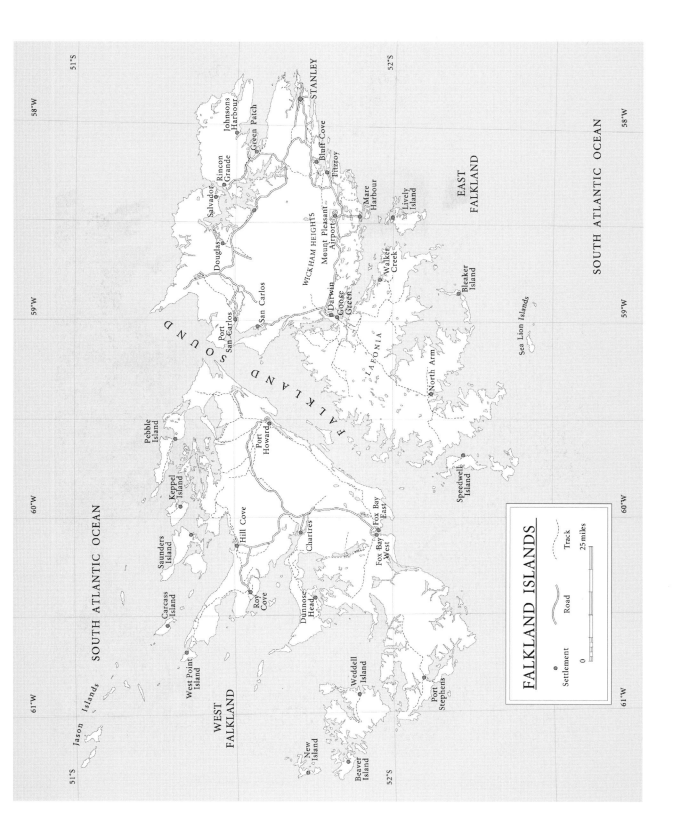

The Falklands Hymn

We entrust to the Lord our lost brothers.
They responded to duty's stern call,
And so far their homes and their loved ones
Paid the price that is highest of all.
Flesh had failed them, but God was their savior;
Bringing rescue from battle's alarms;
Beyond death he is always their refuge,
Underneath, everlasting, his arms

We commend to the Lord those who mourn them,
Loving parents and children and wives,
For whom pride in their selfless commitment
Has been countered by their grief for lost lives.
When so many returned, theirs were absent,
Leaving long years of anguish to face;
May the Lord heal the wounds of bereavement
With the infinite power of his grace

We commit to the Lord now our own lives,
And we vow in our turn to reply
To the call of the weak and the friendless,
Though the cost to ourselves may be high.
When the choosing is hard, may God grant us
The direction that strengthens and calms.
For we trust in the Lord as our refuge,
Underneath, everlasting, his arms.